About Island Press

Since 1984, the nonprofit organization Island Press has been stimulating, shaping, and communicating ideas that are essential for solving environmental problems worldwide. With more than 1,000 titles in print and some 30 new releases each year, we are the nation's leading publisher on environmental issues. We identify innovative thinkers and emerging trends in the environmental field. We work with world-renowned experts and authors to develop cross-disciplinary solutions to environmental challenges.

Island Press designs and executes educational campaigns, in conjunction with our authors, to communicate their critical messages in print, in person, and online using the latest technologies, innovative programs, and the media. Our goal is to reach targeted audiences—scientists, policy makers, environmental advocates, urban planners, the media, and concerned citizens—with information that can be used to create the framework for long-term ecological health and human well-being.

Island Press gratefully acknowledges major support from The Bobolink Foundation, Caldera Foundation, The Curtis and Edith Munson Foundation, The Forrest C. and Frances H. Lattner Foundation, The JPB Foundation, The Kresge Foundation, The Summit Charitable Foundation, Inc., and many other generous organizations and individuals.

The opinions expressed in this book are those of the author(s) and do not necessarily reflect the views of our supporters.

The Monsanto Papers

The Monsanto Papers

DEADLY SECRETS, CORPORATE CORRUPTION,

AND ONE MAN'S SEARCH FOR JUSTICE

Carey Gillam

 ISLANDPRESS | Washington | Covelo

Library of Congress Control Number: 2020944651

All Island Press books are printed on environmentally responsible materials.

Manufactured in the United States of America
10 9 8 7 6 5 4 3 2 1

Keywords: Aimee Wagstaff, agrochemicals, Bayer AG, Brent Wisner, carcinogenic
chemicals, genetically modified organisms (GMOs), Dewayne Johnson,
glyphosate, herbicide, International Agency for Research on Cancer (IARC),
Mike Miller, non-Hodgkin lymphoma (NHL), personal injury lawsuit, pesticide
resistance, plaintiffs' attorneys, Roundup, Tim Litzenburg, weed killer

This book is dedicated to the countless men and women stricken with cancer I have come to know in the course of researching and writing this book, people who have trusted me with their stories of suffering, fear, rage, and yes, hope—always hope.

Enjoy the good times because you never know when the bad times are coming.

—Dewayne Anthony "Lee" Johnson

Photo by Ally Gillam

Contents

Creve Coeur

But man is a part of nature, and his war against nature is inevitably a war against himself.

—Rachel Carson

In English, the French phrase *crève coeur* translates as "broken heart." Legend has it that Creve Coeur Lake, near St. Louis, Missouri, was named in honor of a young Indian princess who fell in love with a French fur trapper. Despite her best efforts, she failed to win his affection, and, as the story goes, the grieving princess killed herself by leaping from a ledge into the lake. Legend says the body of water was filled with so much sadness that it formed itself into the shape of a heart split in two.

That fabled heartbreak proved to be a dark precursor to the saga of real suffering that came to be attached to the area as a company called Monsanto made the city of Creve Coeur its home base. Monsanto Company's growth into a global purveyor of questionable chemicals and altered seeds would lead many to blame it for decades of death and despair.

When Creve Coeur was incorporated in December of 1949, it was a quiet community of fewer than two thousand residents. But by the turn of the century, the city was a hub for innovation and business, with median home prices double the national average. Young professionals and retirees alike were drawn to the suburb for its abundance of parks, restaurants, and highly rated public schools, its low crime rate, and its moderate political views.

The community grew alongside Monsanto, which moved from downtown St. Louis to Creve Coeur in 1957. The company made its home on a sprawling property with sleek black office buildings, glass-topped greenhouses where plant experiments were conducted, and an assortment of high-tech laboratories where teams of scientists labored. Dense groves of trees and guard gates kept curious outsiders at bay.

Monsanto employed more than five thousand full-time staff in the St. Louis area and many more thousands around the state of Missouri and the world. The company was known as a generous benefactor, funneling millions of dollars into community and education programs and research grants at universities. Its name would come to adorn the buildings of many prominent local institutions, such as the Missouri Botanical Garden's research facility, the Saint Louis Zoo's Insectarium and Education Gallery, and various facilities at the area's universities. Washington University, a private research university in St. Louis named for President George Washington, received more than $100 million in research gifts; the Monsanto Laboratory of the Life Sciences was the first building on its St. Louis campus to be named after a corporation. Monsanto's rich donations to biological sciences research at the university sparked fear in the 1980s and 1990s that the integrity of academic research might be compromised. But company and university officials claimed the research remained free of undue corporate influence.

Founded in 1901 by John F. Queeny, whose wife, Olga Mendez Monsanto, was the company's namesake, Monsanto began as a maker of the artificial sweetener saccharin. The company later expanded into manufacturing such things as sulfuric acid, polychlorinated biphenyls (PCBs), plastics, and an insecticide called dichlorodiphenyltrichloroethane, better known as DDT. In the 1960s, Monsanto was a supplier of Agent Orange, a chemical defoliant used during the Vietnam War by US troops to kill vegetation that provided hiding places for enemy soldiers. Agent Orange was eventually found to be linked to cancers, birth defects, and a range of human health problems. Many of the company's other products and practices would later prove dangerous as well. The city of Anniston, Alabama, became so polluted from a Monsanto PCB plant that residents won a $700 million settlement in 2003. Residents said the company knew about the toxic effects of PCBs for decades but did nothing to protect their health or to protect the area's water and soil from contamination.

Monsanto may be best known for its introduction in the 1970s of a weed-killing chemical called glyphosate. Company chemists combined glyphosate with water and other ingredients designed to help the chemical be absorbed into plant tissue, where it would quickly kill the plant. One ingredient, a surfactant called polyethoxylated tallow amine (POEA), was combined with glyphosate in a product Monsanto dubbed Roundup. The formulation poisoned plants so effectively that it became a hot seller not just in the United States but also in many other countries.

Roundup was heralded as much safer than other, older herbicides, and one that people could spray in their own yards with little concern. The company said glyphosate interacted with plants in ways that were not possible with mammals, meaning that people and pets would not be injured by exposure to the chemical. The US Environmental Protection Agency (EPA), charged with regulating pesticides such as Monsanto's glyphosate-based herbicides, also said the product was safe and allowed the company to market it for a wide range of uses, including use on farm fields growing food. Regulatory agencies in other countries echoed the EPA's stamp of approval.

With a green light from regulators, Monsanto was soon marketing Roundup and related products for everything from knocking out pesky weeds in a residential backyard to spraying entire fields of wheat, oats, and other crops to dry them out just before farmers harvested. The herbicide could be sprayed from planes and helicopters, pumped from truck-mounted tanks, or squeezed out of handheld plastic bottles. School districts around the United States sprayed the weed killer on playgrounds and other areas frequented by children. No use was too large or too small for Monsanto's remarkably safe weed killer, it seemed.

By the 2000s, Monsanto was becoming deeply embedded in the big business of agriculture, in large part because of its Roundup products. The company had figured out how to genetically alter different types of widely grown crops, such as corn and soybeans and cotton, so that farmers worried about weeds could spray directly over the crops without drying them out and killing off their growth. These genetically engineered soybeans and corn were impervious to the weed killer. Farmers could spray their fields with Roundup multiple times if needed, and the crops would continue to grow. Use of Roundup and other glyphosate-based products exploded with adoption of these genetically altered crops, making glyphosate the world's most widely used weed-killing chemical.

Monsanto's footprint expanded to include operations in Canada, Mexico, Brazil, Argentina, Uruguay, Chile, Israel, Australia, Europe, and numerous locations throughout Africa and Asia. As Monsanto extended its reach into agriculture, it eventually became the world's largest seed company. At one point, Monsanto's seed portfolio included not just row crops used as ingredients in finished foods but also fruits and vegetables such as tomatoes, melons, onions, carrots, broccoli, and lettuce. Despite Monsanto's global growth, Creve Coeur remained its home base.

But as the company's business grew, so did public distrust. Monsanto became commonly known as "Monsatan" to critics and activists who believed the company was dangerously tinkering with Mother Nature's food supply and polluting the environment with its Roundup herbicides and other chemicals.

So many protests were held outside Monsanto's headquarters that the Creve Coeur city council passed an ordinance prohibiting protesters from standing on the median outside the entrance to the Monsanto campus.

The beginning of the end for Monsanto came in 2015, when the company's assurances about the safety of its herbicides started to unravel. The unwinding revealed numerous corporate secrets, including covert strategies to alter both the scientific record and regulatory assessments of a chemical that by then touched millions of people around the world. Thousands of people suffering from debilitating and deadly cancers came to learn that decades of research linking the weed killer to cancer had been largely discredited and dismissed as a result of actions by Monsanto. And they discovered that the EPA and other regulators worked closely with Monsanto in ways that protected the company's profits much more than public health.

Many hoped lawmakers and regulators would ride to the rescue. But in the end, the victims found that the only way to hold Monsanto accountable was through the courts. An eclectic group of lawyers teamed up to take on the $15 billion corporation and expose its most deeply buried corporate secrets. They spent millions of dollars of their own money building a case; some lost spouses, their health, and large chunks of their personal lives over the years spent gathering evidence. Detractors called them ambulance chasers and accused them of exploiting cancer victims for profit. But no one can deny that without their work, many of Monsanto's distortions would likely never have come to light.

Monsanto is no more—in 2018, the 117-year-old company was absorbed by German conglomerate Bayer AG. But its legacy lives on in lawsuits winding their way through courts in multiple countries.

This is a story about one cancer victim's search for justice in the face of so much injustice, a story of both suffering and determination, and a story about what it took to uncover decades of corporate deception.

CHAPTER 1
Getting Dirty

Before

Sunlight had not yet started to streak its way across the Northern California landscape as forty-one-year-old Lee Johnson pushed himself up out of bed. In the darkness, he pulled on a pair of jeans and a hooded shirt bearing a patch from the Benicia Unified School District. Down the hall, Lee's wife, Araceli, prodded their two young sons into wakefulness. There was no hint that Lee's life was about to take a tragic turn.

Rising early was not just a habit; it was a requirement of Lee's job as a groundskeeper for the school district, which rotated roughly five thousand students through its mix of elementary, middle, and high schools. Lee had been in his current position for only a year but enjoyed a broad job description and a five-figure salary that helped his family claw its way out of near homelessness and into a middle-class lifestyle. They had recently moved into a split-level two-bedroom house in what the young family considered an affluent neighborhood in the city of Vallejo. The beige stucco was not really theirs—just a rental—but it felt like home. The kitchen boasted black marble countertops and maple wood floors, and a small children's park was just a few paces from the front door. Lee loved the tall, leafy trees that lined the streets and the grassy backyard, where a family of squirrels cackled as they chased each other through the branches.

More than anything, Lee treasured the feeling of success he had found and the stability it brought. His youth had been tumultuous—his mother had been young, poor, and often unable to care for Lee. His father had been largely absent, leaving Lee struggling to find his footing. Lee had failed to graduate from high school, instead obtaining a General Educational Development (GED) certificate. Efforts at college classes didn't work out, and Lee seemed to find trouble wherever he turned. He notched multiple arrests, fathered his first son when he was in his early twenties, and bounced from one low-paying job to another, working as a janitor and a roofer and trying to launch a landscaping business. He also attempted, like many in his neighborhood, to make it as a rapper and music producer.

But now all that was in the past, and life was good, solid. Lee's income, combined with what Araceli earned from various part-time jobs, provided enough for an occasional vacation with the kids and a sense of contentment that Lee had long craved. He still wrote music and dreamed of selling and performing his songs, but his focus was on his family, specifically on being as present and engaged with his sons as possible. He did not want them to grow up feeling his absence, the way he had with his own father. Lee had a tattoo inscribed on his forearm reading "Blessings for the righteous." The blessings for his family had finally started to flow, Lee believed.

The work for the school district wasn't easy, but Lee knew that as long as he kept working hard, he could count on a long career with a growing income. He didn't mind starting before dawn or working outside in rain or shine, cold or heat. He found the work satisfying, knowing that every day he made the school surroundings a little cleaner, neater, or safer.

Whether it was trapping rats and raccoons, painting walls, installing irrigation pipe, or applying insecticides to wipe out armies of ants and herbicides to kill off invasive plants, Lee was one of the school district's go-to guys for getting dirty work done. Supervisors had just recently lauded his performance in a written review, highlighting Lee's "positive successful approach" and his "remarkable ability to grasp all aspects of his responsibilities."

On this day—a day he would later be forced to repeatedly recount to doctors and lawyers and to a courtroom full of spectators—Lee's task was supposed to be fairly simple. He would mix up a fifty-gallon drum of weed killer and then spray the concoction over a hilly area between two schools that held baseball and soccer fields. The Benicia district, like many in the United States, did not want its school grounds to appear unkempt, and doing his job right meant Lee needed to stay one step ahead of common California weeds, such as "cheeseweed," which could grow more than two feet tall if left alone.

He did this often, mixing and applying products with macho-sounding brand names such as Roundup and Ranger Pro. Developed by the giant chemical corporation Monsanto Company, the brands were top sellers, largely because the company advertised them as being much safer than rival products, nontoxic to people even though the chemicals were deadly to plants. Some marketers even advised that the Monsanto herbicides were "safe enough to drink." Despite the safety slogans, Lee was wary of these and other chemicals, and he always made sure to arrive at work early enough to don heavy protective gear before beginning a morning of spraying. He also liked to get the wet mixtures on the grounds well before the children would be out playing sports or enjoying recess.

Lee didn't expect the work that day to be too taxing for him. Even as he moved into middle age, Lee considered himself in excellent health. He had grown up playing sports, spending countless summer days and nights at the baseball field just a few blocks from his grandmother's house, where he lived during most of his childhood. As an adult, he was still athletic. He stood five feet nine, with a lean, muscled frame of 165 pounds, and he was blessed with smooth caramel-colored skin that rarely failed to attract admiring attention from women. His mother had named him Dewayne Anthony, but he went by Lee. He frequently dressed all in black, and when he spoke, his voice was low and warm, like a long, lazy slow dance.

His easy ability as a charmer would sometimes spark angry battles with Araceli, who was a decade younger than Lee and fiercely possessive of her husband's attention. Theirs had been a fast and passionate courtship that led to a surprise pregnancy and the birth of their first son, Ali, and then to marriage and another boy, Kahli. Their relationship ran hot and cold, but Lee loved what he called Araceli's spicy personality, her shiny dark hair, and her hazel eyes, which made him think of light brown sugar. He also valued the fact that she worked as hard as he did to support the family financially.

For Araceli, Lee was the love of her life. She wanted nothing more than to raise a family with him. Early in their marriage, when their boys were just babies, Lee couldn't find work, leaving the young family unable to afford rent, so they lived for a while with Lee's mother in her one-bedroom apartment in a complex reserved for senior citizens. They had to sneak in and out of the rent-controlled facility so they would not get caught. But even in the humiliation and struggle to stay out of poverty, Araceli believed in Lee, in what the future could hold for them.

Now her faith in her husband had paid off. But as happy as she was with Lee's solid income, Araceli was often harried by a busy daily routine. Breakfast was a quick bowl of cold cereal or premade pancakes spread with Nutella; then Araceli would load the family into her aging Nissan Altima sedan, drive the roughly fifteen minutes to drop Lee off at his work site, and then make a thirty-minute commute to Napa, where the boys attended elementary school. Born in Mexico, Araceli had moved to the United States with her parents at a young age and spent her teenage years in Napa, where her family worked in the area's famed vineyards. Araceli felt the schools were better and outside influences healthier in Napa than they were in Vallejo, a town long ranked as one of the most dangerous in the state, with a high murder rate and several criminal gangs. As a young man growing up in Vallejo, Lee had sometimes carried a pistol to protect himself. Araceli wanted better for her boys.

On this morning, the couple spoke few words during their predawn commute, and Araceli let Lee out at the highway exit closest to the district offices rather than making the extra turn. She did this often; it was only a short twenty-minute walk for Lee, and he didn't mind. It was better than riding his bike to catch a bus to work, as he did on days when she couldn't or wouldn't drive him.

Lee hopped out of the car, told his boys a quick goodbye, and started the mile-and-a-half walk to his work site at a brisk pace, eager to get the day going. He fast-walked past an aging automotive shop, a liquor store, and a Chinese restaurant and then cut behind a community center to reach the school district office. Although the front of the property had an air of elegance, boasting pink flowering shrubs and an arched entryway, Lee's destination was around back in the district maintenance yard, a grimy lot that no one would describe as anything close to elegant.

Several white district pickup trucks waited there, their beds filled with green hoses, brooms, rubber trash containers, plastic buckets, and other tools of the trade. A rectangular metal building stored the supplies the school district's maintenance workers needed. And across the parking lot was a low metal trailer where workers clocked in and out and ate their lunches. One small storage shed stood apart from the rest of the buildings. A sign hanging on the door read "Danger, Hazardous Chemicals."

Lee was responsible for supervising two coworkers who helped him spray pesticides on school grounds, assigning areas for the guys to treat and making sure they wore their protective equipment. The gear was extensive and included white coveralls with elastic cuffs, chemical-resistant rubber gloves and boots, and heavy goggles. Sometimes the guys tried to get away with skipping the full outfit. Lee got it; the getups made them look a bit like misfit astronauts or some sort of space aliens. But Lee insisted: they had to wear the gear if they were going to be spraying. Despite the full bodysuit, Lee's face was only partly protected by a mask that covered his mouth and nose but left his cheeks exposed. Sometimes, if the wind was blowing, Lee could feel a fine mist of the pesticide drifting onto his face.

Once they had their jumpsuits on, Lee and his team mixed up their weed-killing chemicals for the day. Pulling from large drums of Ranger Pro, Lee and his team mixed the concentrate with water and antifoaming agents before transferring what they called "the juice" into spray tanks. The men would carry the tanks on their bodies like backpacks, using long wands with spray heads to disperse the weed treatment. On this morning, Lee also mixed up enough to fill a 50-gallon tank that was mounted in the back of his work truck. The tank had a motorized engine and was connected to a long hose and a three-foot spray wand that could push the chemicals over a bigger area faster than could a man carrying a backpack sprayer. The truck-mounted sprayer was so heavy that Lee had to use a forklift to get it onto the back of the district vehicle. Using the tank from the truck allowed Lee to cover a lot of ground, and sometimes he would go through 150 gallons in a morning and cover multiple fields. This morning, he wouldn't get that far.

The assignment was to spray weeds around an elementary school, including on a hilly area lying between that school and an adjacent high school. Lee loaded the full tank onto the district truck and drove the ten minutes from the maintenance shed to the school, tuning the truck radio to his favorite jazz station as he drove. When he arrived, he decided to start at the top of the hill and work his way down. Hopping out of the cab, he grabbed the hose reel and proceeded to unwind the 250-foot hose, sweeping the spray wand back and forth as he walked down the hillside. As the sun rose, the day grew warm, but there was little wind, meaning less spray would drift onto Lee's face. It was a good day to spray, he thought. When he was about halfway down the hill, the hose was nearly fully extended, meaning Lee would have to move his truck if he was going to finish the job. He got back into the truck and drove slowly down the slope, not bothering to reel in the hose. He figured that once he was parked at the bottom, he could simply walk back up to the point where he'd left off and spray his way down the last half of the hill.

But just as Lee was slowing to a stop, he heard and felt a jolt from the bed of the truck where the tank full of weed killer rested. He threw open the door and saw that the hose, which had been dragging behind the truck, had somehow become caught in a wide crack in the asphalt. The tension had yanked the hose from its connection to the tank, and a fountain of amber-colored chemical was spewing into the air.

"Oh, shit!" Lee exclaimed, stricken with a fear that briefly froze him in place. He told himself he couldn't panic; the situation could get serious very fast if he didn't stop the toxic flow. He raced around to the back of the truck and clambered into the bed, propelling himself directly into the foul-smelling spray so that he could flip the red switch that shut down the tank motor. His mind was on the pump, but he was vaguely aware of being wet—soaked, in fact. His face, neck, and back felt as if a bucket of water had been poured over him. There wasn't time to worry about that. Even without the motor to drive the pump, the fluid continued running out of the truck bed and onto the ground, making small streams down the hill and toward the property's wastewater drain, which led into a nearby bay where people fished and children sometimes swam. Lee often spent lunch hours there, feeding the gulls and watching sailboats glide by. Letting toxic chemicals flow into the waterway could get him in trouble, Lee knew.

Grabbing a shovel he kept in the truck bed, Lee started piling dirt into a makeshift dam to sop up the wet mess, praying he could stop the flow before it escaped into the drains. The dirt worked like a charm, slowing and soaking up the leak. Lee then carefully reeled the hose back in before stripping off the now-drenched jumpsuit, which was designed to protect the wearer from the light drift of a normal spray job but was not much help for the dousing he had just experienced. Even the shirt he wore underneath the protective suit had become coated in the spray, so he shrugged that off too. He hurried back to the district maintenance shop, where he turned his attention to trying to scrub the chemicals off his body.

There was no shower, but there was a sink in a small bathroom where the guys would wash their hands and faces after particularly dirty jobs. Lee filled up the small sink with hot water and soap and worked to wash the chemicals from his face, neck, and hands. He wouldn't feel fully clean until he could get home and take a long, hot shower, but he did have a spare clean shirt to wear, which he pulled on after drying himself with a handful of paper towels.

Lee spent the afternoon tending to other district chores and trying not to worry about the spray accident. He didn't feel sick, and his smooth dark skin seemed unscathed by the errant chemical bath. Getting dirty was just part of the job, nothing to worry about, he told himself. That night, at home with Araceli and the kids, he didn't even mention the accident. He knew in the back of his mind the chemicals were toxic, but he had also been told repeatedly that Monsanto's products were the safest out there. He pushed the fears to the back of his mind and resolved not to let the incident upset him.

After

Lee wouldn't think about the sprayer accident again until many months later, when an odd-looking scaly lesion popped up just above his right knee. It itched and cracked and oozed. As time passed, the patch near his knee was matched by another on his arm. And another on his torso. Small bumps the size of BB pellets sprouted out of his skin. Lee changed the laundry soap and dryer sheets his family used and tried an assortment of creams, but nothing helped. Dread grew with every new spot that erupted. Eventually, nearly Lee's entire body, including his face and scalp, was covered in painful sores. Some became infected, including one on his head.

As his condition progressed, Lee's once unmarred skin broke open at the slightest touch in some places, and wearing clothing became almost unbearably painful. A lesion even developed on one of his eyelids, making it impossible for him to open the eye without grimacing in pain. The softer the skin where the lesions sprouted, the more searing the pain, Lee learned.

Strangers started to stare when Lee went out. His sons' friends asked if he'd been burned in a fire or suffered from some disfiguring disease. "What's wrong with your dad?" became a common question for Ali when Lee attended a football practice. He took to wearing long sleeves, long pants, and large sunglasses in public, hoping to avoid the pitying glances from strangers.

In the early stages, when the skin eruptions were fewer, flatter, and less painful, Lee could still sometimes tell himself they might just be part of a weird rash. He kept going to work as usual and kept doing his regular rounds, including spraying weed killer. He convinced himself that the skin problems would resolve themselves, just as the bee stings and bloody scrapes he suffered on the job always had. But when the sores spread to his face, Lee had had enough. It was time to see a doctor and, he hoped, find a medicine that would clear it all up.

The Vallejo public health clinic was not a large facility, and the physician who saw Lee was at a loss for how to help him. She pulled out a reference book, and together she and Lee looked through pictures of various skin ailments, hoping to find a match.

"I don't really know what this is," she admitted to Lee.

Lee's next stop was a neighborhood dermatology practice. A lovely dark-haired physician's assistant examined him with a worried frown. Like the public health doctor, she was not certain what she was looking at. The best plan was to biopsy a lesion and send the tissue to the cancer experts at the University of California, San Francisco. They would know what it was, she told Lee.

The results, when they came back, were not good. Lee was told he had squamous cell carcinoma (SCC), a type of skin cancer typically caused by long-term exposure to the sun or other ultraviolet radiation. Overall incidence of the disease has jumped by 200 percent in the past thirty years, killing an estimated fifteen thousand Americans per year.

The doctors emphasized to Lee that the cancer was very serious—unlike some other forms of skin cancer, SCC can metastasize into a patient's lymph nodes and spread quickly. But it can also be very treatable: patients who undergo surgical removal of lesions, as well as radiation and immunotherapy, generally have high survival rates. This was not a death sentence, he was told. Many patients improved significantly with something called photodynamic therapy, a treatment that exposes skin to certain drugs and types of light in a combination that kills the cancerous cells.

Skin cancer made sense, Lee supposed. He did work outside; he always had been active and athletic and enjoyed the California sunshine. It was stunning news, but Lee took it in stride. He was otherwise healthy and active and felt sure he could beat the disease now that he knew what it was.

The next several weeks and months became a blur of doctors, treatments, and more tests, along with mounting medical bills, which Lee struggled to keep up with. There was some dispute over the diagnosis—was this really SCC or something more insidious? The doctors did biopsies of his skin and his lymph nodes and took extensive scans in a probe for more complete answers. Lee had health insurance through the school district, but it didn't pay for everything, and deductibles and co-pays added up fast, even as it seemed to take far too long to find answers.

Eventually, doctors would determine that though the lesion on Lee's thigh was SCC, Lee also had mycosis fungoides, a type of non-Hodgkin lymphoma that shows up on the skin but can spread through the body, including to the lungs and brain. It begins when certain white blood cells, called T cells, become cancerous. The exact cause of mycosis fungoides is not known, though it does tend to afflict men twice as frequently as it does women, Lee learned.

Through it all, Lee wondered about the sprayer accident. It had been less than a year from the day he was drenched in the pesticide to the day the lesions started showing up, and he could not think of anything else that might have triggered the disease. He started trying to find answers online, researching information about the toxicity of Monsanto's products, but as far as he could tell there was no one else like him—no one who had developed this type of cancer from using a Monsanto weed killer. He called a poison control hotline, but if there was information linking cancer to the chemicals he had been using, Lee wasn't finding it.

In November of 2014, Lee called Monsanto directly after finding a phone number for the company on the internet. A woman who worked as a product support specialist listened to Lee describe his accident with the tank sprayer and his concerns that it might be the cause of his cancer. She promised to try to find someone who could call him back with answers to his questions, documenting Lee's description of this sprayer accident and his skin lesions in an email to one of Monsanto's medical experts. "His entire body is covered in this now and doctors are saying it is skin cancer," she wrote. "He is just trying to find out if it could all be related to such a large exposure to Ranger Pro. . . . He is looking for answers."

Lee never did receive a call back. With no proof to back up his suspicions, he continued to work as he could, continuing to spray even as he underwent treatments for his cancer.

Lee's doctors did not seem to share his curiosity about a cause. One of his doctors would later testify in court that she had not spent much time trying to figure out what had triggered Lee's condition because her focus was on how to get him better.

By late 2014, Lee had a team of doctors working to rein in the cancer with an aggressive treatment plan that often felt harder to bear than the disease itself. The lesion near Lee's knee was surgically sliced off. He underwent a round of radiation, and then another. Immunotherapy was next. An alternative to traditional chemotherapy, immunotherapy uses biological substances to try to strengthen the body's immune system to fight cancer. The treatments made Lee so sick some days that he couldn't get out of bed, couldn't eat, couldn't make it to watch his kids play sports. Family trips to the beach became a thing of the past. Even a dinner out with the family became too hard for Lee to bear. His skin, still marred from the lesions, became even darker after the radiation, and looking into the mirror above his bathroom sink, Lee didn't recognize himself.

Many nights, Lee would cry quietly into his pillow, trying not to wake Araceli or the boys. At other times, he seemed to be in shock, retreating into himself. The exhaustion and pain took a toll on his once razor-sharp attention to detail, leaving him feeling as if lost in a fog. Araceli worried that he was depressed, and she noted that each day, her husband seemed to be thinner, quieter, fading away.

One day as Lee struggled to dress himself, Araceli saw that his clothes hung off his wasted frame. His feet were so swollen and covered in the oozing sores he called "stingers" that he cried as he tried to pull on his shoes.

"I just want to die," he told her, sobbing.

Later, much later, Lee would remember that period—as hard as it was—with longing. Though the days and nights were often filled with pain, frustration, and fear, those months also represented a cushion of time when Lee still could envision a long future, a time when he believed that he could regain his health and watch his children grow up.

There were periods when the treatments seemed to be succeeding and he would feel good enough to go to his job, to take his boys to the park, or to work on writing a song he planned to perform one day.

But then there was another work accident, another accidental dousing of weed killer when a backpack sprayer he was using tore and leaked herbicide down his neck and back. Lee emailed his doctor to alert her to the exposure. "Hopefully it doesn't send my current situation into a frenzy," he wrote.

Lee's fear soon became a reality as the lesions that had seemed to settle and soothe came back with a fury, spreading pain like wildfire across his flesh, leaving him more scarred. And more scared. Lee was now fully convinced that his cancer was connected to the chemicals he'd been spraying, and he refused to continue his work applying the weed-killing chemicals. The school district provided some money for a while but eventually ended disability payments.

The loss of income hit the family hard. The rental house with the smooth marble countertops, leafy trees, and large backyard was now a luxury of a past life, and the family squeezed into a tiny two-bedroom ground-floor apartment near a busy highway. It was cramped and dark, and Lee hated it. Weeds overran the dirt patch near the front door, and paint peeled off the siding of the complex. Only weeks after they moved in, the family came home one night to find the kitchen window broken. Burglars had taken their television and the boys' video gaming system, along with other trinkets.

Lee's medical file noted that by September of 2015, Lee's skin was "getting new thicker plaques with some ulcerations." Old lesions were rising back up at the same time that new ones were growing. The worst was happening. Lee's cancer had progressed into what his doctors referred to as "large cell transformation disease."

There were some new treatments offered through clinical trials Lee could try, but "it definitely was not a good sign," one of his doctors would later recount. "He was heading in the wrong direction." Median survival for patients in that condition was one and a half years.

Lee's vision of a long and bright future started to fade into something small and dim. He realized with a sad irony that his skin was so ravaged that the "Blessings" tattoo on his forearm seemed to be slowly disappearing. He would not be there to watch his boys grow up after all.

Lee was dying.

CHAPTER 2

Railroad Avenue

Nearly three thousand miles stretch between Lee's California home and the Virginia office of attorney Mike Miller. While Lee was searching for answers about what was causing his declining health, Mike was starting to ask questions about Monsanto's popular products. He wondered—just as Lee did—whether there might be evidence tying the weed killers to cancer.

The sixty-two-year-old lawyer had made a career of holding corporations accountable for products that were sold as safe but later were proven to be quite the opposite. He had no inside knowledge of connections between Monsanto's herbicides and cancer, but he had seen news articles here and there and was aware of multiple scientific studies that raised some serious concerns, including studies that observed a specific link to non-Hodgkin lymphoma, a type of blood cancer that can be deadly. Mike had never tried a case involving a pesticide before, and he didn't know a lot about Monsanto, but he decided he wanted to know more.

Mike and his wife, Nancy, ran their practice, The Miller Firm, out of the tiny town of Orange, Virginia. Just a dot on the map between the bustling cities of Richmond and Washington, DC, Orange was a quiet community steeped in Civil War history and civic Southern pride. The people were friendly, the real estate was cheap, and the entire town was contained within about three square miles, meaning no tedious, time-wasting commutes in rush-hour traffic. It was the kind of town where a busy lawyer could walk a couple of blocks for a quick lunch of deep-fried chicken livers and made-from-scratch cornbread at the Country Cookin café.

For many years, Mike had based his practice in the upscale suburb of Alexandria, Virginia, making a reputation and a small fortune representing people who had been harmed by medical malpractice, faulty medical devices, or dangerous drugs peddled by pharmaceutical companies. Litigation over fen-phen diet pills was one of the many cases he had thrown himself into. The pills had been marketed as a safe aid for people who were trying to lose weight, but they were pulled from the market after scientific studies showed they could cause heart valve defects. After years of battling, the drugmaker paid out billions of dollars to settle litigation brought by Miller and other attorneys. Another big win had come from Mike's representation of people who had taken the drug Zyprexa. Zyprexa was approved to treat adults suffering from certain psychotic disorders, but its manufacturer, Eli Lilly and Company, was accused of marketing it to calm unruly children and cantankerous elderly patients—uses that were not approved by federal regulators and that caused serious side effects in these vulnerable populations. The company eventually paid $1.42 billion to settle multiple civil lawsuits and a criminal probe.

Mike's move out of Alexandria came after he met Nancy, a trim blonde lawyer with blue-green eyes who had her own firm in Mississippi. Nancy was blessed with a flawless complexion, a bright smile, and a hearty laugh that could make a stranger feel like a friend almost instantly. She was divorced, with two young children, but had a youthful enthusiasm and energy that drew a range of suitors. Like Mike, Nancy was active in fen-phen litigation, and it was over the course of many meetings and trial proceedings that the two fell in love. Mike was fourteen years older and had six children himself, as well as two grandchildren. Unlike Nancy, his age and long years of hard work showed in his lined face and graying hair. But the two found they shared a passion for their legal work as well as a desire to embrace adventures when they could carve out time off.

Nancy had grown up on a working cattle ranch in Mississippi and wanted a rural lifestyle that would allow for land and horses, and the couple's combined legal victories meant the blended family had the financial resources to live about anywhere they chose. After canvassing the Virginia countryside, they purchased a sprawling 365-acre farmstead, which Nancy populated with unwanted ponies and older horses that were not much good for riding but made for lovable "lawn ornaments," as she called them. On weekends, Mike enjoyed picking up his guitar for an impromptu performance for the kids.

Orange became the home for their law practice primarily because it was a mere fifteen-minute drive from the farm but also because it was there that Mike found an abandoned pool hall that he was sure would make a perfect office space. The building, at 108 Railroad Avenue, had a unique charm and more than enough room for Mike, Nancy, and the eight other lawyers and support staff the firm employed. It wasn't the easiest to find; its main entrance opened onto a stretch of railroad tracks that intersected the town, and young attorneys showing up for job interviews sometimes complained about getting lost. But The Miller Firm wasn't looking for local clients anyway. Mass tort cases—nationwide claims involving dozens, hundreds, or thousands of plaintiffs—were the focus.

Mike and Nancy spent more than a year refurbishing the century-old two-story structure, which had also once served as a hotel and a courthouse. They kept the high tin ceilings and exposed brick walls and turned the old bar top into the firm's reception counter. They decorated a large conference room with an expensive wool rug over the polished wood floor and filled a bookcase with medical and legal journals. They hung a picture of the Statue of Liberty on one wall. The second floor held more offices along with a small apartment for use as needed. When freight and passenger trains rumbled by, as they did multiple times a day, the entire building shook and its windows rattled.

Mike outfitted his office with an old wooden desk that on a typical morning would be covered with stacks of legal files and a copy of the *Washington Post*, which he would read before starting work. With his graying goatee, dark-rimmed glasses, and natty pinstripe suits, Mike was the embodiment of a veteran litigator.

Still, after more than thirty-five years of arguing cases, Mike was starting to contemplate what retirement could look like. He and Nancy owned a second home and sixty-four acres on the eastern side of the Hawaiian island of Maui and had turned the land into an organic coffee plantation, where caretakers cultivated red and orange bourbon coffee varieties. The Hawaii home also was a haven for Mike to practice kiteboarding, one of his favorite hobbies. He also was a trained pilot and enjoyed the solitude of cruising through the skies. There was not nearly enough time, Mike felt, for him to enjoy the life he had earned. The type of litigation he pursued required long hours, and when a case was nearing trial, there was no such thing as a weekend break or a night off. Big cases could take years to resolve and often required the firm to bear hefty up-front costs. Many firms like his had to take out loans or seek investors to provide the funding required to prepare for a big case. It was hard work, this big business of plaintiffs' law. Nancy wanted to see Mike slow down, move from litigator to mentor.

But Mike knew he was not ready to walk away quite yet. Though critics pegged plaintiffs' attorneys as unprincipled parasites who exploited individual tragedies for their own personal gain, Mike felt a real sense of satisfaction in representing the "little guy"—people who had suffered injuries or had lost loved ones at the hands of powerful corporations and lacked the means to seek justice without a good attorney by their side. He didn't mind the money, of course. He made a lot of money. When and if there was a victory, attorneys' fees could tally in the six and seven figures.

It was 2014 when Mike's caseload started to ebb. The pharmaceutical litigation that had consumed his life for more than a decade was settling down, and his young associate attorneys were hungry for a new case, as was he.

Mike knew the name Monsanto, and he knew the large St. Louis–based corporation had a top-selling herbicide called Roundup that was so effective at killing weeds it had become the most widely used herbicide in the world. He also knew that concerns were starting to grow about the safety of the chemical agent in Roundup and other branded herbicides. The active ingredient was a substance called glyphosate, which Monsanto had patented in 1974. Glyphosate was used in a variety of herbicide brands, some designed for people who wanted to treat weeds in their backyards and other, stronger potions for use in farm fields, schoolyards, parks, and almost anywhere else someone might want to eradicate undesired plants. Monsanto made billions of dollars from the sale of these herbicide products, even after glyphosate's patent expired and competing glyphosate-based products came to market.

The company and the US Environmental Protection Agency (EPA), which regulates pesticide use, had long maintained that glyphosate-based herbicides were very safe and could be used without worry. Scores of scientific studies paid for by Monsanto and by other companies that made the herbicides backed up the assurances of safety.

But a separate body of scientific research had grown over the years indicating that the herbicides might not be as safe as the company and the regulators said. Some scientists were warning of a cancer risk, specifically a risk of non-Hodgkin lymphoma.

The Roundup case could be similar, Mike thought, to some of the big pharmaceutical litigation he had spent years waging. One of the cases

Mike was most proud of was a legal challenge he led against the Takeda Pharmaceutical Company, the maker of a diabetes drug called Actos that was found to cause bladder cancer. With more than thirty million Americans suffering from diabetes, Actos made billions of dollars for Takeda—largely because it was seen initially as much safer than other remedies. But as scientific evidence of the cancer risk grew, thousands of people filed product liability lawsuits accusing Takeda of failing to warn of the risks. After unsuccessfully trying to defend itself in court, Takeda agreed to pay $2.4 billion to settle the claims. Through the course of the litigation, Takeda was found to have destroyed files, and it was revealed that the company knew even before the drug was approved that a study of rats dosed with the drug showed an association with bladder cancer. That case, like so many others Mike had worked on over the years, left him firmly convinced that when corporate profits were at stake, the facts about dangerous products were often buried. He wondered whether that might be true for Monsanto and its glyphosate-based herbicides.

Through his work with Actos, Mike knew that when it came to cancer hazards, one organization was seen as the chief authority. The International Agency for Research on Cancer, known as IARC, is part of the World Health Organization (WHO) and is solely devoted to studying cancer research and encouraging international projects aimed at preventing cancer worldwide. IARC, based in Lyon, France, doesn't do new research; the group's scientists analyze existing published research about substances that people are widely exposed to and for which cancer concerns may exist.

IARC had announced in June of 2013 that after reviewing the body of published research, agency scientists classified pioglitazone, the generic name for Actos, as "probably carcinogenic to humans."

The finding from such a prestigious group was a game changer for the Actos litigation, helping Miller and other lawyers cruise more easily to courtroom victories.

So in 2014, when IARC said its scientists would start assessing the growing concerns about cancer connections to glyphosate-based herbicides, Mike alerted his young associates to keep an eye on the IARC review. It was not typical for IARC to classify a substance as a probable carcinogen or known carcinogen. The agency's scientists most often found that substances it reviewed were "not classifiable" regarding carcinogenicity.

Months passed. But one afternoon in March of 2015, news agencies out of Europe started churning out the news: the IARC scientists announced that their review of years of research made it clear that glyphosate, the weed killer Monsanto had been selling for decades, was a probable human carcinogen. They found a particular association between glyphosate-based herbicides and non-Hodgkin lymphoma, one of the most common types of cancer in the United States and one that kills thousands of people each year.

In a lengthy report, the IARC scientists said they found evidence of cancer causation in studies of people exposed to the weed killer not only in the United States but also in Canada and Sweden. In the research from Canada, some association between the weed killer and non-Hodgkin lymphoma was seen in people who were exposed more than two days per year. One study of people exposed to glyphosate-based formulations through aerial spraying found chromosomal damage in the blood cells of those people and noted that the markers for the damage were significantly greater after exposure than before. The scientists said they also saw evidence of cancer causation in experimental studies on animals. One such study had found that a glyphosate-based formulation promoted skin tumors in mice.

The IARC scientific report was a plaintiffs' attorney's dream. On top of that, glyphosate-based herbicides were so widely used that the potential pool of plaintiffs would be massive. And with roughly $15 billion per year in annual sales, Monsanto had very deep pockets.

Mike called a quick meeting of his team. Aside from Nancy, all the firm's attorneys were men, and all were younger than Mike. They didn't have his trial experience, but they shared his enthusiasm for courtroom challenges. The associates took their seats, settling into the blue leather chairs that ringed the expansive conference room table, and looked at him expectantly. Mike explained the details of the IARC decision and its relevance to Monsanto's herbicide business, pausing for a moment to look around the room. "We're getting in, boys," he announced.

The next several weeks turned into a blur of action as the firm started putting together its game plan. News stories about the IARC cancer classification were racing around the globe, leading thousands of people to wonder if their own cancers were due to their use of Monsanto herbicides.

The IARC decision could not carry a case, Mike knew. Someone on the team would need to dig deeper into the science. They would also need to know everything they could find out about Monsanto, its history, how it developed and marketed its products, and how the company worked with regulatory agencies such as the EPA.

Mike assigned the task to Jeff Travers, a quiet young associate attorney who had joined the firm in 2008. Jeff hated the travel that nationwide litigation entailed, and he was so self-conscious that conversations with other professionals sometimes left him stammering to complete a sentence. "Charisma" was not an adjective people generally used to describe Jeff.

He had come to the legal profession a bit later than his colleagues, tending bar for several years after graduating from college before finally deciding to give law school a try. His office, on the second floor of the firm, was as far away as possible from the noisiness of the first floor and the bellowing trains outside the firm's front windows.

But while Jeff may not have been a very good trial attorney, he was a hell of a researcher. Not only did he know how to pull together key evidence that big cases required, he was a genius at compiling the legal briefs that documented arguments aimed at winning a case. Writing a brief is a tedious and time-consuming task but one that is an incredibly critical element of courtroom battles. In a typical trial, lawyers might need to file hundreds of briefs on very tight deadlines. The Miller Firm relied heavily on Jeff for this work. He had such a sharp grasp of details that colleagues speculated he must have a photographic memory. If a piece of evidence existed that could help make the case for a client, Jeff could find it. And once he had his teeth into an assignment, he didn't let go.

While Jeff set about finding evidence, the firm went about finding clients—farmers, landscapers, gardeners, or anyone else who had developed non-Hodgkin lymphoma after regularly using Monsanto's weed killers. That meant advertising. Lots of advertising. Mike called in an agency to shoot a video in both English and Spanish to run on the firm's website. Mike and Nancy also set up a web page to solicit clients with a contact form and a 1-800 number. And they employed a search engine optimization expert to make sure their ads rose to the top of the pack in internet searches. The ad was carefully worded to offer would-be plaintiffs sympathy along with a possible day in court:

Truth be told, this herbicide does an amazing job in eliminating weeds when applied to lawns, crops, and landscaping areas. But at what expense? Many view Monsanto as the world's most evil corporation because of the information they withheld. Their negligence put the lives of many in jeopardy. If you're a victim of RoundUp's effects, you're not alone. At The Miller Firm, we understand the turmoil this has caused you and your family. If you are experiencing the effects of this toxic herbicide, we encourage you to explore your options to get the help and support you deserve.

Within days, dozens of people were swamping the Miller law offices with stories of their exposures and their cancer diagnoses. Other law firms were also posting advertisements. Some were even deploying representatives to fan out through farm country, holding town-hall-style meetings in small towns in Nebraska, Kansas, Iowa, and Missouri. At these meetings, the law firm reps explained to farmers and their families how herbicides they had been spraying on farm fields for years might be the cause of sickness and suffering in their households. If they were sick, or knew someone who was, legal assistance was only a phone call or an email away, the families were told.

By October of 2015, a little more than six months after the IARC classification, several lawsuits had been filed against Monsanto in different cities around the United States. All were filed by people diagnosed with variations of non-Hodgkin lymphoma. One was brought by a twenty-four-year-old woman who grew up as the child of migrant farmworkers; another was filed by a landscaper who formerly had been a farmworker. The lawsuits accused Monsanto of knowing that glyphosate was a health hazard but engaging in yearslong deceptive campaigns to mask the dangers of the company's herbicides.

Research by the Miller law firm's attorneys had turned up news articles and scientific studies dating back several years that described concerns about glyphosate and ties to cancer, contrasting sharply with Monsanto's insistence that the scientists were wrong and glyphosate's safety was undisputed.

So many inquiries from potential plaintiffs were coming into The Miller Firm by late 2015 that Nancy could only screen the calls and emails before passing them out to the associate attorneys for deeper scrutiny and follow-up. One of the attorneys she designated to help with the flood of potential clients was a relatively new young associate named Tim Litzenburg. With a flop of streaked sandy-blond hair, a lanky frame, and a languid air, Tim did not look like a litigator, nor did he act like one. In fact, he liked to say he had gone to law school "almost as a lark." After graduating with a bachelor of arts degree from a private liberal arts college in Virginia, Tim had spent the summer painting houses and pondering what he wanted his future to hold. At the time, he was fascinated by lawyer and politician John Edwards, who made a career as a well-known plaintiffs' attorney representing children and families injured through medical malpractice. Edwards's fame had propelled him to become the Democratic nominee for vice president in 2004, the year Tim graduated from college. When Tim decided to try to follow in Edwards's footsteps, he had no way of knowing that Edwards would later become widely disgraced as an adulterer and serial liar.

Tim attended the University of Richmond Law School, and after graduating in 2008 he joined a personal injury law firm in Richmond before applying to and being hired by The Miller Firm in June of 2012. He was only thirty years old and still learning the ropes of the plaintiffs' bar, but, like Mike and Nancy, he was drawn to defend individuals against injustice, whatever that might look like. Mike and Nancy saw big potential in Tim, but they determined that for all his passion, Tim was not at his best in front of a jury. He had a hard time commanding a courtroom and, in Mike's view, didn't understand instinctively how to amplify the emotional aspects of his arguments to elicit sympathy from a jury. Tim could not even be counted on for writing briefs. He had learned to type using only two fingers and was the first to admit that writing briefs was not his thing.

But Tim was very good at working with clients. People who became plaintiffs were often frightened, confused, and frustrated as they navigated the thorny path of product liability litigation. Often, they were injured or sick or had lost a loved one, and Tim had a way of offering comfort along with legal guidance. Nancy knew that Tim could provide the careful handling needed with these cases, so she handed off a large number of the intake forms to him for review. Each person who called or emailed in response to the advertisement had to be scrutinized to determine if his or her situation fit the type of case Mike was building. Only those with non-Hodgkin lymphoma who had been exposed to

Roundup or other glyphosate-based products multiple times would be accepted as clients. Younger people would make better clients than older individuals, and the firm would need to carefully screen anyone who had a history of other cancers and compromised immune systems.

~

Back in California, Lee had never heard of The Miller Firm, but he was growing increasingly angry about his loss of good health and was spending long hours on the internet searching for any information he could find about Roundup, Monsanto, and ties to cancer. When the Miller law firm's advertisement popped up on his screen with its toll-free number, Lee scrolled quickly through the firm's message. One line stood out—"If you're a victim of RoundUp's effects, you're not alone."

As he read the words, Lee froze. He didn't want to be a victim. But he was suffering, and he and his family were in turmoil. Was he a victim? Sitting with his laptop in the dark and cramped apartment, where he was spending far too many days moving from bed to sofa and from sofa back to bed, Lee felt both brief relief and fresh anger. He eyed the short online form and the black button at the bottom of the web page that read "Get Help Now." What "help" might mean Lee wasn't sure, but he knew he wanted to find out. A click on the button would whisk his details straight to the law firm. Forget that, he thought. He wasn't waiting for someone to read an email. He grabbed his phone and dialed.

CHAPTER 3
Making a Case

Lee's phone call to The Miller Firm was one of scores of similar calls and internet inquiries the firm was juggling in those months that followed the classification of glyphosate as a probable carcinogen by the International Agency for Research on Cancer (IARC). Like others who reached out to the firm, Lee was asked a few questions and then told that someone would get back to him. He feared no one would call him back, as had happened with his call to Monsanto. But within a week, an energetic attorney who introduced himself as Tim Litzenburg was in touch, saying he thought Lee had an excellent case, and The Miller Firm was very interested in signing him as a client.

The file was one of many assigned to Tim, but the young lawyer still set about getting to know everything he could about Lee, his use of Roundup, and the progression of his cancer. Over the phone—during that first call and many that followed—Tim quizzed Lee about an array of factors important to his case, such as Lee's health before the Roundup exposure, other pesticides or chemicals he might have been exposed to in the past, any family history of cancer, and any drug use or other habits that could impact his health. Tim told Lee that he would need to have his medical records and employment records, and he would need to talk with Lee's doctors, his coworkers, and his wife. A lawsuit could be filed right away, Tim explained, but making a case and actually taking that case to trial could be a long, slow ordeal, and Lee would have to agree to have his life scrutinized by teams of lawyers he might never even meet.

Tim didn't meet every potential client in person, but Lee's case seemed extraordinary. His accidental dousing followed by the devastatingly rapid onset of cancer made for a compelling legal case, Tim thought. He couldn't learn everything he needed to know all the way across the country. He had to meet Lee in person. And his wife. The couple needed to be fully prepared for what could be an arduous process.

Lee knew very little about Tim other than he was a white guy with a slight Southern drawl. And Lee didn't like bringing new people to the apartment, with its sagging orange sofa, scuffed walls, and stained beige carpet. Ever since he was a child, living mostly with his grandparents as his mother struggled for stable housing, Lee had craved order amid chaos. He abhorred the clutter that came with squeezing a family of four into a living space where the kitchen, dining area, and family room were all essentially one small shared rectangle.

So, for that first meeting between lawyer and client, Lee and Tim met at an Applebee's chain restaurant not far from Lee's apartment. The two had already spent long hours on the telephone discussing Lee's declining health, and Tim knew from the photos in his medical file that Lee's skin was grotesquely deformed by the cancerous lesions that covered him from head to toe. But he still was taken aback when he saw Lee in person for the first time. Though Lee was wearing long sleeves and pants, it was impossible to hide the patches distorting his face, neck, and hands. He looked like a man who'd been burned in a fire, wounded in a war he'd never signed up to fight.

Lee was wary at first. What could this young white Southerner actually do for him? But the fact that Tim was willing to take time away from his own family and travel all the way from Virginia to California meant something to Lee. Clearly, there was no way Tim could save his life. But maybe there was a way, Lee thought, that Tim could make his suffering mean something. Maybe there was a way to hold someone responsible.

As the two sat together in the noisy restaurant, Lee realized he was impressed. Tim was smart, and he was quick with answers to all of Lee's questions. He was also different from what Lee had expected. Tim seemed truly interested in Lee as a person, not just as someone he might make money from. And Tim seemed youthful and hip, in much the way Lee had once seen himself. Lee would later describe Tim to a friend as a "great dude," a "solid man's man."

Though they had already had many phone conversations, in their initial meeting Tim had Lee walk him through the tank sprayer accident and its aftermath once again. Details such as dates and times of the exposure would be important in making a case that Roundup had caused Lee's cancer, Tim knew, and Lee's memory was worrisomely fuzzy. The illness and chemotherapy had taken a toll on his once sharp mind.

One thing Lee was clear about, however, was that he could not afford months, maybe years, of legal work on his behalf. He knew lawyers charged hundreds of dollars per hour, and he and Araceli were barely scraping by. But Tim explained that the legal representation was on a contingency basis, meaning Lee would not need to pay even a penny for his representation—unless he won. If that were the case, the legal team would charge Lee for the accumulated expenses plus a fee of 40 percent of whatever a jury or judge might award him.

"Don't worry, man. We've got this," Tim told Lee.

Lee was at first a bit stunned by the hefty cut the deal would give the lawyers, but he figured he had little to lose. If he actually won his case, even after paying the lawyers he might be able to collect hundreds of thousands of dollars, he guessed. That kind of money would help keep his family stable and maybe make it possible for Araceli to cut back on her hours. If they got enough money, they might even be able to buy a house before Lee died, and maybe there would be enough to pay for his boys to go to college. Lee knew it was crazy to hope for something like that. But it was possible, he told himself. He decided not to talk to Araceli too much about it. There was no reason to get her hopes up. Lee signed the contract for The Miller Firm to represent him, and on January 28, 2016, *Dewayne Johnson v. Monsanto Company* was filed in the Superior Court of California for the County of San Francisco.

To Lee's surprise, the lawsuit barely mentioned him at all. Other than citing his name, age, occupation, and cancer diagnosis, the suit focused on allegations of wrongdoing by Monsanto. The initial filing didn't even mention his accidental dousing. The meat of the fifty-page petition dealt with the years of scientific studies that linked the chemical glyphosate to cancer, IARC's finding of glyphosate as a probable carcinogen, and Monsanto's years of marketing and advertising claims about the safety and efficacy of its products.

Importantly, the allegations, as laid out by the attorneys in the lawsuit, not only blamed Monsanto's herbicide for Lee's cancer but also accused the company of hiding the dangers in order to protect its profits: "Monsanto assured the public that Roundup was harmless. In order to prove this, Monsanto championed falsified data and attacked legitimate studies that revealed its dangers. Monsanto led a prolonged campaign of misinformation to convince government agencies, farmers and the general population that Roundup was safe," the lawsuit stated.

Monsanto, the suit claimed, "risked the lives of consumers and users of its products, including Plaintiff, with knowledge of the safety problems associated with Roundup and glyphosate-containing products, and suppressed this knowledge from the general public."

The company's motive was simple—"to maximize sales and profits" regardless of the cost to the "health and safety of the public," according to the lawsuit.

Lee was not the first to sign up with The Miller Firm. Just a month prior to filing Lee's lawsuit, Mike Miller had joined with a lawyer in Missouri to bring a lawsuit on behalf of a woman named Phyllis Kennedy, whose husband, Van Kennedy, had died of non-Hodgkin lymphoma after using Roundup for years to kill weeds around the couple's property. Much of the language in the Kennedy lawsuit was nearly identical to that in the Johnson lawsuit. Eventually, roughly five thousand Roundup users stricken with non-Hodgkin lymphoma would retain Mike and Nancy's firm to make legal claims against Monsanto. All would claim that Monsanto had worked to suppress scientific evidence of the risks of Roundup and similar herbicides it sold, risking the health, the lives, of its customers.

What Tim didn't tell Lee, but what Tim and everyone else at The Miller Firm knew, was that actually winning a claim against the giant Monsanto corporation was going to require much more than a sympathetic cancer victim who had been doused in Roundup and much more than the IARC cancer classification and the scientific studies it was based on. The lawyers would need to dig deep into what they colloquially referred to as "corporate conduct." Essentially, they would need to find out what Monsanto executives knew about their weed killer's potential link to cancer, and what they did—or did not do—with that knowledge.

That type of research required access to internal corporate records such as emails, product reports, strategic marketing plans, studies conducted by the company's own scientists, and any communications with regulatory agencies responsible for vetting the company's products. If the lawyers were to prove that Monsanto knew its products were dangerous and worked to cover up the risks, they would need to sift through decades of corporate records. They would have to get inside the heads of Monsanto scientists and marketing executives and trace relationships with regulators and lobbyists. Mike Miller and his team wanted to know everything the company knew—and then some. Roundup had been on the market more than forty years, since 1974, so the trail they had to follow was long.

In legalese, the search for information is called "discovery." In reality, the work is less about discovering new information than about digging up long-buried information hidden inside the halls of some of the world's most powerful corporations. In the discovery process, lawyers question witnesses under oath in depositions, submit written questionnaires to the other side, and, perhaps most important, request documents, which the opposing side is then compelled to turn over.

Members of the public often trust that regulators fully understand the risks posed by the products and practices they oversee and that they make sure consumers are warned about those risks. But sadly, Mike and his team knew that was just not the case. An assortment of product liability lawsuits over the past forty years demonstrated that, for a variety of reasons, regulatory oversight had not always been as rigorous as it needs to be. And without an ability to count on regulators for protection from products that carry unseen dangers, consumers too often have had to rely on lawyers, lawsuits, journalists, and the occasional whistleblower to get answers about products that cause illness and death.

The key to unraveling troubling untruths about many public health problems often comes down to revelations found in internal corporate documents. In case after case, the words and deeds of company scientists and executives as memorialized in confidential business records have been critical to holding corporate wrongdoers accountable. It was just such a trove of internal corporate records that pulled back the curtain on many tobacco industry secrets, for instance.

It took a combination of lawsuits brought by cancer victims and the guilty consciences of whistleblowers to expose the internal workings of cigarette makers. One key case was brought by New Jersey resident Rose Cipollone. Cipollone, a smoker, sued three prominent cigarette makers, the Liggett & Myers Tobacco Company, Philip Morris, and the Lorillard

Tobacco Company, in August of 1983, about a year before she died. The case ended up going all the way to the US Supreme Court, which found 7–2 for Cipollone. The justices ruled that even though cigarettes came with certain warnings, individuals could bring claims based on fraudulent or inaccurate statements in company advertising and could pursue damages against companies for conspiring to mislead people about the health hazards of smoking.

In 1994, an anonymous whistleblower leaked thousands of pages of confidential internal documents of the Brown & Williamson Tobacco Corporation, including scientific studies that exposed the addictive qualities of nicotine along with health problems associated with exposure to tobacco smoke. Brown & Williamson, then the third-largest tobacco company in the nation, sought to have the records withheld from public view, but the company was unsuccessful in court and the records ended up posted in a public database maintained by the University of California, San Francisco, and shared in numerous newspaper articles.

Hundreds of lawsuits had been filed by smokers against cigarette makers before the 1980s and 1990s, but the tobacco companies had been able to keep the bulk of their confidential records out of the public view and routinely won those cases. After the release of the internal records, there was an explosion of litigation as lawyers and multiple states sued to hold the industry accountable for the smoking-related illnesses and deaths of hundreds of thousands of Americans. Minnesota officials, in particular, went after the tobacco industry's internal document trove, which eventually helped the state win a settlement of more than $6 billion.

By 1998, roughly thirty-five million pages of formerly secret documents from within seven cigarette makers were part of the public record. The damning documents included letters, memos, and other communications written by corporate scientists, consultants, lawyers, top executives, and other employees. The documents helped attorneys make cases showing that the companies knew tobacco was dangerous but failed to warn the public and even denied the danger existed.

The World Health Organization found the revelations so important that it issued a sixty-page report describing the events as "the story of how a powerful industry was forced by US courts to reveal its internal documents, documents that explain what nine tobacco companies knew, when they knew it and what they concealed from the public about their dangerous product."

Similarly, the Actos litigation that Mike and his firm were involved in helped expose internal secrets held by the Takeda Pharmaceutical Company about the dangers of its diabetes drug. Documents the lawyers obtained through discovery provided evidence that Takeda misled the US Food and Drug Administration (FDA) and the health-care community about the safety of Actos, in part by hiding the side effects seen in clinical trials.

So as The Miller Firm started interviewing potential Roundup cancer plaintiffs, the lawyers knew they had to get their hands on Monsanto's internal files. Companies rarely were happy to turn over what they usually deemed "confidential business information," and some would fight bitterly to keep such records private. But the lawyers also knew that if they could convince a judge that internal communications could help prove allegations of product liability or corporate knowledge of harm, the records would have to be turned over.

Miller's team had already started reading through digitalized documents archived by the US Environmental Protection Agency (EPA) that dated back to the 1970s, and one revelation struck the lawyers immediately as important evidence. They saw that there had been a Monsanto-funded study conducted from 1980 to 1982 in which four hundred mice were divided into groups and given different doses of glyphosate. Some mice received no glyphosate at all, for observation as a control group. The study, which was referred to simply by the surnames of the authors—Knezevich and Hogan—was submitted by Monsanto to the EPA in August of 1983. Monsanto claimed it showed no adverse health effects, but several EPA scientists disagreed. Some of the mice exposed to glyphosate developed rare kidney tumors, while mice that were not given glyphosate did not develop tumors at all.

Eight members of the EPA's toxicology branch had been so worried by the kidney tumors that they stated in a March 1985 internal agency document that they were classifying glyphosate as a Category C oncogen, a substance "possibly carcinogenic to humans." The records showed that Monsanto fought back against the classification and wrestled with EPA officials for the next few years until the agency ultimately sided with Monsanto and made the official finding that glyphosate was "not likely" to be carcinogenic.

The lawyers were astonished—the EPA had known since 1985 that there were some cancer concerns about glyphosate, yet Monsanto and agency officials repeatedly told the public the opposite.

There was something else. As they did the research, the legal team found news reports from the 1970s about a scandal involving a laboratory called Industrial Bio-Test Laboratories (IBT). Three IBT officials were convicted of fraud for submitting false data on substances that showed adverse effects in order to make them appear safe. One of the people convicted was a Monsanto scientist named Paul Wright who left the company to work for IBT at the time it was doing testing for Monsanto. He was then rehired by Monsanto.

Evidence of fraud and deceit—exactly what the plaintiffs were looking for. The EPA documents and the news reports certainly made it appear as though Monsanto had spent many years figuring out ways to hide scientific data that showed its products caused harm and to fight against any science that questioned the safety of its herbicides.

Now the lawyers needed to look inside Monsanto. The Kennedy lawsuit, filed in Missouri, provided the perfect opportunity for The

Miller Firm's lawyers to start asking Monsanto for documents that the firm could then use for all of its plaintiffs' cases. The first order of business was to decide what to ask for. Though they would have liked to search Monsanto's computers and record storage facilities themselves, the law allowed the plaintiffs' attorneys only to give Monsanto a set of search terms and parameters to guide the company in searching for, and turning over, records that met the criteria.

The discovery process is crucial to any case, for both sides. Defendants can ask for private records detailing such things as a plaintiff's medical history, insurance payments, financial status, or other information that they might find useful in countering claims against them.

For Mike and Nancy, as they prepared to tackle Monsanto and the issue of Roundup safety, the first order of business was to call up Mike's friend Art Crivella. Art was a genius in data management and ran a company in Pittsburgh, Pennsylvania, that specialized in "discovery analytics"—taking enormous caches of documents and using artificial intelligence to seek out those most useful to his clients. The Crivella firm was a dream come true for plaintiffs' attorneys such as Mike. Best of all, the documents that went into the Crivella system could be easily shared and searched by teams of attorneys spread around the world. Just one lawsuit could involve millions of pages of documents, far more than a lawyer, or even an entire firm of lawyers, could read through and analyze. Art's system did the work for the lawyers, so for firms like Mike and Nancy's, which handled cases for thousands of plaintiffs, Art's services were essential. Art and Mike had done so much business together over the years that it was not uncommon for Art to be invited to the Millers' Virginia farm, where he joined in family jam sessions, playing drums to Mike's guitar. Like Nancy, Art was a horse lover. He owned six of them, including a polo pony for his teenage son and a trained show jumper for his daughter.

So when Mike and Nancy made the short trip to Washington, DC, for their first meeting with Monsanto's lawyers, they took Art with them. Jeff Travers and Tim Litzenburg also tagged along for the "meet and confer," in which they would make their first request for discovery documents.

Monsanto employed several law firms around the country for different legal projects, but for high-profile matters that required delicate handling, Hollingsworth LLP was the company's first choice. Headquartered in the historic Franklin Square area of the nation's capital, the firm oozed power and prestige, stacked with eighty attorneys who specialized in defending pharmaceutical companies, insurance and financial institutions, and corporations defending against product liability claims.

In a courtroom, the firm's founder, Joe Hollingsworth, cut an imposing figure: he was tall and solemn faced, his mostly bald head was set off by strikingly bushy eyebrows, and he had a focused stare that could rattle an inexperienced opposing counsel. But he also could offer a friendly grin and a warm handshake to friends and courtroom foes alike.

Hollingsworth's ability to win big cases for big clients had kept his name a regular on the annual list of Washington's Super Lawyers. In one notable victory, his firm had secured a controversial win for DynCorp International in a case brought by more than three thousand people from Ecuador. The plaintiffs were farmers who alleged they had been poisoned when DynCorp—acting as a contractor for the US Department of State—sprayed glyphosate-based herbicides on their land from the sky as part of an effort to wipe out drug crops in neighboring Colombia. DynCorp had applied the chemical aerially across tens of thousands of acres of foreign property as part of the program.

The Ecuadorans said that in addition to medical injuries, they had suffered hundreds of millions of dollars in damages because DynCorp's spraying had destroyed crops, killed livestock, and polluted water supplies. But, arguing in federal court in Washington, DC, Hollingsworth and his law firm partners Eric Lasker and Rosemary Stewart were able to beat back the allegations and secure an important victory for DynCorp.

The Hollingsworth firm celebrated the victory, stating, "The Dyn-Corp ruling is a welcome and much needed rebuke to international activist efforts to demonize U.S. industry through unfounded legal actions arising from international operations."

Hollingsworth's legal legend was built over decades of work defending corporations against mass product liability claims. His lengthy client list included a company making hernia repair mesh that was alleged to cause infertility; a chemical company found to have contaminated water supplies in Tennessee through the improper disposal of toxic chemicals; and a pharmaceutical company whose cancer therapy was alleged to cause long-term injuries to patients.

Hollingsworth did not attend that first meeting with the Miller team. It was March 29, 2016, one year after the international cancer scientists' classification, and though several hundred lawsuits were percolating in numerous courts, the cases were not seen as much of a threat.

Monsanto had vehemently rejected the IARC cancer classification for glyphosate and had spent the better part of 2015 working to refute the work of the IARC scientists. The company reminded its detractors that the EPA and regulatory agencies in Europe and elsewhere around the world had found no cancer risk with its herbicides. Monsanto's reputation for product safety was still solidly intact, the company and its attorneys believed.

When Mike, Nancy, and the others arrived at the Hollingsworth firm in Washington and were led into the spacious conference room, the attorney greeting them that day did so with a smile. Rosemary Stewart was the matriarch of the practice, a veteran litigator in her late sixties who was known not only for her sharp legal mind but also for the genuine warmth that she projected.

Stewart had co-led the defense of DynCorp with Eric Lasker, so she was deeply familiar with the history of glyphosate. In winning the DynCorp case, she and Lasker convinced the judge to disqualify the plaintiffs' sole expert witness, who would have testified that the health problems suffered by the Ecuadoran farmers were directly due to the aerial spraying of their properties with glyphosate. Without an expert to make that causal connection for the plaintiffs, Stewart and Lasker won a summary judgment, a hard-to-get ruling meaning the judge found in their favor before the case could be decided by a jury.

At Stewart's side for the meeting with the Miller team was Jim Sullivan, another of the Hollingsworth firm's partners. Sullivan was the firm's specialist in what in legal circles is known as "e-discovery," meaning evidence that existed and could be delivered in electronic format. Paper records have become increasingly limited as people communicate more through email, text messaging, and other electronic means. And, importantly, electronic information is usually accompanied by metadata that can help link records, people, and events together. Knowing how to negotiate the search for, and sharing of, documents for litigation purposes is crucial for both sides.

After politely listening to Mike describe the claims and the evidence his team was requesting from Monsanto, Stewart told the group they were welcome to whatever they needed. Monsanto had nothing to hide. "You're not going to win," she said. "Roundup doesn't cause cancer."

"That's what we're here to find out, Rosemary," Mike said, grinning. "So your client isn't going to mind letting us take a look for ourselves."

Over the course of the next couple of hours, Art laid out the search parameters for the records The Miller Firm was seeking. Art was trained as an economist and a mathematician, and before starting his own firm he had worked for military contractors, helping design guided missile technology. In his mind, words were more than mere expressions of thought; they were pieces of data that held the keys to unlocking corporate secrets. When he was hired for document analysis by a law firm, he told his clients to envision his software as a giant vacuum cleaner sucking up vast quantities of text and then sorting, scanning, and shaping the material into meaningful packages of information. In his work for The Miller Firm, the data would all go into a patented Knowledge Kiosk, an electronic database referred to simply as Crivella, that would receive Monsanto's documents and then analyze them to provide guidance about records that might be most relevant to the case. Art had trained Jeff and other Miller firm attorneys how to delve into the database to pull out what they needed, and he had secure systems in place so they could easily share them back and forth. His work didn't come cheap. Art's typical fee for help on a case was in the millions of dollars. But he had proven the value of his system in hundreds of other court cases, working for both defense and plaintiffs' law firms. Mike didn't blink an eye at the cost.

Art's company had handled about 170 million pages of information while working for lawyers involved in a medical device product liability case, so Art was confident he could handle Monsanto's forty-year history with Roundup. The initial search inside Monsanto's records would encompass about one million keywords and was likely to produce between sixteen million and twenty million pages of records, Art told the Hollingsworth lawyers.

The Miller Firm's attorneys already had a stack of scientific studies that showed cancer links to glyphosate, to Monsanto's glyphosate-based formulation, or to both, that had been published in various medical and scientific journals over the years. And they knew about the 1983 mouse study and the IBT fraud.

They also knew what the company's public messaging around these issues looked like; what The Miller Firm wanted from Monsanto in discovery was to see if its public declarations matched its private communications. The plaintiffs' lawyers wanted—needed—to see how the company's executives and scientists reacted to cancer warnings; the extent of their own testing of their products; how and what they communicated to regulators; and what real basis they had for their rock-hard public assurances that their products were safe.

The records the Miller team sought included emails between those executives and scientists, public relations reports, and notes from employees about any schmoozing with the EPA and lawmakers. Even PowerPoint presentations and text messages from employees' cell phones would eventually be included in the discovery documents.

Stewart and Sullivan agreed that Monsanto would start producing documents right away and that the initial wave of documents would include the files of five employees involved in the safety assessments of glyphosate: Donna Farmer, a senior toxicologist at Monsanto; Steve Adams, regulatory affairs manager for the company's chemical business; Dan Goldstein, a company scientist involved in "outreach" to the public; William Heydens, chief of regulatory science; and toxicologist David Saltmiras. The request for their files extended to any of their assistants or "deputies." Importantly, The Miller Firm's lawyers also asked for the names of fifty-two employees Monsanto had internally interviewed about the litigation matters.

Jeff laid out the terms of the discovery demand in a follow-up letter The Miller Firm sent to Monsanto's lawyers after the meeting:

We agreed that Monsanto will begin providing us an initial production of documents within 30 days from clearly relevant sources including: 1) EPA registration files; 2) Scientific Studies and Articles related to the safety and efficacy of glyphosate; 3) Roundup Labels; 4) Material Safety Data Sheets; 5) corporation communications regarding glyphosate.

The team wanted to make sure the files specifically included records that dealt with Monsanto's marketing of its Roundup and other glyphosate-based herbicide products. But Stewart and Sullivan balked at that. They argued that marketing information was not relevant to the question of whether or not the product could cause cancer. They told Mike and the others that they would ask the court to bifurcate any trial, meaning they would ask that the plaintiffs prove Monsanto's products caused cancer before delving further into allegations that Monsanto might have known about and hidden cancer risks.

The Monsanto attorneys had another bit of bad news. They informed Mike and his team that Monsanto officials had not felt the need to keep all of the company's old emails, and therefore many that the Miller team wanted could have been destroyed. The company had placed a "litigation hold" to retain documents only after the filing of the first Roundup lawsuit a few months prior, they explained.

Mike was angry but not necessarily surprised. He expected Monsanto to put up a fight, despite Stewart's pleasant demeanor. Trying to bifurcate the case was a slick move, he realized. If Monsanto could keep out evidence that it had tried to hide unfavorable research and present its own scientific studies showing no cancer risks to counter the ones that did show cancer risks, the company might be able to create enough doubt with judges and juries to stop the lawsuits in their tracks.

The courts would have to sort out the question of bifurcation, but right now Mike wanted his hands on whatever internal records he could get. Both sides agreed that The Miller Firm's attorneys could request more as they became more familiar with the internal workings of Monsanto.

Both sides knew that discovery was a process much like pulling on a thread. With each slight unraveling, more can be seen through the thick shroud that often keeps corporate secrets hidden from public view. Companies often try to fight discovery requests, arguing that internal conversations and strategy discussions are confidential. But both sides also knew that those arguments rarely worked with a judge if a case was deemed valid enough to proceed to discovery.

That day, as the Miller team laid out their request, Monsanto's lawyers appeared to be thoroughly unfazed. Aside from the unwarranted digging around in the company's confidential marketing programs, Mike's discovery request was no problem, Stewart reiterated. The company was an open book.

Sitting at the conference table with the group, Jeff watched the proceedings but said little, quietly taking notes on a lined yellow legal pad. He tried not to show any emotion, but he was stunned. It was clear to him that Monsanto's attorneys had no idea of the magnitude of the legal battle that lay ahead.

Art also was astonished by the casual confidence of the Monsanto attorneys. "They don't seem to know what's coming, do they?" he said to Mike after the meeting.

It took only a few weeks for the first run of the discovery production to churn through the Crivella analysis. Jeff had been trained on the Crivella system to run his own searches, so he could sift and sort through the documents the system pointed him to. Reading through that first series, he could see the case starting to take shape. He printed out a bundle and hurried to Mike's office.

"You're going to want to see these," he said, laying the stack on Mike's desk.

As he started flipping through the pages, Mike began to grin, and then the grin grew wider. They didn't just have a case—they had a big case. It was going to be a case that called for punitive damages, tens of millions, maybe hundreds of millions, of dollars, he calculated quickly. Monsanto might not think its paper trail carried liability, but in Mike's eyes these Monsanto papers showed a corporate culture that lacked any real concern for its customers, prioritizing instead the dollars that were rolling into the company in profits. If Mike and his legal team could get these records in front of a jury, the company would have a very hard time defending what looked like decades of deceptive messaging about the safety of its weed killers.

Some of the emails dated back more than a decade; others were recent. Mike could see that the company had been dealing with many concerns about glyphosate and Roundup not just since the IARC classification but back to the early 1980s.

There were emails discussing concerns about the presence of formaldehyde in Roundup, as well as another cancer-causing substance referred to as N-nitroso. There were also emails about the company's disappointment when a scientific expert who had been brought in to help the company counter outside studies showing that glyphosate-based products could cause cell mutation did not come up with the solid defense Monsanto had hoped for. It appeared to Mike, as he read through a series of the emails, that the scientist, a mutagenicity expert named James Parry, had other concerns about the company's products and had recommended that the company undertake new studies to get a better idea of the risks. The emails appeared to show that Monsanto did not want to do those studies.

"We simply aren't going to do the studies that Parry suggests," Monsanto toxicologist William Heydens wrote in a 1999 email. In other emails, Mike could see that the company instead focused on seeking out a different expert who could be "influential with regulators."

One email that immediately caught Mike's attention had been written in November of 2003 by Donna Farmer, the manager of Monsanto's toxicology program and the scientist responsible for the company's glyphosate-based products worldwide. She was responding to correspondence from India in which Monsanto employees reported growing concern about Roundup use. The India team wanted guidance on what reassuring messages they could deliver to tamp down what they referred to as "agitation."

And there, in that one email, Mike could see a gaping hole in Monsanto's public assertions that Roundup was proven safe. He read it again slowly. Monsanto scientist Donna Farmer was explaining to her colleagues that an important distinction existed between glyphosate and the branded formulations, which contained mixtures of glyphosate and other chemical agents. "For example you cannot say that Roundup is not a carcinogen . . . we have not done the necessary testing on the formulation to make that statement. The testing on the formulations are not anywhere near the level of the active ingredient," she wrote.

It was only one email, but Mike knew there would be more gold to dig out of the discovery database, which was growing by the day. For Lee Johnson, and the scores of others stricken with cancer who were filing lawsuits, Mike saw these papers as the leverage they needed. They were going to make Monsanto pay.

CHAPTER 4
Joining Forces

The Miller Firm's lawyers were not the only attorneys seeing the potential for large-scale litigation against Monsanto. Others who specialized in drug and medical device litigation also recognized a disturbing familiarity in the emerging Roundup cancer concern. They had seen many products long heralded as safe by companies and regulators later turn out to be not just unsafe but deadly.

In Denver, thirty-nine-year-old attorney Aimee Wagstaff and her law firm partner Vance Andrus already had their hands full with cases ranging from lawsuits against makers of talcum powder, suspected of causing ovarian cancer, to injury claims brought by thousands of women who received vaginal mesh implants to treat incontinence. Aimee had not followed the quiet buildup of years of troubling scientific studies linking Monsanto's herbicides to cancer, but news that the International Agency for Research on Cancer (IARC) had classified the weed-killing chemical as a probable human carcinogen got her attention. She wanted in on what she was certain would be big litigation.

Though they were business partners, Vance and Aimee could not have been more different. Vance was approaching seventy years of age and was in every way a creature of his Cajun roots. He had spent most of his life and legal career in the Deep South of Louisiana before moving to Denver to be close to his adult son Cameron, who was also an attorney. Vance relished hosting dinnertime roundtables of young lawyers during which he regaled them with stories of legal battles won and lost and of the injustices he saw growing up in the racially divided South. And he had notched enough victory laps in his legal career to allow himself frequent leisurely vacations with his wife.

In contrast, Aimee was still making a name for herself as a "products and pills girl" in the national network of plaintiffs' attorneys. She was known for a competitive streak and a brutal take-no-prisoners attitude that regularly had her pushing hundred-hour workweeks preparing for and trying cases. It was not uncommon for her to leave her longtime companion and the home they shared for weeks at a time as she pursued a case.

In a courtroom, Aimee's broad smile and neat brunette bob gave her an approachable, friendly air that often helped her win the trust of jurors, and her restrained and respectful demeanor was appreciated by the judges she faced. When dressing for court, she favored long skirts and dark jackets, in keeping with a conservative appearance. But outside the courtroom, Aimee preferred jeans or sweats to business suits, rarely wore makeup, and often laced even casual conversations with strings of raw profanity and dark humor. She was bighearted and loyal to a fault to friends, family, and coworkers, but she was also known as the kind of woman not to mess with. She kept a black gag gift "Fuck" button on her desk that loudly brayed out various salty phrases when pushed. And atop a bookcase laden with black binders, Aimee kept a bottle of Don Julio tequila. Vance liked to describe his much younger law partner as fearless, with a "constitutional inability to kiss ass."

Aimee had grown up in a sleepy, upscale suburb of Kansas City with a schoolteacher mother and a father who ran his own law firm.

Her grandfather had also been an attorney, and her brother was also pursuing a legal career. But from the time she was a child, Aimee had balked at following a prescribed path—defying her parents' attempts to set curfews and spending countless Saturdays in school detentions for flouting classroom rules. She was a straight-A student but one who constantly sought to challenge the system. She once led a sit-in at her junior high school to protest the poor fare on the school lunch menu. After college, where she was a standout scholarship soccer player, Aimee worked for two years as a sailing instructor at resorts in Florida and in Cancun, Mexico, rather than immediately jumping into law school, as her family expected. But once she had her law license in hand, Aimee found she had a passion for the work as long as she was taking on controversial cases and seeking justice for people she believed to have been wronged. And even as she maintained a caseload that left her with little free time, Aimee hosted an annual retreat in Aspen as a forum for women involved in mass tort litigation to network, mentor one another, and enjoy a bit of a break from the grind with group hikes and cocktail parties. She called her organization Women En Mass.

Like the attorneys at The Miller Firm, Aimee had never worked on a case involving Monsanto or pesticides, but she had helped lead three nationwide cases consolidated in what in legal jargon is known as multidistrict litigation (MDL), which had collectively garnered more than $200 million in jury verdicts and more than $1 billion in settlements. MDLs are structured to allow cases around the United States to be joined together for the purposes of discovery and pretrial proceedings, but in contrast with class action suits, each case has its own trial. Aimee was particularly proud to have helped lead an MDL brought on behalf of women who had been diagnosed with a deadly form of cancer after undergoing gynecology surgeries involving a tool that was found to spread cancerous tissue in the body rather than excising it as intended.

It was a winter day, and Aimee was ensconced in the firm's cavernous conference room, poring over research about Monsanto and its long history as a purveyor of chemicals, when she saw a notice of Mike Miller's first case filing, the Kennedy lawsuit he had brought in Missouri. The notice caught her by surprise; she had not expected The Miller Firm's fast entry. Aimee's friend and fellow mass tort attorney Robin Greenwald of the New York City firm Weitz & Luxenberg had just filed a similar case, and the two women had already agreed to join forces in what they expected would become a large Roundup MDL. Like Aimee, Robin was a highly regarded attorney—she was former assistant chief of the US Department of Justice's Environmental Crimes Section. Robin had honed her skills suing petroleum companies for environmental contamination, but she had no experience in the world of farm chemicals and pesticides.

Aimee knew Mike and Nancy Miller from crossing paths with them on medical device litigation, and she quickly gave Mike a call, explaining that she was planning to move for MDL status for the Roundup litigation and would like his firm to be part of the team she thought would be necessary to take on Monsanto. There was power in numbers, and even though Aimee had never litigated against Monsanto, she felt intuitively that it would take the top legal skills of many seasoned plaintiffs' attorneys working in concert to win against the century-old company.

Roundup brought in roughly $4 billion a year in sales for Monsanto and was the linchpin to so-called Roundup Ready seeds, which the company had genetically engineered so that crops such as corn and soybeans would not die when hit with Monsanto's herbicides, though any weeds threatening to crowd the crops would die. The special crops were a hit with farmers and amounted to many more billions of dollars in sales each year for Monsanto. Additionally, the company marketed its glyphosate-based weed killers to farmers to spray on non–genetically engineered crops such as wheat and oats shortly before harvest to help dry them out. Both practices were known to leave weed killer residues in the food made from the sprayed crops. If the public understood that Monsanto's herbicide could cause cancer, regulators would be called upon to limit its use, and Monsanto's herbicide and seed businesses could be decimated.

This was not just one product, Aimee realized. This was Monsanto's billion-dollar baby, and she knew the company would do whatever it could to fight to keep it. "We are taking on their biggest product," she told Mike. "We need to work together."

Unaware of the strategy being plotted by Aimee, Mike, and Robin, Los Angeles attorney Michael Baum was doing his own research on the potential for Roundup litigation. But he wasn't looking at cancer; he was looking at butterflies. There was mounting evidence that widespread Roundup use was contributing to a marked decline in the monarch butterfly population, and environmental scientists were warning that the monarch could disappear almost entirely by 2036. He wasn't sure, but Michael thought there might be a lawsuit in the situation.

He did not really need a new case to chase. Michael was managing partner of Baum Hedlund Aristei & Goldman, a firm so large it sprawled across the ninth and tenth floors of a Wilshire Boulevard office building, and he was on the back side of a career that had brought him wealth as well as the respect of his peers in the plaintiffs' bar. He was sixty-three, drove a Jaguar, and owned a home in the tony beach community of Malibu, and when he was not working he often could be found trying to balance his lean five-foot-eleven frame on a boogie board in the ocean. He liked to match dark business suits with colorful striped socks, and underneath the cuffs of his crisp white dress shirts Michael wore couplets of braided leather bracelets more commonly seen on surfers than on lawyers.

His office was a reflection of the fact that Michael was one part harried lawyer and one part aging hippie. Asian artwork, including a praying

Buddha sculpture, was scattered among the furnishings, as were books and postcards from exotic travels. A faded leather sofa sat underneath floor-to-ceiling windows that offered a view of waving palm trees and a hint of the distant ocean. One entire wall of Michael's office was covered with framed certificates of recognition, including a National Association of Distinguished Counsel certificate ranking Michael among the "Top One Percent" of members. Another touted both his legal skills and his ethics. A University of California law diploma, as well as his undergraduate English degree diploma, hung near a framed sign that read, "In every job that must be done there is an element of fun." A dartboard affixed to the back of his office door offered distraction from the stacks of legal files surrounding his long, black glass-topped desk.

Baum Hedlund's focus was on representing people with personal injury and wrongful death claims, primarily stemming from pharmaceutical product dangers and commercial transportation accidents—aviation disasters were the firm's specialty. Pesticide problems, such as Roundup's danger to monarch butterflies, would be new territory for the firm, and it wasn't clear who the plaintiffs would be. But Michael believed that practicing law came with a larger duty. He described his view to outsiders as striving to "make money delivering blows against the empire" in whatever form that came.

On the wall just outside his office hung a large framed quote from anthropologist Margaret Mead: "Never doubt that a small group of thoughtful, committed citizens can change the world. Indeed, it is the only thing that ever has."

In his quest to explore how his firm might help save the butterfly, Michael had been working closely with one of Baum Hedlund's newest and youngest attorneys, Brent Wisner. Brent was the son of a longtime family friend and had been contemplating joining a corporate defense firm before Michael lured him to join the plaintiffs' side instead.

Brent was barely thirty years old and still new to the profession after earning a law degree at Georgetown University and clerking for two years for a federal court judge in Hawaii. He had grown up in Topanga, a community situated in the Santa Monica Mountains between Los Angeles and Malibu, known as an enclave for a bohemian lifestyle and populated by artists, filmmakers, and musicians. Brent's father was a screenwriter, and as a child Brent had tried his hand at acting, an experience that made him adept at working a courtroom much as if it were a stage. In Michael's eyes, Brent was the epitome of the "Topangan" legend, someone who cared about more than personal success, who shared his desire to use the law in pursuit of the sort of justice that lived up to the Margaret Mead credo.

It was late October of 2015 when Robin McCall, a slender blonde who managed Baum Hedlund's public affairs office, approached Michael and Brent about a relative who was dying of non-Hodgkin lymphoma. Anthony "Jack" McCall, a second cousin to Robin's husband, was sixty-nine years old and had been diagnosed with a rare and aggressive form of the disease. Doctors had told the family Jack might not live very long, and as they wrestled with their grief, Jack's wife, Teri, and son Paul began searching for answers about the cause of the disease. When they read the news about the IARC link between the weed-killing agent in Roundup and non-Hodgkin lymphoma, they were sure the weed killer had to be the culprit. Jack had sprayed Roundup regularly for years throughout the orchards on his farm. He hadn't used any other pesticides and had only felt comfortable using Roundup because it was advertised as being very safe. Before Jack was diagnosed, the family dog, which had romped beside Jack as he sprayed, had died of cancer. Now Jack was sick. Very sick.

Jack and Teri called Robin one day, as they were driving to one of Jack's many hospital appointments, to ask whether anyone in the big Los Angeles law firm where she worked would consider representing them in a lawsuit against Monsanto. Robin knew that Michael and Brent had been researching Monsanto's weed killer, and she took the information to them. The two attorneys were aware of the IARC classification and knew there were lawyers around the country examining the litigation potential. But they did not know how much or how strong the evidence might be against Monsanto. They would have to do more research.

Jack died the day after Christmas in 2015, and an anguished Teri pushed again for Robin's help in finding an attorney. Brent and Michael still were not sure there was a case to be made, so Robin sought help elsewhere, trying to find a firm that would take Teri's wrongful death claim. Teri could not find any California firm willing to take the case.

Until Michael talked to Mike Miller. The two lawyers knew each other from work on the Actos litigation, and once Michael learned that The Miller Firm was building a case against Monsanto, he felt pulled to join in. Taking on Monsanto over one of its top-selling products would be hard for one firm alone, but combined forces might just have a chance. If they could pull it off, beating Monsanto would likely make history in the annals of plaintiffs' law, and it might just serve up a bit of that global justice Michael always pined for. Michael decided the butterflies would have to wait. He called Brent into his office and told him to go ahead and sign Teri as a client.

Short and baby-faced with bright bluish-green eyes, Brent looked even younger than he was and, when not working a courtroom, often came across more as a good-natured fraternity brother than an experienced litigator. He had been captain of the sailing team during his undergraduate years at the University of California, Los Angeles, and though he had lost some of the solidness of an athlete in the ensuing years, he maintained a charisma that caused friends and strangers alike to see him as a leader—someone they could, or should, trust. And those who knew Brent well understood that once he set his mind to a task, it was virtually impossible to deter him. On March 9, 2016, Brent filed *Teri Michelle McCall v. Monsanto Company*. The Baum Hedlund firm was officially on the Roundup case.

Neither Brent nor Michael was familiar with the details of Lee Johnson's story, but they knew Mike had filed Lee's lawsuit just a few hours' drive north of them, in San Francisco, two months prior. Mike let Michael know he had a meeting with Monsanto's lawyers coming up at the end of March. They should probably meet before then and start to craft a plan of attack. The ball was rolling, and there was no time to waste.

With Michael and Brent on the West Coast and Mike and Nancy and their team on the East Coast, it made the most sense to meet in the middle, so they all gathered in Denver at Aimee and Vance's firm for two days of strategizing about who would take which depositions, how to coordinate and share document reviews, and how best to shepherd the several thousand potential cases they believed were inevitable. Aimee's colleague Robin Greenwald flew in from New York to round out the group.

They were an unlikely and eclectic team—a combination of LA flash, New York sophistication, Southern stubbornness, and midwestern salt of the earth. None had any experience with the pesticide industry, and none had ever challenged Monsanto, a company known for its ruthlessness in legal matters.

But they all were standouts in the plaintiffs' bar, and by joining forces they thought they had a good shot at winning enough cases to at least cover their costs and possibly secure damages for some of the many cancer victims, such as Lee Johnson, who believed their lives had been shortened because of Monsanto's products. It remained to be seen if they had the skills, the brains, and—most important—the evidence to take on one of the world's biggest chemical and seed corporations.

~

The next few months became a blur of filing new cases, juggling deposition schedules and document reviews, and keeping up with court filings and hearings. And though the litigation was still relatively new, the team was starting to realize that they were not dealing with a typical opponent. Monsanto seemed to have one trick after another up its sleeve, and lawyers suspected that the US Environmental Protection Agency (EPA) was working to help Monsanto in its defense.

Their concerns mounted in late April of 2016 when an eighty-seven-page report appeared unexpectedly on the EPA's website. Titled "Glyphosate—Report of the Cancer Assessment Review Committee," it was signed by a longtime EPA official named Jess Rowland and concluded that glyphosate, the active ingredient in Monsanto's herbicides, was "Not Likely to be Carcinogenic to Humans." The report flatly contradicted the IARC conclusion that glyphosate was probably carcinogenic.

The timing was excellent, as Monsanto had key court hearings coming up in the litigation. And even more importantly, Monsanto executives had started negotiating a potential $64 billion sale to the German pharmaceutical giant Bayer AG and needed all the help they could get to reassure Bayer executives that the mounting Roundup litigation was going nowhere.

The document appeared on the EPA's website on Friday, April 29, but was pulled down and disappeared from public view by the following Monday with an apology. The agency said the document was not final and should not have been posted. It would not say who had posted it or why.

Despite the quick withdrawal, Monsanto issued a press release about the report, presented it in court hearings held that month, and touted it as evidence that the litigation had no merit. Monsanto's chief technology officer, Robb Fraley, tweeted to his several thousand Twitter followers, "This is the EPA's highest ranking for product safety—they also do nice job of explaining all of IARC's mistakes."

Monsanto's chairman and chief executive officer, Hugh Grant, made an even bolder statement:

> *No pesticide regulator in the world considers glyphosate to be a carcinogen, and this conclusion by the U.S. EPA once again reinforces*

this important fact. Glyphosate has a 40-year history of safe and effective use. Unfortunately, last year's inconsistent classification by IARC generated unwarranted concern and confusion about this important agricultural tool. This rigorous assessment of the data by EPA builds on the sound conclusions of both the European and Canadian regulatory authorities and once again makes it clear that glyphosate does not cause cancer.

The legal team was caught off guard by the surprise boost of unofficial EPA support for Monsanto, and they found it noteworthy that shortly after the mysterious leak of the cancer assessment report headed by Jess Rowland, Rowland left the EPA for retirement. They couldn't prove it, but they felt certain the leak had been no accident. Monsanto had friends in high places and had no reservations about calling on them for help.

~

By the summer of 2016, dozens of lawsuits had been filed by at least ten different firms in what the attorneys dubbed "Roundup Products Liability Litigation." All were brought on behalf of cancer victims, some still struggling with the disease as Lee was, and others who had already lost the battle, such as Jack McCall. And all accused Monsanto not just of having information that its Roundup and other glyphosate-based herbicides caused cancer but also of intentionally covering up the risks in order to protect sales.

Many of the claims were filed in courts within the St. Louis, Missouri, metropolitan area because of the proximity to Monsanto's corporate headquarters in the St. Louis suburb of Creve Coeur. Though it was essentially Monsanto's hometown, there was no home turf advantage in the eyes of the plaintiffs' attorneys. The city of St. Louis was known in legal circles as a hot spot for product liability and personal injury litigation, in part because of demographics that included a large low-income African American population, simmering racial tensions, and blue-collar resentment of corporate wealth that never seemed to trickle down quite far enough. Plaintiffs' attorneys saw Missouri and St. Louis in particular as one of the best places in the nation for landing speedy trials and massive jury awards. From a corporate defense view, St. Louis was a judicial hellhole that companies tried to steer clear of in litigation. As the Roundup litigation was building, St. Louis was already awash in lawsuits brought by people from around the United States alleging that asbestos exposure had caused them to suffer from mesothelioma, a cancer affecting the lining of the lungs and heart.

An oddity of Missouri law allowed out-of-state plaintiffs to combine their claims with those of local plaintiffs, and Mike and the rest of the team quickly determined they should direct as many cases as possible to the state. Another benefit would be the ability to subpoena Monsanto executives to testify at trial. The attorneys had little power to force witnesses to appear for a deposition or trial if it was far away from where the witnesses lived or worked. And while they could certainly travel to Monsanto to depose company officials ahead of trial, there would be no way to require them to be at trial unless the trials were held in Missouri.

In addition to the cases already filed, each of the four firms had several hundred more plaintiffs signed, some in state courts and some in federal. For the federal cases, the team determined it made sense to formally establish an MDL. A class action suit wouldn't work. Each plaintiff had developed non-Hodgkin lymphoma, yes, but different plaintiffs had different types of the cancer and had been exposed to different Monsanto products in different ways over different periods. An MDL would allow for many of the cases to be grouped together for the pretrial work and still provide for individual trials or trials in small groups.

Setting up a Roundup MDL required a hearing before the United States Judicial Panel on Multidistrict Litigation (JPML) in Washington, DC. The team filed their motion for consolidation on July 27, 2016, laying out a detailed argument asking that the MDL be established and assigned to a federal judge. The MDL would not handle all the cases; many would remain in state courts. But an MDL would allow the lawyers to streamline their gathering of evidence, taking and sharing of depositions, and other important and time-consuming activities that have to take place before a trial.

In a motion Aimee drafted to make the case for an MDL, she pointed out that because Monsanto was claiming there was no evidence at all that its herbicide caused cancer, the plaintiffs' lawyers needed broad pretrial discovery of Monsanto records. It did not make sense for the different individual plaintiffs to have to make separate requests for the same records from the company when one joint discovery effort would be more efficient.

Monsanto, Aimee told the panel, was resisting releasing all of the internal records the plaintiffs wanted, and there should be one federal judge in charge of ruling on the discovery demands to avoid a mishmash of different rulings by different judges in different courts. The Southern District of Illinois was the perfect venue for an MDL, she wrote in her motion. The courthouse sits a mere twenty miles from Monsanto's headquarters, and the proximity would give plaintiffs subpoena power over Monsanto executives to force them to testify at trial. Also, the venue would allow for easy coordination, she argued, of the numerous lawsuits filed in the state courts in neighboring Missouri.

Each of the lawyers had a different idea about the best place for an MDL. Mike suggested to the court that Hawaii might be a good location. Brent suggested Los Angeles, where the Baum Hedlund firm was based and where Teri McCall's lawsuit and others were pending.

The one place Aimee and the rest of the plaintiffs' legal team did *not* want the MDL to be located was in the Northern District of California, in front of Judge Vince Chhabria. Chhabria had never overseen multidistrict litigation before, and two lawsuits already filed there were not going the plaintiffs' way. One of the cases in front of Chhabria was brought by a man named Edwin Hardeman, who had been diagnosed with non-Hodgkin lymphoma after using Roundup for twenty-six years to control weeds and poison oak on property he and his wife owned in Sonoma County, California. The other was brought by Elaine Stevick of Petaluma, California, who was diagnosed in 2014 at the age of sixty-three with multiple brain tumors. Elaine blamed her repeated use of Roundup on an overgrown property she and her husband spent years renovating for her cancer.

Monsanto had asked Chhabria to sharply limit the types of documents the plaintiffs' lawyers could make Monsanto hand over as part of pretrial discovery, and Chhabria had agreed. He sided with Monsanto's argument that until and unless plaintiffs could show solid evidence that Roundup caused cancer, the company should not have to share internal records or answer questions about other matters, such as its marketing and media strategies. It was Chhabria's position that discovery at this early stage should focus on studies and data Monsanto possessed involving any health issues associated with its herbicides, and little more. The plaintiffs' attorneys believed that the evidence that might resonate most with a jury would not be dry discussions of the statistical significance of data and scientific theories on such things as genotoxicity, but evidence of deceptive intent. They had already seen enough to feel certain they had only scratched the surface of Monsanto's secrets.

To make their case in person, Aimee, Robin, Brent, and Mike traveled to Washington, DC, to appear before the seven-member judicial panel. Each was allowed to address the judges, who were clad in formal black robes, for no more than six minutes.

What they wanted the judges to see was that although there were currently about two dozen lawsuits filed in fourteen different federal district courts by ten different law firms, the number would quickly become unwieldy because more cases were in preparation. Already, chaos was developing as disputes between plaintiffs and Monsanto were receiving conflicting rulings from different judges in different venues.

"It doesn't make any sense for dozens and dozens of districts around the country to have to wrestle with these legal issues over and over again," Robin told the panel. Along with the Southern District of Illinois, the Central District of California was another good option for placing the MDL, she said.

"We really are not opposed to any of the districts which our plaintiffs' counsel are recommending today," she said. "Roundup is ubiquitous in the United States, around the world actually."

And though she didn't say it directly, Robin tried to get the message about Chhabria across—the plaintiffs' trial team was fine with an MDL established almost anywhere, as long as it was not with Chhabria.

His decision to allow what was referred to as a bifurcation of the evidence was not appropriate, Robin told the panel, and several other judges had ruled differently in other pending Roundup lawsuits. "We believe that this case should really go to a judge that will look at this issue anew."

Monsanto didn't agree that centralization was needed at all. Joe Hollingsworth, head of the Washington, DC, firm representing Monsanto, explained the company's position in a lengthy filing to the judicial panel explaining that there were too many individual facts that would differ from plaintiff to plaintiff, including what formulation of Roundup each person had used, to make an MDL useful. Hollingsworth suggested the parties could simply work cooperatively with "informal" coordination to keep the multitude of cases moving forward.

Monsanto was already providing internal records related to the question of whether or not Roundup could cause cancer, and other matters, he told the panel. The company had recently turned over 2.8 million company documents to Miller and other members of the plaintiffs' legal team, a sign of how cooperative the company intended to be, he said.

If an MDL was formed, it would merely "derail" and slow the litigation, not speed it up, according to Hollingsworth. The current tally of twenty-five federal lawsuits was easily manageable without an MDL, and even the assertion by the plaintiffs that thousands of additional cases would eventually be filed against Monsanto over the Roundup cancer claims did not change the company's position that no centralization was needed.

Hollingsworth also laid out a bit of Monsanto's defense to the panel, telling the judges that IARC's classification of glyphosate as a probable carcinogen was not going to be strong enough evidence for plaintiffs to win their cases. IARC was not a regulatory agency, and its classification was not supported by any regulatory agency, including the EPA.

"IARC has classified a variety of everyday substances and exposures as 'probable' or 'known' carcinogens, including bacon, hot dogs, and red meat; alcoholic and certain hot beverages; salted fish; shift work; and frying food," he told the panel.

Covering his bases, Hollingsworth said if the panel did decide an MDL was in order, Monsanto wanted it set up in the Northern District of California with Chhabria, precisely because of Chhabria's "extraordinary" ruling to separate and limit the evidence.

The plaintiffs' desire to have the MDL in Illinois was a bad idea, he said. The judges in the southern district of the state were not familiar with the issues in the litigation because cases had only recently been filed there. Plus, he pointed out, the judges there were already burdened with stacks of unrelated cases to manage, and nearly 40 percent of the district's civil cases were over three years old and still unresolved. If there had to be an MDL, Chhabria and the Northern District of California were the best choices, Hollingsworth told the panel.

After considering the arguments for and against, the JPML panel members agreed with Hollingsworth and Monsanto, ruling that Judge Chhabria and the Northern District of California were the best choices, given Chhabria's handling so far of the two cases pending there.

"The Northern District of California is both convenient and easily accessible for all parties, and we are convinced that the district has the necessary judicial resources and expertise to efficiently manage this litigation," the panel's chair, US District Judge Sarah Vance, wrote in an order transferring twenty-one cases to the new MDL. "Furthermore, centralization in this district allows us to assign this litigation to the Honorable Vince Chhabria, a skilled jurist who has not yet had the opportunity to preside over an MDL."

The forty-six-year-old Chhabria had a stellar record. Born and raised in California, he obtained his law degree in 1998 from the University of California, Berkeley, School of Law, graduating with honors. He had served as a law clerk for two federal judges and for US Supreme Court Justice Stephen Breyer and worked as an associate for two law firms before joining the office of the City Attorney of San Francisco. He worked there from 2005 to 2013, when he was nominated by President Barack Obama for the federal bench.

Still, the decision to turn the Roundup MDL over to him was a blow. Aimee, Mike, and the rest of the team worried about Chhabria's oversight. It was not just his rulings on evidence that bothered them. He had never handled an MDL before, a particularly challenging task. And, more worrisome, early in his career Chhabria had worked as an associate for a law firm named Covington & Burling, known as a powerful and politically connected defender of a variety of corporate interests, including Monsanto.

Covington & Burling was perhaps best recognized for its zealous work on behalf of the tobacco industry. In 1997, a judge in Minnesota found that lawyers at the firm had willfully disregarded court orders to turn over certain documents pertaining to claims that the tobacco industry had engaged in a forty-year conspiracy to mislead the public about the health impacts of smoking and to hide damaging scientific research from public view. Shortly before Obama selected Chhabria for his federal judgeship, an array of former Covington & Burling attorneys took spots in the administration, including Attorney General Eric Holder and Deputy Chief of Staff Daniel Suleiman. Chhabria's stint at Covington & Burling had been more than a decade before he became a federal judge, but the connection made the plaintiffs' attorneys uneasy.

~

It wouldn't matter who the judge was if the evidence was not strong enough to make a compelling case that Monsanto was in fact to blame for the suffering of so many cancer victims. Each plaintiff's case would hinge on what the lawyers could uncover from years of obscure scientific studies, decades of archived regulatory files, and the company's internal records.

By this time, the discovery database Mike had set up with Art Crivella was opened up to Aimee, Robin, Brent, and several other lawyers at the lead firms, including Jeff Travers and Tim Litzenburg, so they all could pore through the records as they built their case strategies. Individualized icons distinguished various folders. One folder was identified with the icon of a skeleton clad in a black shroud. The shrouded figure was lettered with the name Monsanto.

Though Chhabria was limiting the evidence in the federal court cases, that was not the situation with the state proceedings. Monsanto was compelled to turn over many types of records, not only those that dealt with experiments and scientific analysis of potential cancer ties to its herbicides but also documents related to its interactions with regulators and outside scientists and its public relations tactics. Many of the records Monsanto turned over were mundane—discussions of routine meetings, plans for product testing, and regulatory submissions. But some were, in the eyes of the plaintiffs' lawyers, jaw-dropping evidence of the type of corporate conduct that could enrage a jury. The legal team felt certain, just as Mike had when he first laid eyes on the document trove, that Monsanto's own words would be the company's undoing.

In addition to communications about the lack of cancer testing on formulations such as Roundup, there were emails discussing concerns about an ingredient in Monsanto's Roundup products that was linked to tumor promotion in some of the company's own studies. There were emails discussing how to overturn the 1980s-era EPA finding that glyphosate was possibly carcinogenic due to the large study that showed tumors developing in mice exposed to glyphosate but no tumors in mice that were not exposed. There were emails in which Monsanto employees analyzed studies done by international scientists that found potential health problems tied to Monsanto herbicides, and laid out plans to counter those studies to avoid any loss of sales.

Tim and Jeff spent more time than the others trolling through the database. They were astonished to see language that suggested the company was not just countering negative information reported by independent studies but was actually trying to secretly infiltrate scientific journals with favorable studies promoting the safety of its herbicides. These papers appeared to be written by authors who were independent of the company, but Monsanto's emails showed they actually were written at least in part by company scientists.

Tim and Jeff saw one email string as particularly outrageous. In it, Monsanto scientist William Heydens discussed a plan to write scientific journal articles to refute IARC's glyphosate classification. Heydens told colleagues that they could "ghost-write" specific sections. As Jeff read the words, his eyes widened. The email went on. Heydens explained how the ghostwriting would work, suggesting to his colleagues that they could pay third-party scientists to "have their names on the publication," but Monsanto would actually be "doing the writing." The outside scientists would "just edit & sign their names so to speak," Heydens wrote.

In the same email, Heydens pointed out that Monsanto had done the same thing for a study published in 2000 that backed up the safety of the company's products. "Recall that is how we handled Williams, Kroes & Munro," Heydens wrote. The revelation was significant because the Williams 2000 paper, which concluded that Roundup was not a health risk, was considered so authoritative that it was cited by the EPA in confirming the safety of glyphosate.

Scouring the discovery documents, the lawyers found more—emails from 1999, when the Williams paper was actually being written. The emails showed substantial involvement in the paper, not just from Heydens but also from several other Monsanto employees.

The paper was titled "Safety evaluation and risk assessment of the herbicide Roundup and its active ingredient, glyphosate, for humans," and its conclusions left no room for doubt about the absolute safety of Monsanto's herbicide: "The use of Roundup herbicide does not result in adverse effects on development, reproduction, or endocrine systems" in people or animals. "It was concluded that, under present and expected conditions of use, Roundup herbicide does not pose a health risk to humans."

The Williams paper came at a critical time for Monsanto because by the end of the 1990s, Roundup was facing increasing scrutiny by independent scientists who were finding growing evidence that the products could cause cancer.

The internal corporate files showed that after the paper was published, in April of 2000, a woman named Lisa Drake, Monsanto's government affairs specialist, emailed Heydens and several other colleagues to congratulate them and thank them for all the hard work they had done on the paper. She emphasized that the Williams paper would be critical to Monsanto's growth plans.

"This human health publication on Roundup herbicide and its companion publication on ecotox and environmental fate will undoubtedly be regarded as 'the' reference on Roundup and glyphosate safety," Drake wrote in the email, dated May 25, 2000. "Our plan is now to utilize it both in the defense of Roundup and Roundup Ready crops worldwide and in our ability to competitively differentiate ourselves from generics."

Another employee happily suggested that the Monsanto employees who had helped with the so-called independent Williams paper all receive logo polo shirts as a "token of appreciation for a job well done."

Reading the more than decade-old communications, Tim felt both elated at the find and a bit sick to his stomach. If the Williams paper was secretly the work of Monsanto, what other scientific literature declaring glyphosate safe had been directed by the company? Just how far did the deception go?

It was not just Heydens who talked about ghostwriting, the lawyers found. Multiple examples of the practice were cited in the company's internal documents. One internal document showed a Monsanto scientist named David Saltmiras citing his work in ghostwriting papers as a reason for praise in his annual performance review. Another showed company scientist Donna Farmer talking about cutting and pasting information into a paper that did not carry her name or that of any other Monsanto employee when it was published. Instead, the final version listed only seemingly independent scientists as authors of the work, which concluded that there were no harmful impacts from glyphosate on the reproductive health of people and animals exposed to the weed killer.

It was clear to Tim, Jeff, and the other lawyers who read the emails that Monsanto recognized claims about Roundup's safety would be much more credible if the information did not appear to be authored by Monsanto. So the company created a false aura of credibility through a variety of strategies that involved a lot of money, time, and secrets. That type of duplicity would not sit well with jurors, the lawyers were certain.

There was something else. A September 2015 email between Monsanto employees discussed the EPA official Jess Rowland—the man who oversaw the agency review that said there were no cancer concerns with glyphosate. A full seven months before the review was "accidentally" posted to the EPA website, it appeared that Monsanto had known Jess Rowland would be helpful to the company's position. The email from one Monsanto official to colleagues in the company noted that "Jess" would soon be retiring and "could be useful as we move forward with ongoing glyphosate defense." And indeed, just after the very helpful glyphosate review showed up temporarily on the EPA website, Rowland did retire, finding consulting work with the chemical industry.

It was shocking to see the cozy relationship between Monsanto and the EPA laid out so clearly in the employees' own words. Yes, the team agreed, they had more than enough to proceed to trial. The question now was which case, which person stricken with cancer, would be the first to tell their story to a jury.

CHAPTER 5
Going After Goliath

Before he curled his aching form onto the ragged orange sofa in his cramped Vallejo apartment, Lee made sure the blinds covering the sliding glass door were closed. He used to crave the light, relishing how young and strong he felt working outside with the sun's rays warming his skin. Darkness made him feel small and weak, and so tired. But these days, Lee wanted the blinds closed, the sun and the world outside sealed off. He could hardly bear to look at his face in a mirror, hating the thickened patches of diseased skin. Driving his car was also hard because his hands on the steering wheel were in easy view, and the lesions that leaked and burned made him want to tear the flesh from his body. He started wearing gloves to hide his hands. And he closed the blinds.

More than the light, Lee was shutting out his wife. He didn't want Araceli to go with him to his treatments, to see him weak and sick, sometimes crying from the pain and exhaustion. She was working so many hours to keep the family finances intact that Lee was often on his own to prepare meals and manage the laundry—when he felt well enough to do so. The heated physical chemistry the two had enjoyed was fading. He didn't see how Araceli could be attracted to him now, how any woman could. Lee had grown up believing the man was supposed to be the leader in a marriage, and it angered him that his marriage, like his health, was deteriorating. Yet he didn't know how to beat back the disease, and he felt incapable of drawing close to his own wife.

He had thought there might be an escape, an answer to his prayers for a cure. Doctors at Stanford University had enrolled Lee in a clinical trial of an experimental chemotherapy, and it had actually slowed the advancement of the disease. But nothing could truly stop the cancer from spreading, the doctors told him. All he could hope for was that the treatments would buy him extra time.

He wondered about his lawsuit against Monsanto. He talked to Tim Litzenburg on the phone every now and then, and he knew the lawyers were working on the case. But he worried he might never get to tell his story in court, to hear Monsanto's answers to the many questions he had that all seemed to boil down to really just one question: Why? Why had the company advertised the herbicides it sold as so safe? Why didn't he know when he was spraying it for the school district that it could potentially cause cancer? Why was he dying?

~

As Tim, Mike Miller, and Jeff Travers worked to compile and catalog the evidence to be used at trial, they and the other members of the legal team were also working to sign more plaintiffs as clients and to encourage more law firms to collaborate.

They could not take just anyone who had used Roundup and later was diagnosed with cancer. They needed to carefully screen prospects for winnable clients. Aimee Wagstaff put together a "Roundup Case Criteria" memo laying out what lawyers should look for when trying to sign new plaintiffs—and what they should avoid. The strongest cases were landscapers who had been relatively young when diagnosed.

Landscapers tended to use the same product repeatedly and in large volumes and would likely keep records about their use.

And only people who were diagnosed with non-Hodgkin lymphoma (NHL) at least a year after first using Roundup or other Monsanto glyphosate-based herbicides should be considered as potential clients, the group decided. It takes time to develop cancer, and a shorter span between exposure and diagnosis might be a hard sell for a jury. They could not have too long a span, either. So anyone who had not used Roundup in at least the past thirty years was out.

Additionally, anyone who had been diagnosed with HIV or AIDS would be automatically rejected because HIV infections were known to increase the risk for NHL. And anyone who had prior chemotherapy treatment for another disease would have to be turned away because some types of chemotherapy were believed to involve an increased risk of developing NHL.

The hunt for plaintiffs in mass litigation is often criticized as predatory, in part because plaintiffs don't always go looking for lawyers; quite often it's the opposite. An entire legal marketing industry exists solely to track down potential plaintiffs and feed them into networks of law firms, where the cases are referred to as "inventory." The more plaintiffs signed, the more money in fees when—if—cases are won or settled.

But in the eyes of the plaintiffs' attorneys, the more people they represent, the greater potential impact courtroom victories may have. Many cases become causes, legal actions taken to right wrongs or implement protections for people who have nowhere to turn but the courts when lawmakers and regulators fail to do their jobs. For Michael Baum, Aimee, and the others, the Monsanto litigation was squarely in line with the principles of the professional organization they belonged to, the American Association for Justice (AAJ). The AAJ maintains that civil justice is the most powerful tool to hold corporations and institutions accountable when they cause harm, even if those companies and institutions are among the most powerful on Earth. The group calls such work "going after Goliath," referencing the biblical story of battle between the Israelites and Philistines in which a young boy named David slayed a giant, heavily armed soldier named Goliath with a single stone launched from a slingshot. The parable seemed fitting for the fight they were picking with Monsanto, but the team knew they would need much more than a single stone.

Part of building the case and preparing for a trial, whoever the first plaintiff might be, involved taking depositions—lots of depositions. This question-and-answer process was much like putting a witness on the stand in a trial, except no judge or jury was present. Only the witness, someone to transcribe the meeting, and opposing legal counsel were typically present. Depositions were vital to trial preparation because they often elicited important testimony, including new facts that might help the plaintiffs when their cases did get to trial. And, depending on how far the witness lived or worked from where the trial was scheduled to take place, the deposition might be the only opportunity to present that person's version of events to a jury.

One of the depositions Mike most looked forward to taking was that of longtime Monsanto toxicologist William Heydens. Heydens was a Monsanto "lifer," someone who spent his entire career—more than thirty years—attached to the company. Even when going through graduate school, Heydens had worked part-time at Monsanto. He rose through the ranks over the years, eventually becoming the company's lead scientist for product safety assessment strategy, which meant when Monsanto wanted to market Roundup and other products for a new use, Heydens and his team developed the types of studies that had to be done to back up the company's assurances that the product would be safe. It was an important job, one of the most important jobs in the company when it came to Roundup.

Heydens was also the author of several emails Mike and his team had received through discovery, including the email strings that discussed ghostwriting scientific papers, a practice Mike and the team were certain a jury would find scandalous. In the emails, Heydens had discussed paying scientists outside of Monsanto to "edit & sign" their names to papers that Monsanto scientists would write about Roundup as a means to shore up the belief that the weed killer posed no health threat.

Though ghostwriting is a commonly accepted practice in the literary world, where memoirs authored by celebrities and politicians often are created by professional writers, in the scientific arena using a scientist's name on work actually produced by someone else is widely regarded as unethical. The practice can be helpful to the company doing the ghostwriting because declarations about the safety of chemicals or pharmaceuticals appear more credible if seen as coming from authors who are not employed by the company selling those products. But while it may serve corporate interests, the practice damages scientific credibility and can mask the potential dangers of harmful drugs and chemicals to an unsuspecting public. Publishers of scientific journals have tried to curb the practice, but it has become so common that some legal scholars argue that those engaging in ghostwriting articles should be sued for fraud under the Racketeer Influenced and Corrupt Organizations Act.

Ghostwriting appeared to be a common tactic within Monsanto, according to emails the Miller team was seeing. Several Monsanto scientists had discussed writing papers about the company's products while looking for third parties who would agree to serve as outside authors to make the papers appear more credible. Some of the most damning emails were written in early 2015, as Monsanto was steeling itself for the soon-to-be-issued classification of glyphosate by the International Agency for Research on Cancer (IARC). Monsanto's scientists had written to one another—in emails Mike now possessed—about the likelihood that IARC would classify glyphosate as either a possible or a probable human carcinogen. From the look of the correspondence, Monsanto was both fearful of such an outcome and determined to fight it. In one email, Heydens had written to several colleagues about the "potential vulnerabilities" the company had as a result of multiple unfavorable research findings in studies of people and animals exposed to the weed killer. That same email discussed a need to find allies and arrange funding for a "fight" against IARC.

It looked to Mike as if one big part of fighting back against IARC was ghostwriting a set of new scientific papers. In an email dated a month before the March 2015 IARC meeting was to take place, Heydens had written to other Monsanto scientists with an outline of the types of papers that should be written and suggestions for the individual outside scientists Monsanto might enlist to appear as authors. Mike could hardly wait to get Heydens under oath and answering questions about just who the company was trying to fool with what Mike saw as Monsanto's secret scientific manipulations.

It was late January of 2017 when Mike got his chance. The deposition was scheduled to take place in the law offices of Husch Blackwell in St. Louis, Missouri, not far from Monsanto's headquarters. The videographer hired to record the testimony set up a dull gray backdrop for the Monsanto scientist to sit in front of as he took a seat at the head of a long conference table. Lawyers for Monsanto lined one side of the table, and Tim, Mike, and Nancy Miller took the other side. The Miller team had flown in from Virginia the night before, taking a private plane and checking in at the posh Four Seasons Hotel in St. Louis. The three had celebrated Tim's thirty-fifth birthday with a quick dinner after their arrival and then spent the rest of the evening preparing for the deposition.

Mike and Tim were hoping that Monsanto didn't know what they had found in the morass of pages turned over so far in discovery and therefore would have had a hard time preparing their senior scientist for what was coming.

The camera was rolling as Mike opened with a series of simple questions asking Heydens to describe his tenure at Monsanto. "How long have you been an employee of the Monsanto Corporation?" he asked.

The scientist had a serious air about him, clad in a dark business suit and conservative tie, with his graying hair neatly parted and smoothed back. Mike appeared equally formidable in a sleek slate-gray suit and a favorite yellow tie knotted around the neck of his crisp white shirt. With his dark-rimmed glasses resting low on his nose as he read from a prepared list of questions, Mike showed no hostility for Monsanto's scientist, nodding his head in agreement as Heydens explained his education, his job title, and the responsibilities that had spanned his thirty-three years at the company.

"One of your main jobs at Monsanto is to defend glyphosate, right?" Mike asked, adjusting his glasses. Heydens looked directly at the camera and answered firmly, "My main job at Monsanto is to ensure that glyphosate is reviewed using sound science."

"You've heard the phrase 'ghostwriting' before, haven't you?" Mike asked, swiveling in his chair to look directly at the scientist.

"Yes, I've heard that term," Heydens said, nodding, without a hint of nervousness.

"And ghostwriting is considered unethical by scientists, isn't it, sir?" Mike persisted.

"I think you'd have to define what ghostwriting is first before you could decide whether it's unethical or not," Heydens replied. Under his own personal definition, Heydens continued, ghostwriting occurred when someone made a "significant intellectual contribution" to a paper "without being recognized" as doing so.

Mike pushed the point: "That has been an issue in the scientific community for some time, hasn't it, Dr. Heydens?" he asked. But Heydens didn't budge: "I really am not aware the degree to which that has been an issue," he said. "That's just not an area I pay much attention to."

Outwardly Mike showed almost no reaction, though internally he felt a rush of adrenalin. Heydens's answer was nothing short of incredible, given the internal Monsanto emails Mike's team found in the document dump the company had made into Crivella. Ghostwriting was not an area Heydens paid much attention to? Really? The internal Monsanto emails showed that Heydens himself had suggested to other Monsanto scientists that they "ghost-write" scientific papers. He had actually used the term. And multiple other Monsanto scientists working with Heydens talked to one another about engaging in the practice as if it had long been an accepted and common strategy for the company. Was it possible that Heydens did not realize the lawyers had these internal files? Mike wondered. Well, if Heydens was going to hang himself, Mike was more than happy to provide plenty of rope. The video of Heydens's testimony would be invaluable when shown to a jury.

Mike proceeded with his questioning. He knew from reading an internal Monsanto action plan that in 2015 the company had hired a consulting firm called Intertek to act as an intermediary between Monsanto and a group of outside scientists for the preparation of papers supporting Monsanto's claims of safety regarding its herbicides. Under the plan, Monsanto would pay Intertek, and Intertek would then contract with the scientists who would be listed as authors on the papers that Monsanto wanted created. The goal was to contradict IARC's finding of a cancer connection to glyphosate. A series of papers authored by Monsanto's scientists would obviously be considered biased by members of the public and the media, but papers by independent scientists could carry more authority and help counter the negative attention generated by the IARC decision, the company hoped.

Monsanto had not hidden the fact that it had asked for the papers; the company's chief executive officer, Hugh Grant, had told the press about hiring Intertek. But he said while some Monsanto scientists would provide information and data for the project, the scientists enlisted by Intertek would do their own work, and the findings of the papers would be truly independent of Monsanto influence.

As Monsanto had hoped, the series of papers was published in September of 2016 in a respected scientific journal called *Critical Reviews in*

Toxicology, and—as Monsanto had intended—the papers declared the IARC finding about glyphosate's cancer ties was wrong. The authors concluded that the data did not support IARC's classification of glyphosate as a probable human carcinogen, and in fact the data showed the chemical to be unlikely to pose any carcinogenic risk to people.

No Monsanto scientist was included in the group of sixteen authors listed, and to underscore the independence of the papers, a statement accompanying them in the journal told readers this: "Neither any Monsanto company employees nor any attorneys reviewed any of the Expert Panel's manuscripts prior to submission to the journal." The statement also said that none of the authors had been directly contacted by Monsanto.

The papers worked just as Monsanto hoped they would and were widely shared by media and by organizations friendly to Monsanto. The papers helped Monsanto create enough doubt that IARC's credibility became a topic in the press.

But as Mike sat across the table from Monsanto's top scientist, he knew the papers had not been written independently at all and, in fact, that Heydens had actually suggested the team "ghost-write" parts of them. Mike also had copies of the drafts and finished product and several emails showing just how much time Heydens himself had spent working on the so-called independent Intertek papers. He wouldn't call Heydens a liar on tape, but he could make sure the jury got that point.

"Now, you're aware, sir, that Monsanto funded the Intertek panel reports on whether Roundup was carcinogenic, right, sir?" Mike asked Heydens.

"We funded that project to determine if glyphosate was carcinogenic. It was not a study of Roundup," Heydens replied with hesitation.

"The truth, Dr. Heydens, is you ghostwrote that report, isn't it?" Mike pressed, staring hard at the scientist.

Heydens did not waver. "That is not correct."

Mike continued to lead him into the trap he was trying to lay. "Are you, William Heydens, listed as an author on this report?"

"No, I am not," Heydens replied, looking down at the table and the stack of papers in front of him.

"Did you write any parts of this report?" Mike asked.

It was just the slightest of moves, but Mike thought he saw the scientist's smooth delivery start to crack.

Heydens looked down at the table and his papers as he answered. "I provided, um, a little bit of historical information that—when I say 'historical information,' I mean historical information relative to things about Monsanto and registrations going way back to the, uh, '70s that none of the authors would have known anything about. So that is some information that I did provide," Heydens said in a stilted voice, waving his hands slightly as he spoke. "I also provided a minimal set of—a few comments at one point in the process, well after the paper had been written and was well on the way to being finalized."

"Did you communicate directly with the authors of this paper about this paper?" Mike asked, sounding almost scolding.

"I was not in communication with the authors when they were doing their conclusions and—doing their evaluations or conclusions," Heydens said, shrugging. "That was—that was their paper to write, and they did that."

Mike continued: "You did, in fact, review the article before it was published, true?"

Heydens shrugged again. "I received—there were times I remember that I received them, but I never provided comments and asked for changes of any content. I basically never responded. I received them and just filed them off because I did not want to be part of influencing this project at all," Heydens said, shaking his head back and forth.

"Dr. Heydens, you wrote 28 proposed edits to this paper before it was published. That's the truth, isn't it, sir?" Mike insisted, growing stern as he punched the words out across the table.

Heydens appeared increasingly uncomfortable. "I don't know if that number is correct or not," he said. "My recollection was the only information that I—there was at one point in time when the different scientists actually started reviewing each other's work and they were commenting on each other's work. And there was at one point in time that I recall that I made some comments on some of their comments, provided that information back. . . ." He looked down at his hands.

The questioning was going just as Mike had hoped it would. Seated at Mike's left shoulder, Tim was silently celebrating as well. They had already scored some key points and had many more cards to play.

Mike directed Heydens to open a copy of the article they had been discussing as it was published in the journal *Critical Reviews in Toxicology* and to look at the "Declaration of interest" section.

"It says, 'Neither any Monsanto Company employee nor any attorneys reviewed any of the Expert Panel's manuscripts prior to submission to the journal.' Do you see that, sir?" he asked Heydens.

"I see that that's written there," the scientist replied.

"That's absolutely false, isn't it?" Mike prodded.

Heydens blinked but wasn't giving an inch. "I don't know that it's false, quite honestly," he responded. "I don't know what they meant by that. They wrote that. I had nothing to do with what was put in here, and so you'd have to try and decide what they might have meant. As I look at this now, I think perhaps what they meant was we didn't—there was—nothing was provided from the company. But, you know, exactly what was meant when they wrote this, whoever wrote that, only he or she knows what was meant by clear that."

Time to circle in closer, Mike decided. When a jury viewed this exchange, he wanted it to be crystal clear that Monsanto had ghostwritten these papers, a deception aimed squarely at manipulating the scientific record in a way that Mike hoped any reasonable person would see as not just unethical but an admission that the company had something to hide when it came to the safety promises surrounding its herbicides.

After all, if glyphosate and Roundup were completely safe, there should be plenty of actual independent scientific reports stating as much. There would be no need for Monsanto to ghostwrite anything.

Mike resumed his questioning. "The planning for it began back in 2015, right, sir? . . . It was, fair to say, something you guys wanted to initiate after IARC to sort of explain your position on the science, generally speaking?"

"This was something that we wanted to initiate not to explain our view of science," Heydens answered. "It's something that we wanted to explain the best sound science way to look at the data, which is exactly the way these panels approached it, these scientists approached it."

Time to pull out more Monsanto emails, Mike thought. "All right. Here's Exhibit 3:5, a series of e-mails between you and others in May of 2015 concerning post-IARC activities to support glyphosate. This is—one of the e-mails here is from you. . . . It's concerning a meeting that you folks had had that day. . . . And some things that you were going to do is publish on animal data cited by IARC, right, sir?"

Heydens paused and drew in a deep breath before answering. "Really what this is, these are—these were ideas that we had at that point in time. We hadn't established which—exactly which ones," he said, keeping his eyes on the table and the documents in front of him. "This was more the things that rose to the top as possibilities as part of our overall brainstorming on the topic."

Time to tighten the noose just a bit, Mike thought. "And you wrote, sir, on the publication on animal data cited by IARC, there would be a manuscript to be initiated by Monsanto as ghostwriters, right, sir?" he asked, stressing the word "ghostwriters" as he stared at the Monsanto scientist.

Heydens did not meet his gaze, continuing to keep his eyes lowered to the table. "That is written there, that's true, but, um, that's not—but again, as I said, this was, was just thinking early on in the process, and that's not what happened. Ultimately, a totally different paradigm was used."

Mike was not about to drop the point. "And you knew that it would be more powerful if it looked like it had been written by outside authors, right?"

"No, that's not correct," Heydens insisted, appearing not to realize the trap he had just stepped into.

"Let's see what it says here." Mike wielded a yellow sharpie over a printout of a Monsanto email written by Heydens to his Monsanto colleagues. "You say, 'It was noted this would be more powerful if authored by non-Monsanto scientists. . . .' See that?"

Bam. Score another point for the plaintiffs' team, Tim thought as he watched the exchange.

Too late, Heydens realized he had been snagged by his own words. But he wasn't ready to crack.

"Oh, yeah, I see that," he answered casually. His eyes widened slightly as he looked earnestly into the videographer's camera. "So I sort of misunderstood your question. The idea here really is—I mean, you know, obviously it would be real easy for Monsanto to write a scientific paper, but really it would hold more weight, uh, if we selected or, you know, if the panel was put together by independent experts who are experts in the field, people that have done these evaluations for 30 or 40 years and have reputations in the international scientific community."

As the day wore on, Mike prodded Heydens on email after email detailing how Monsanto's hidden hand had helped dictate what was published as independent work. Mike even forced him to admit—in an ironic twist—that Heydens himself had reviewed the wording attached to the Intertek papers declaring that no review had been made by Monsanto scientists.

Mike also used the emails to press Heydens on statements that appeared to refer to ghostwriting of a significant scientific paper known as Williams, Kroes & Munro that had been published in 2000 and had helped convince regulators of the safety of Monsanto's herbicides. Heydens had written in an email to colleagues that he would "strangle" the authors if they "ask for any rewrites" of all the work Heydens had done on the paper. Just like the Intertek papers, the Williams paper listed only the outside scientists and did not publicly list Heydens or any other Monsanto scientist as an author.

"Dr. Heydens, the truth is, you ghostwrote the Williams article in 2000, and you ghostwrote the Intertek article in 2016, correct?" Mike demanded.

"That's absolutely false," the scientist shot back. "Did not ghostwrite the 2000 paper and did not ghostwrite this 2016 paper."

The sparring continued as Mike's questioning of Heydens extended over two days, with rebuttal questioning by Monsanto's attorney. The whole deposition would never be seen by a jury, but hours of the best exchanges would be made available. Mike would have preferred to put Heydens and other Monsanto employees on the stand live at the upcoming trials, but he knew that would not be likely. Witnesses could not be forced to travel far from their homes or workplaces to testify in civil trials, and Mike felt certain Monsanto would not be volunteering its people for live testimony. The depositions would have to do.

~

By the summer of 2017, the plaintiffs' attorneys had completed several depositions of Monsanto executives and felt they were nearly ready to go to trial. There was so far no smoking gun—no internal memo indisputably tying the company's products to cancer. But the legal team had what they saw as strong evidence that the company had long been aware of concerns about the potential cancer risks of the Roundup formulations that combined glyphosate with certain surfactants. There were reports about how rapidly the glyphosate formulations were absorbed into human skin; how the chemicals could accumulate in bone and bodily organs. And there were many questionable emails between Monsanto and EPA officials that the lawyers were convinced showed unethical collusion with the regulators.

The team even had started getting help from an anonymous tipster. Mysterious brown envelopes with no return address began showing up at Aimee's office in Denver and at The Miller Firm in Virginia. Inside one envelope was a single sheet of paper containing typed suggestions for specific documents the legal team should request from the EPA. Another listed several EPA and government officials the team should look into. The envelope was postmarked in New York. One of the anonymous tip sheets came in via fax. The team thought they might finally have a way of tracking down the tipster and hired a private investigator to determine where the fax originated. After a little sleuthing, the team learned the fax had come from a retail printing and copying store in the Washington, DC, area. They were able to convince the retailer to turn over video recorded on store security cameras at the exact time and day the fax was sent. The footage did capture images of the person sending the fax, but the visual was too grainy to allow a sharp look at the person and caught him only in profile as he leaned over the fax machine. The lawyers could tell their secret tipster was a Caucasian man who was wearing a light-colored shirt with a dark jacket and a hat pulled low over his head. But it was not enough to help them track him down.

Though they failed to figure out the identity of the source, the team was still thrilled by the information. One of the mailings in particular was shocking. It was a copy of a letter dated March 4, 2013, that appeared to have been written by a thirty-year career EPA scientist named Marion Copley. In the letter Copley accused the EPA's Jess Rowland of playing "your political conniving games with the science" to favor pesticide manufacturers such as Monsanto. Rowland was the official who oversaw the EPA's cancer assessment for glyphosate and the one who retired from the EPA shortly after the helpful leak of the draft cancer assessment report to Monsanto. In the correspondence, Copley wrote that it "is essentially certain that glyphosate causes cancer." Copley accused Rowland of having "intimidated staff" to change reports so they favored companies such as Monsanto. If the Miller team could prove the letter was authentic, it would be powerful evidence for the plaintiffs in court. There was one big problem, though. Copley had died from breast cancer at the age of sixty-six in January of 2014. Without Copley to confirm that she had written the correspondence, the team likely wouldn't be able to use the letter. They reached out to her husband, who still lived in the DC area, but he wanted nothing to do with the messiness of the litigation and refused to let the attorneys go through Marion's computer to see if they could find a trace of the letter.

Even if they couldn't do much with the Copley letter, the legal team felt great about where they were. There were scores of documents that showed that rather than acting to warn consumers or change the formulas as concerns mounted, Monsanto had instead worked to suppress the concerns and manipulate the scientific literature. Mike could hardly wait to get it all in front of a jury.

With the evidence against Monsanto coming together, the hunt for Roundup plaintiffs was in full swing. To help spread the word, the legal team arranged a daylong Roundup Litigation Conference for June 29 in Chicago. The goal was to educate other lawyers about the evidence already in hand and the status of both the multidistrict litigation set up under Judge Vince Chhabria and a multitude of state cases that were proceeding separately from the MDL. Small firms that had cancer victim clients but were uncertain about their ability to take their cases to court alone would be encouraged to refer their cases to the lead firms. Mike and Nancy, Aimee, Michael, Robin Greenwald, and Brent Wisner would do the bulk of the work, and the small firms would receive referral fees.

The conference was also very much about the business of the plaintiffs' bar—generating large numbers of plaintiffs, which could lead to big payouts if and when the litigation succeeded. A group called Consumer Attorney Marketing Group printed up glossy green brochures outlining various "creative capabilities and options for your Roundup campaign." For a fee, the marketing group would produce commercials to solicit cancer patients who had used Roundup, retrieve medical records from prospective plaintiffs, and handle other tasks to "ensure that your firm gets the most cases possible within your budget."

It was a hot and sunny summer day in Chicago, but inside the darkly tapestried, air-conditioned meeting room on the eighth floor of the InterContinental Chicago Hotel, the temperature was pleasantly cool as the legal team took turns laying out the twists and turns of the litigation and what lay ahead. The gathering was small but diverse, with lawyers showing up from Arizona, Florida, Oklahoma, and elsewhere to explore how they might get involved in the legal fight. They sat quietly taking notes at long tables bearing water pitchers and dishes of mints in shiny green and blue wrappers. On a large projection screen at the front of the room, Aimee, Michael, and the others took turns sharing a slide show of key documents and data they had gathered so far.

Aimee told the group that Monsanto had already scored some major points against the plaintiffs' lawyers, starting with the "sandbagging" when the unfinished EPA cancer report was briefly publicly posted to the internet, declaring Monsanto's herbicide not a cancer risk. When the lawyers deposed the EPA's Jess Rowland, who was the author of the report and appeared cozy with Monsanto, Rowland had denied any wrongdoing and claimed not to remember anything about how his draft report was briefly posted at a critical time for Monsanto. The fact that Rowland left the EPA shortly after the leak and found work consulting in the chemical industry was something the lawyers felt certain was no coincidence.

Another blow had come just that month when an explosive story published by the international news agency Reuters rocketed around the world. It alleged that the chairman of the IARC group that classified glyphosate as a probable carcinogen had withheld critical research information about glyphosate from his fellow scientists. The information that this scientist—Dr. Aaron Blair of the National Cancer Institute—withheld reportedly showed that glyphosate did not cause cancer, the story stated. Had the scientist simply been more open and honest, the story suggested, the classification potentially could have been different.

Bolstered by press statements from Monsanto and its lobbyists, the article sparked widespread concern about the integrity of the IARC review. Monsanto and its allies were pushing members of the US Congress to probe the validity of the organization's cancer classifications, even suggesting that Congress strip funding from the international cancer agency.

The lawyers were certain that Monsanto had somehow engineered the story. The company had deposed Dr. Blair early in 2017, and the Reuters reporter who wrote the piece, a health correspondent based in London, declared in her article that the narrative was based in part on that deposition of Blair. And even though the reporter attributed the material for her story to "court documents," the deposition had not actually been filed in court, meaning the reporter most likely got it from Monsanto, the lawyers knew. More importantly, it was clear to the lawyers that the reporter had mischaracterized the statements Blair made in the deposition. All one had to do was read the deposition to see the truth, but the reporter had not provided such a link, and the deposition was not publicly available. Most readers would simply assume the story was true, that the IARC classification was flawed. It was a slick move by Monsanto. The lawyers were learning that the company didn't only work behind the scenes to manipulate the scientific record; it also appeared to have ways of manipulating international media.

"Monsanto fights hard, fights dirty, fights every step of the way," Michael told the group, dressed in his typical casual lawyer attire—a dark blue suit and blue button-down shirt.

The best way to fight back was to continue to dig through the company files turned over in the discovery process and bring as many damning documents as possible into the public domain. Monsanto officials were going to have a very hard time explaining away the internal discussions that repeatedly seemed to show more concern about sales than about protecting public safety, he said.

In fact, Michael explained, in just a few weeks, if all went as planned, the team would be releasing to the world what they had started referring to as "hot dox"—portions of Monsanto's internal files that the company had provided in response to discovery requests. Monsanto had been pressing to keep most of the discovery documents it turned over sealed from public view, and the lawyers knew that a document release was likely to raise the ire of Judge Chhabria. The judge had been keeping a tight rein on what the lawyers in the case could and could not do with the evidence they were compiling. But Michael, Brent, and Tim believed that the public had the right to know about important issues divulged in the documents—sooner rather than later. They were not yet sure how or when they could get the documents into the public spotlight, but they were working on a plan.

"The documents show internally they understood they had a cancer problem," Michael told the group. "It's our job to help the world find about this stuff."

When it was Tim's turn to lay out more aspects of the case, he compared the Roundup litigation to lawsuits that brought to light the health hazards of smoking. He had spent the past few months tracking a web of payments made by Monsanto to third parties. It looked to him as though those payments bought pro-Monsanto messaging on social media, in news outlets, and through seemingly independent health and science organizations. These third parties were supposed to defend the safety of Monsanto's products and attack anyone who agreed with IARC or expressed concerns about the herbicides—but appear to be doing it without Monsanto's backing. Just as with the ghostwriting of scientific literature, Tim saw Monsanto's deceptive tactics as posing dangerous consequences to public health.

"We'll look back in twenty years and we'll all know it is terribly carcinogenic," he said. "We're going to slap some new tires on the wheels of justice."

Tim's confidence was shared by most of the team, but there were some lingering doubts. Their case was strong, but was it strong enough? A look at the history of litigation brought against Monsanto showed that the company rarely lost. With deep pockets and some of the nation's biggest and most talented law firms at its disposal, the company had demonstrated that it would fight long and hard against anyone who dared challenge its products and practices.

This legal fight, challenging the safety of a widely used consumer product that regulators around the world solidly backed as safe, was clearly not going to be easy. Nor would it be fast. It would cost millions of dollars, thousands of working hours, weeks and months of time in courtrooms around the country, and many missed holidays and family events for the lawyers involved. A loss on this grand a scale for the legal team would be painful, even potentially crippling. Would it be worth it? Could they actually win?

After the presentations concluded, the team gathered in a small cocktail lounge to relax. Waiters crisscrossed the room offering trays of hors d'oeuvres to the hungry group of lawyers as they talked through the events of the day and the uncertainties ahead. They did not yet have a lead plaintiff designated, nor did they know who their first judge would be or where the first trial would take place. Many other firms around the country had taken a look at the cases on file and decided not to join in the litigation because of the cost and risk involved. If there was a time to turn back, now was the time. But Mike, Tim, Aimee, Brent, and the rest of the team knew they were going forward.

As Aimee looked around the table at her fellow lawyers, she saw the doubt in their eyes and a need for reassurance. She lifted her margarita glass in a semi-toast. "We're going to win! We are, you know." She smiled and took a long, satisfied drink of icy tequila. "We're really going to win."

CHAPTER 6

In the Interests of Justice

As the summer of 2017 wore on, the number of plaintiffs signing up to sue Monsanto had grown to include several thousand people: young and old, rich and poor, some suffering significant debilitation from non-Hodgkin lymphoma (NHL) and others fortunate enough to have responded well to chemotherapy and other medical treatments and be living near-normal lives. But all wanted to see Monsanto held to account.

Among the newest group of plaintiffs were a husband and wife in their seventies from Livermore, California, who both had been stricken with devastating forms of NHL after thirty-five years of spraying Roundup products around their properties. Married fifty years, Alva and Alberta Pilliod had once envisioned spending their retirement years traveling and enjoying adventures with their grandchildren. But in 2011, Alva was found to have a type of NHL that had spread into his pelvis and spine, leaving him in sometimes unbearable pain even after treatments abated the spread of the cancer. Four years later, Alberta was diagnosed with NHL that had struck her brain. She nearly died during her multiple hospitalizations and was left with extensive balance and vision problems that made navigating each day difficult. When the couple filed their lawsuit in June of 2017, Alva was seventy-five and Alberta was seventy-three. Every day was an exhausting and agonizing struggle.

And then there was Elaine Stevick and her husband, Christopher. Elaine was diagnosed in December of 2014 at the age of sixty-three with multiple brain tumors due to a form of NHL called central nervous system lymphoma, the same type Alberta Pilliod had. Before she had gotten sick, before there were any worries that a weed killer might cause cancer, Chris had jokingly called Elaine the "Queen of Roundup" because she used it so frequently.

The couple had purchased an old Victorian home on overgrown property in Northern California in 1990, and while Christopher worked on renovating the interior of the house, Elaine's job was to spray Roundup over the weeds and wild onions that smothered the grounds. She never wore gloves or other protective clothing. She didn't think there was any reason to worry. Both the Pilliods and the Stevicks were clients of The Miller Firm, just as Lee Johnson and so many others now were.

Michael Baum's firm and Aimee Wagstaff's firm also had stacks of case files. One of Aimee's newest clients had a particularly heartbreaking story. Sharlean Gordon had been only thirty-nine when she was diagnosed with NHL in 2006. Chemotherapy didn't work, and radiation treatments left her without control of her bowels and so unsteady on her legs that she became nearly wheelchair-bound. A stem cell transplant put her into remission, but the quality of her young life had been ruined. While in remission, she had continued using Roundup for many years, not knowing of the science showing a connection between the chemical and cancer. Her stepfather had died from NHL, so she knew the viciousness of the disease. Ironically, or perhaps not, her stepfather had been the one who showed her how to spray Roundup around the family's aboveground pool. She often had worn just a swimsuit, shorts, and flip-flop sandals when spraying the herbicide because, as her family believed, Roundup was totally safe.

There were so many people with cancer, and there was so much anger over the growing belief that Monsanto had known all along that its products could be dangerous. Several lawsuits had multiple plaintiffs, and the litigation by now was lodged in multiple venues, from the federal court in San Francisco to the St. Louis County court in Monsanto's hometown in Missouri. But the legal team still did not know who would or should be the first plaintiff to go to trial.

Tim Litzenburg had not been in touch with Lee for a while. He felt for the guy; he knew Lee had been going through a lot of painful treatments and was struggling emotionally with not being able to work. Lee had been on disability leave from the school district, but that was running out, meaning the little bit of monthly income and the health insurance Lee counted on were going away. The guy's life was unraveling. A better lawyer, a better friend, would be in closer touch, Tim thought. He felt guilty; he should go visit Lee again. But there were so many clients, so many sick people.

And to be honest, Tim was distracted. His own life was starting to unravel a bit too. His marriage of eight years was ending. The couple had separated in 2016, and the effort to finalize the divorce was wearing him down. He had a young son and daughter he hardly ever seemed to be able to find time for, and he desperately needed a break from work, but the cases couldn't wait. He felt as if he lived on an airplane, spending almost every other week flying back and forth from Virginia to California to Missouri for hearings and case management meetings. He started taking anti-anxiety medication to deal with the stress.

When he wasn't on a plane or in a meeting, Tim continued to spend several hours each day trying to untangle the spiderweb-like network of Monsanto allies who received money and marching orders to help defend the company's herbicides. Some of the connections were easy to see; others were convoluted and confusing. Tim was obsessed with trying to figure it all out, spending hours at a time squirreled away in his second-floor office in Virginia listening to the trains rattle by while he constructed an organizational chart of the covert links detailed in the Monsanto files. From what he could tell, the records showed that the company had designed an invisible network of front groups, university professors, farm group leaders, scientists, and others who would promote Monsanto's agenda without anyone knowing they were collaborating with the company. Monsanto knew and discussed in several emails how messaging from "independent" third parties carried more credibility than if it came from the company directly. Tim saw that company money secretly flowed into a group called the American Council on Science and Health, for instance, and ACSH scientists in return published articles on websites and in prominent newspapers where they might help influence public opinion. ACSH had been particularly vocal in attacking the scientists of the International Agency for Research on Cancer (IARC) after they classified glyphosate as a probable carcinogen in 2015. ACSH didn't disclose that it was working with Monsanto money when the group published a series of assaults on the IARC scientists claiming their findings were not based on science.

In one internal Monsanto email thread, a company executive had written to colleagues about ACSH's pro-glyphosate propaganda and the need for more funding of ACSH. In all caps, he wrote, "You WILL NOT GET A BETTER VALUE FOR YOUR DOLLAR than ACSH."

Monsanto had multiple teams of employees and contractors, including a "reputation management" consultant firm in Washington, DC, that worked with third parties such as ACSH to push Monsanto propaganda all over the world without it appearing to originate with the company. One group secretly funded by Monsanto would often quote another group secretly funded by Monsanto, creating a covert echo chamber that magnified the company's messaging.

Another strategy laid out in internal company email chains called for the company's consultants and public relations teams to create "third-party content" such as op-eds that defended the safety of Monsanto's glyphosate-based herbicides. The op-eds could not look like they came from Monsanto, so the teams recruited doctors, nurses, and others in medical, health, and scientific professions to personalize and put their names on the articles as authors. The commentary pieces were then to be "placed" by Monsanto's public relations experts in newspapers and with online consumer, social media, and news sites. Two major American daily newspapers—the *Washington Post* and *USA Today*—were top targets for placement of these third-party pieces, the internal Monsanto emails showed.

It all was brilliant. Of course most people would think Roundup was safe, Tim thought. Yep, it was an absolutely brilliant strategy. Also sneaky and deceptive. A jury might even see it as sleazy.

It would be great if someone on the legal team could get Monsanto's chief executive officer on the stand and ask about all of this. Why, Tim would ask him, why did the company need to go to such extraordinary lengths to convince people its products were safe? If they really were safe, why would there be such a need to enlist all these third parties and spend all this money—millions of dollars, from what Tim could tell? In his files, he dubbed his work the "Monsanto Dark Money Project." If he could ever get it all in front of a jury, he was sure it could go a long way toward showing a truly sinister side to the company.

As Tim labored away in Virginia, buried in documents, Lee was struggling with the seesaw of cancer treatment. The doctors had tried various cocktails and concoctions and radiation, but it all made him so sick that sometimes he felt as though death would be a welcome escape from the pain that seemed to splinter his bones, sear his flesh, and rob him of sleep. Trying to eat enough to nourish his frail figure was a struggle in itself as nearly every bite of food he tried to consume came back up in violent vomiting episodes. So many days were spent feeling as if he could not bear another. The treatments also left him with neuropathy, a type of nerve damage that causes weakness, numbness, and pain in hands and feet. For Lee, the pain was worst in his feet. Sometimes it felt like they were on fire, and all he could do was cry.

And then, respite would come. He would start to feel better, almost normal, though he wasn't sure he really remembered normal. But he could eat, could walk, could dress himself and go outside with his boys. During these good periods, in between the treatments, he even could work a little. Lee could usually count on his best friend, Daryl Waters, to find him a few hours of odd-job labor at the medical cannabis business where Daryl was employed.

Lee appreciated the work. He had been on temporary disability leave from the Benicia Unified School District for over a year when, in April of 2017, the district changed his status to permanent disability. That meant the $630 per week he had been getting dropped to $290 per week. And even that small amount of money—a fraction of his prior salary—was due to end in September of 2017. Lee already owed a little more than $100,000 in medical bills. He wasn't sure what he was going to do when the payments ran out. The part-time jobs Daryl found him wouldn't solve the money problems, but they helped.

Daryl loved Lee, and vice versa. The two had met in their early twenties in a music studio, writing raps. Sometimes after hours in the studio, they would take off after midnight and drive to Lake Tahoe to shoot craps at a casino there, returning home after dawn. As they moved into middle age, Lee had helped Daryl landscape his house and Daryl had helped Lee navigate tensions with Araceli, just as he had provided a listening ear to Lee's earlier struggles with the woman he had impregnated in his twenties. Lee rarely saw his oldest son, who by now was in his twenties and had an assortment of his own struggles, and Daryl knew how much that tore at Lee's heart.

When Daryl first learned of Lee's cancer, he felt certain that Lee would beat it. Lee always figured out a way to overcome his obstacles. But now Daryl wasn't so sure. On good days, Lee seemed almost like his old self, and he would assure Daryl that he could survive the disease. But the number of days they could consider good were becoming fewer and fewer.

In April, the same month Lee learned his benefits were running out, his oncologist told him that his battle to beat the cancer was failing. Tests showed a significant increase in his skin lesions, which meant the cancer was gaining momentum despite the experimental chemotherapy he had been receiving. By June, the news was even more dire. Lee's doctor told him the disease was affecting 80 percent of his body. It was time to get his affairs in order. The doctor was clear: Lee would not live to see another year.

It never occurred to Lee to reach out to Tim. He knew Tim was his lawyer, but he also knew Tim had lots of clients. So he was surprised on one hot summer day to get a call from him. Lee was hiding out in the apartment, shades pulled, when his cell phone buzzed. Tim was on the other end, telling Lee he had a status conference in California to attend, and that had prompted him to take a look at the latest medical reports that had been added to Lee's file. He was shocked by what he saw. He had known Lee's condition was dire but had not expected the disease to spread so quickly. If Lee was ever going to get his day in court, it needed to be soon.

Tim explained to Lee that they would file a motion for trial "preference," essentially a request to a judge to let Lee jump ahead of other people with cases pending in that court. The California Code of Civil Procedure has a specific provision to allow for a speedy trial for people who doctors believe will die within six months. The language of the law leaves the decision up to a judge, stating that the court must be satisfied that "the interests of justice will be served by granting preference."

There was no reason for Lee to read the motion, and Tim hoped he wouldn't have to. His throat felt thick as he read over the final version.

Though he had always known Lee might die before his case could get to trial, seeing the words on paper made him want to weep.

A subhead to the motion, printed in boldface type, almost seemed to leap off the page: "Setting This Case For An Earlier Trial Is In The Interests of Justice," it read.

Good cause exists to grant this motion because Plaintiff has terminal epidermotropic T-cell lymphoma (a non-Hodgkin lymphoma) and his medical condition is such that there is substantial medical doubt that he will live more than six months and granting a trial preference is in the interests of justice under the circumstances. Because of his terminal cancer and grave condition, if this motion is not granted, he will be deprived of justice because he is unlikely to survive long enough to see the day that his case goes to trial.

To strengthen the motion, Tim added details about Lee's condition pulled from his medical file: "Mr. Johnson's cancer has spread throughout his skin and lymph nodes in the past two years, and has proven resistant to a number of different chemotherapies, as well as radiation therapy." He typed one sentence in bold for extra emphasis: "Mr. Johnson's current condition raises medical doubt of survival beyond six months."

To make sure the judge had little room for doubt, Tim enlisted the opinion of a medical oncologist named Chadi Nabhan to look over Lee's medical history and the latest test results. Nabhan was chief medical officer of Cardinal Health in Chicago and considered an expert on NHL. Tim attached to the motion a report from Nabhan concurring that Lee's life expectancy was six months or less.

"Waiting to set this case for trial sometime after Mr. Johnson is dead is not in the interests of justice," Tim wrote in the motion. He wanted the court to set a trial date of December 11, 2017. "California courts have long recognized that 'justice delayed is justice denied,'" he added.

As he finished the motion, Tim's heart tightened. He loved the law and thrilled at the power it gave him to do things such as this, give a poor and sick man the chance to point a finger of blame at a powerful corporation in a public setting. But practicing the type of law he did also meant he was constantly mired in human suffering. There was a saying among those who represent plaintiffs in personal injury cases—"No one comes to a plaintiff's attorney because they had a healthy baby." No one needs a personal injury attorney unless they've suffered something—the loss of a child, a limb, a loved one. Some particularly cynical practitioners referred to themselves as "merchants of misery." There were no feel-good stories to savor in this business. Even when cases were won, big money awards ordered, sick people would still be sick. Dying people would still die.

Tim filed the motion on July 21 in the Superior Court of California for the County of San Francisco, asking Judge Curtis Karnow to set a trial as soon as possible. He felt good about Judge Karnow so far. The judge had already given Lee's case a big lift by rejecting Monsanto's request to bifurcate, or separate, any future trial into two segments. Monsanto wanted to separate evidence about the company's ghostwriting and other questionable conduct from evidence about the science surrounding glyphosate-based herbicides. Separating the trial into two segments, in which a jury must first determine whether or not the company's products caused cancer before the jury could hear evidence of how Monsanto attempted to cover up the evidence and manipulate the scientific record, could make a victory for Lee extremely difficult. Very few judges ever agreed to bifurcate trials in the way Monsanto had requested.

And Judge Karnow already knew of Lee's declining health from discussions in a prior case management conference between the parties. It was Karnow who had set July 21 as a deadline for the preference motion. If Lee's health was truly deteriorating as quickly as Tim said it was, the judge did not want to waste any more time. He wanted to see the medical evidence for himself. Monsanto's attorneys also had a right to see the medical files, the judge said. Karnow told Monsanto that if it was going to oppose the motion, it needed to do so by August 14, and he set a hearing on the matter for August 29.

After filing the formal motion for trial preference, Tim crossed his fingers and awaited Monsanto's response. He felt certain Monsanto would oppose his request. But what could they say? Lee was dying. How would the company justify its opposition to a speedy trial?

Three weeks later, on August 14, Monsanto's attorneys filed their twenty-page response, and, as Tim expected, the company was firmly opposed to a speedy trial for Lee. The company's lawyers questioned the authenticity of the medical records Tim cited in his motion, and they cited their own medical expert, who asserted that Lee likely had well more than six months to live. In fact, he could probably survive until "at least November 2019," Monsanto's expert declared. The company also asserted in its response that Lee's doctor, a woman named Thach-Giao Truong, did not have enough expertise to predict Lee's life expectancy. And the company argued that as recently as April, Lee had been riding a bike, playing basketball, and gardening. He was, according to Monsanto, "generally healthy." The opposition motion filed by Monsanto also took issue with the report from medical expert Chadi Nabhan, stating, "Dr. Nabhan presents litigation-driven advocacy, not sound science."

There was "no good reason why Mr. Johnson's case should cut to the front of the line," Monsanto's attorneys wrote in their opposition.

Tim thought he had a good chance the judge would agree with him and set a trial before the end of the year, but he worried about Monsanto and the many tactics he knew the company was ready to deploy. Monsanto had already tried to pull the case out of the Superior Court of San Francisco and have it placed with the federal multidistrict litigation, or MDL, under Judge Vince Chhabria, who favored bifurcation and was openly skeptical of the strength of the allegations against Monsanto.

Lee's case had been remanded to the state court shortly after Monsanto got it sent to federal court. But Tim wouldn't put it past the company's lawyers to try again. It might make sense to try to find a compromise with Monsanto, he thought.

Helping Tim on the preference issue was Miller Firm associate Curtis Hoke, who had obtained his law degree in California and was licensed to practice there, unlike Tim, who was handling Lee's case pro hac vice, a Latin term meaning "for this occasion." This common practice allows a lawyer who is not admitted in a certain jurisdiction to practice there for a particular case. Tim and Curtis decided it might be best to cut a deal with Monsanto. Along with Monsanto, The Miller Firm had named Monsanto's West Coast salesman, Steven Gould, personally as a defendant and had also named California herbicide distributor Wilbur-Ellis Company as a defendant. They could drop those defendants and agree to a trial date six months later than the desired December 2017 date and avoid potentially losing their preference motion, they decided.

As Tim and Curtis mulled over the situation, Mike Miller decided he needed to be more active in the case as it headed for trial. Mike also was granted pro hac vice admission for Lee's case in California. Mike agreed with the idea of withdrawing the motion for a trial in December if Monsanto's attorneys would agree to a trial the following June. Mike wanted to make sure they had plenty of time to gather evidence. They already had several depositions of Monsanto scientists that would be helpful for their claims and hundreds of internal emails and memos that would also be useful. But Mike wanted more. Discovery orders were still in place, and Monsanto was having to turn over additional files on a regular basis. Mike wanted to make sure they had as much ammunition as possible before going head-to-head with the company's lawyers in court. The first trial would no doubt be closely watched—not just by media in the United States but also by European news outlets. Glyphosate concerns were growing in Europe, and regulators there were wrestling over proposals to ban the herbicide from the market. Yes, Mike told Tim and Curtis, they had to win this first trial. They could not afford to rush it. The world would be watching.

After a little back-and-forth between The Miller Firm's attorneys and Monsanto's counsel, both sides notified the judge that they had a deal. "Plaintiff and Monsanto agree and request that a trial date be set in this case for June 2018 and that the trial date remain even in the event that Plaintiff passes away prior to that date," read the joint stipulation, filed eight days before the scheduled hearing on the preference motion.

Judge Karnow issued the order, setting Lee's trial to begin in roughly ten months—on June 18, 2018, at 9:30 a.m.

It wasn't exactly what they had hoped for, but Tim, Curtis, and the rest of the Miller team felt they had achieved an important victory. The Roundup litigation had its first trial on the calendar. And Lee would get his day in court. If he lived that long.

CHAPTER 7
Corporate Secrets

As Tim focused on getting a trial date set for Lee Johnson's case, Aimee, Brent, Mike, and the others were bracing for a brawl with Monsanto over a different issue. The plaintiffs' attorneys wanted to unseal many of the Monsanto files that had been turned over through court-ordered discovery so they would be available for public scrutiny. But Monsanto was doing everything in its power to keep that from happening.

Monsanto's attorneys made their position very clear: there was no reason the company's internal communications and other records should be available to anyone but the lawyers for the cancer patients suing the company. To make sure of that, before Monsanto turned over the required documents, they were stamped as "confidential." That designation meant that though the lawyers for both sides could read every word of the documents, most of the pages had to be blacked out—redacted—if they were attached to any motions or other public court filings. That way, anyone who might be poking around in court files, such as reporters, other lawyers contemplating filing their own lawsuits, or even interested lawmakers, would not be able to see through Monsanto's shroud of secrecy.

Aimee and the rest of the legal team had expected this fight and were adamant that Monsanto had no legal right to keep the records sealed from public view. It would be understandable for Monsanto to seal documents that related to patented formulations of products or other types of "trade secrets." But the documents Monsanto was designating as confidential had nothing to do with marketplace competition and everything to do with avoiding public outrage at the company's actions, the plaintiffs' legal team believed. Embarrassment was not a legal reason to keep documents sealed. The revelations in Monsanto's files related to public health, and the public deserved to have the information as soon as possible. It was as simple as that. They just needed to convince a judge.

The debate was typical for this type of product liability litigation. It has long been part of the game for companies sued over their peddling of dangerous chemicals, drugs, medical devices, and an array of consumer products to try to keep a tight seal on internal documents they have to turn over to plaintiffs' attorneys. Many find success, escaping public scorn by convincing judges to keep company emails and other records hidden from the public, even those that could have alerted people to health and safety risks. Internal documents from drugmaker Purdue Pharma that showed deceptive marketing regarding the safety of OxyContin painkillers were sealed by judges in litigation dating back to 2001, for instance. It was only when the death toll attributed to Oxy-Contin addictions rose to staggering heights that public outcry and investigative journalists forced the records into public view. Similarly, a judge agreed to seal records showing that General Motors Company knew that reinforcing the roofs of its cars and trucks was needed to save lives in rollover crashes, and it took a decade before the records were released, after which the federal government upgraded its standards for roof strength in vehicles.

The Roundup case was filled with evidence of corporate misconduct the public needed to know about, the plaintiffs' team assessed. Among the close to one million documents the company had so far turned over were pages and pages of internal communications that portrayed a company that was not at all interested in public health but was solely focused on protecting its profits even in the face of mounting scientific concerns. These files would enable the plaintiffs' team to make a case to a jury that Monsanto had been suppressing years of scientific information about the dangers of its herbicides at the very same time it was promoting what the company pledged was the safety of those very same weed-killing products. They could use the Monsanto records to paint an ugly portrait of an organization that had been tinkering with the scientific literature, cozying up to regulators, and using secret collaborations with front groups and other third parties to make consumers and policy makers believe Monsanto products were safe.

There was an extraordinary amount of detail in the files. The internal records provided examples of how Monsanto scientists had been alerted to a number of concerns about the company's weed-killing formulations over the years, including warnings about science that showed the products might be genotoxic—damaging to human cells. The records also showed that Monsanto officials knew of scientific evidence that the ingredients could promote tumor development in test animals and significantly raise the risk of cancer in humans. Even more, the records revealed that while the company was running advertisements showing consumers spraying Roundup without any protective gloves or other gear, Monsanto was warning its own employees to wear not only gloves but also protective bodysuits and face masks when spraying its herbicides on company test plots.

It was more than outrageous. It was almost criminal, from Aimee and Mike's viewpoint. Consumers deserved to know the truth, they believed, at the very least to be adequately warned of the risks. Millions of people were still using Roundup and other Monsanto glyphosate-based brands, and most still believed they did not need to take precautions when they sprayed the chemical concoctions.

Sure, many of these "Monsanto Papers," as the legal team had started calling the discovery documents, could be introduced during the trials that would eventually take place. But to wait a year or more to let the world learn about Monsanto's covert activities to hide the risks of its products just seemed wrong.

As Aimee and her colleagues pondered which documents to fight to unseal, Monsanto attorneys Joe Hollingsworth and his co-counsel, Eric Lasker, were working not only to keep the company's records sealed from public view but also to block as many discovery requests as possible to keep Monsanto from having to turn records over in the first place. The company lawyers insisted that legal precedent gave the public almost no right to view discovery materials unless they were being used in a public judicial proceeding such as a hearing or at trial.

Aimee and the group didn't care much for Hollingsworth, and they found Lasker even less likable, if that were possible. In private, they had taken to referring to Lasker as "Mario" because he reminded them of the popular Mario Brothers cartoon character. Despite the image, Lasker could be a formidable opponent, the team was learning. He had a long history of legal work defending clients in cases involving medical and environmental issues, and he had developed skill in defending corporations against personal injury cases. Neither he nor Hollingsworth was going to bend on the designation issue, as unreasonable as Aimee and the group thought the two were being.

Many of the discovery requests were running through the federal court in San Francisco, where Judge Vince Chhabria was overseeing the multidistrict litigation that was created in October of 2016 as a means for moving multiple cases forward. Within just days of getting the assignment, Chhabria could see that the casework was going to be contentious at every turn. In many court cases, opposing lawyers might appear as bitter rivals at trial, but behind the scenes they would often treat each other collegially, trading emails back and forth with efficiency and professionalism as they bargained over the nuts and bolts that construct the framework of large-scale litigation. Just as a parent will tell two squabbling children to work out their differences, judges often encourage plaintiffs' and defense attorneys to work together as much as possible to resolve disputes without judicial intervention. That was not going to work with these lawyers.

Less than three weeks after the multidistrict Roundup Products Liability Litigation was filed in his court, Chhabria had his first full-on fight to referee between the lawyer groups. Aimee had asked Monsanto's lawyers to provide files from several more Monsanto employees as part of the discovery process, but Monsanto's attorneys not only had refused the request for what were called "custodial files" but also had refused to discuss any potential compromise. They completely ignored three emails Aimee sent them about the issue and even refused to state their position in a joint letter to the judge requesting a ruling on the dispute, as was protocol. As the co-leaders for the plaintiffs' legal team, Aimee, Mike, and Robin Greenwald wrote to Judge Chhabria to say that Monsanto's attorneys not only were rebuffing requests to turn over files from some of its European employees but also were rejecting proposals to meet and discuss the matter.

Sitting at her desk one cold winter morning, Aimee pondered Monsanto's unwillingness to make even minimal efforts to cooperate in what should be routine procedural matters, and she realized she was angry, really angry. The actions by Monsanto's lawyers were simply stunning. Though she had spent several years engaged in court battles against other large corporations, Aimee had never experienced, or expected to experience, the level of arrogance she felt from the Monsanto lawyers. To *ignore* her team's formal requests to meet, to refuse to confer, and to decline requests even for something as basic as jointly briefing the judge on a dispute—it was more than hubris and more than a lack of professional courtesy. This was an intentional insult, a strategy that frustrated and delayed the process and could wear down the will of the plaintiffs' legal team if they weren't careful. Aimee realized this was going to be an even longer and harder fight than she had steeled herself for. She was already working on the Roundup case night and day, seeing her marriage fray just as Tim's was, and becoming emotionally tied to clients whose lives had been irreparably damaged by cancer. There was no way she was going to let these assholes get to her. Bring it on, Mario, she thought.

By December of 2016, the dispute over the custodial files was some-what resolved as Judge Chhabria agreed with Aimee and the other plain-tiffs' lawyers on some of their requests for additional files but agreed with Monsanto's lawyers on others. What remained unresolved, however, was the continued conflict over the confidential designations Monsanto kept stamping on most of the files it did turn over.

Aimee, Mike, and the rest of the team wanted to fight almost all of those designations, but in complex mass litigation, as the Roundup cases were becoming, taking time to battle over hundreds or thousands of pages of documents would take away time the lawyers could be using to prepare their case. New plaintiffs were signing up to join the litigation against Monsanto almost every day, and the plaintiffs' lawyers were already scrambling to keep up with court deadlines for filings regarding deposition schedules and more.

The lawyers did not need the discovery documents unsealed for their own use; after all, they could read everything, confidential or not, and use what they needed to put their cases together. But they couldn't shake their belief that if the contents of the documents were known to the public, some lives might be saved.

Chhabria had never run multidistrict litigation before, but he had no intention of letting the ongoing battles between the opposing teams of lawyers consume time he needed for the other cases on his calendar. In an attempt to keep the lawyers from running to him with every disagreement over the designation issue as they had with the custodial file requests, Chhabria decided to lay down a list of rules for both sides to follow before they could engage him. It was a rigid step-by-step system that had to be followed to the letter. And if they didn't, he would make sure there would be hell to pay.

Chhabria's December 2016 court order had something for both sides. It granted Monsanto the benefit of the doubt, allowing company officials to designate as many documents as they wanted as confidential so long as the Monsanto officials believed the records were, in fact, confidential. The judge said his order did not "confer blanket protections" for all Monsanto documents and that the company should be sure it was following "applicable legal principles" in making confidential designations to the documents it handed over.

If the lawyers for the cancer victims wanted to challenge the confidentiality Monsanto asserted, they would be allowed to issue a challenge for up to five hundred documents in one thirty-day period. But each challenge had to follow certain steps. Under Chhabria's ordered protocol, if Mike, Aimee, Brent, or any of the other plaintiffs' attorneys wanted to challenge the confidentiality of documents, they first must notify Monsanto's lawyers in writing of each document they were trying to "de-designate" and explain in writing the basis for their belief that the designations were not proper.

Both sides must then talk to each other directly "in voice to voice dialogue," within fourteen days of notification of the de-designation effort. If Monsanto's lawyers were not persuaded that the designations should be lifted, they then would have to explain the specific basis for keeping sealed each of the documents the plaintiffs' lawyers wanted unsealed.

If the two sides could not resolve the matter, the judge would intervene. But to obtain his intervention, one of two things had to happen. Either the lawyers for the plaintiffs had to file a motion formally challenging the confidentiality designations to the judge, or Monsanto had to file a motion asking to "retain confidentiality."

And in what would later become an important provision, Judge Chhabria said that the burden for resolution of the challenges to document confidentiality would be squarely on Monsanto. He wrote in his order the following:

> *If the Parties cannot resolve a challenge without court intervention, the Designating Party shall file and serve a motion to retain confidentiality . . . within 30 days of the initial notice of the challenge or within 21 days of the parties agreeing that the meet and confer process will not resolve their dispute, whichever is earlier. . . . Failure by the Designating Party to make such a motion including the required declaration within 30 days (or 21 days, if applicable) shall automatically waive the confidentiality designation for each challenged designation.*

Aimee, Mike, and Robin wasted no time in testing Judge Chhabria's protocol. They did as his December order stated, identifying roughly two hundred documents they believed Monsanto had no legal reason to keep sealed. Among those were internal emails in which Monsanto employees discussed interactions with the US Environmental Protection Agency and former EPA official Jess Rowland, who had led the cancer assessment for glyphosate within the agency. To the plaintiffs' attorneys, the emails looked like clear evidence of collusion. The public should see these documents. And Rowland should answer questions about them. The lawyers were convinced Rowland had tight ties with Monsanto and helped the company every chance he got. He was the one who had leaked the report to Monsanto in April of 2016 during a pivotal time in the litigation, they believed. And though they couldn't prove it yet, they suspected that when he left the EPA shortly after the leak, Rowland had gone to work for chemical industry interests affiliated with Monsanto.

Not surprisingly, Rowland did not want to be deposed, and the EPA also wanted to keep him from having to give sworn testimony. An EPA lawyer told the plaintiffs' attorneys that Rowland's testimony would not be in the "best interests" of the EPA.

Monsanto lawyers Hollingsworth and Lasker also did not want Rowland deposed, and they definitely did not want the company's internal emails about Rowland available for public scrutiny or any of the other internal records plaintiffs wanted unsealed. In a February 2017 brief filed with Judge Chhabria, they argued that Aimee, Mike, and Robin were trying to remove the confidentiality designation of the EPA and Rowland documents only to garner public sympathy for the people suing the company. If the public saw the emails, it would harm Monsanto's credibility and taint any potential future jury pools, they said. The "reputational and privacy interests of Monsanto, and its interests in fair and efficient court proceedings, could be damaged if plaintiffs are permitted to use raw discovery material to launch a public, out-of-court attack," they wrote in a brief to Chhabria.

Monsanto had by that point produced nine hundred thousand documents totaling roughly ten million pages, and the plaintiffs' lawyers should be allowed to challenge the confidentiality of those records only when there was a "litigation need," Hollingsworth and Lasker argued for Monsanto. "The process of resolving confidentiality challenges disconnected from relevance and litigation need inevitably would be time consuming and expensive for the parties and Court," they wrote in their brief.

Mike, Aimee, and Robin fired back, countering that Monsanto had stamped as confidential more than eight million of the ten million pages turned over, and their review found clear abuse of the designations. They believed that Monsanto should not be allowed to curtail public access to discovery materials that affect public health. "Secrecy offends the principles of transparency and public oversight undergirding our judicial system," the three attorneys wrote in their brief to Judge Chhabria. One phrase they capitalized and put in boldface type for extra emphasis: "Public Health and Safety Interests Outweigh Monsanto's Privacy Interests."

They reminded the judge of the rules laid out in his December court order specifying the process Monsanto must follow to keep records sealed. That order made no mention of a requirement that plaintiffs show a "litigation need"; rather, the burden was to be on Monsanto to show specific reasons why the company wanted to keep each of the documents sealed.

The ruling from Chhabria did not come quickly. It was not until March that he weighed in, but for the plaintiffs the judicial decision was worth the wait. Chhabria rejected Monsanto's efforts to keep the Rowland documents sealed, with the exception of one document. He said that the "potential embarrassment" to Monsanto was not a sufficient reason to keep the communications cloaked, and there was no credible argument that the documents contained trade secrets. Several other documents related to the EPA could also be unsealed, he said.

In stern language, he reminded both sides they should not play with his patience. Going forward, plaintiffs must be sure that a document they wanted to release was relevant to the litigation when they asked for it to be unsealed. And Monsanto lawyers should know they would be sanctioned if they continued filing "unreasonable or unsubstantiated declarations" regarding sealing documents, Chhabria warned.

It was not much of a victory, but it was still something to celebrate for Aimee, Mike, and Robin. Finally, the public would be able to see at least a little of what they were seeing. They did not want to push Chhabria too hard. They weren't going to publicize Monsanto's internal documents on a law firm website or email them to news organizations. But they would now at least be able to file several revealing documents as open exhibits attached to their briefings and motions, and these would then be available in the court docket, where reporters or anyone savvy enough to navigate court files could read and copy them. And they were not about to waste any time.

The ruling came down on a Monday, and by Tuesday Aimee, Mike, and Robin had filed exhibits into the court docket that included multiple email strings written by Monsanto officials. Many dealt with the company's plans to counter the concerns international cancer scientists had about glyphosate. Among the unsealed documents were emails from Monsanto officials discussing their interactions with the EPA's Rowland.

As the lawyers had hoped, members of the news media were eager to see the emails. One email in particular sparked outrage when it was dug out of the court files by a reporter for the Bloomberg news agency and published for all the world to see. The email had been written by Monsanto regulatory affairs official Dan Jenkins, who was sharing with colleagues a comment he said Rowland had made to him. He wrote that Rowland was trying to stop a probe into glyphosate safety planned by a federal agency outside of the EPA called the Agency for Toxic Substances and Disease Registry, referred to as ATSDR. Monsanto's files showed the company had been very worried that the ATSDR review would agree with the determination by the International Agency for Research on Cancer (IARC) that glyphosate was probably carcinogenic, and the company had been trying to enlist the EPA's help in stopping the planned review. Rowland was, as ever, trying to be helpful, according to the Jenkins email. Jenkins quoted Rowland as saying, "If I can kill this I should get a medal." Jenkins warned his colleagues not to get their hopes up, however, writing, "I doubt the EPA and Jess can kill this; but it's good to know they are going to actually make the effort."

Also among the unsealed documents was an email string in which a Monsanto official wrote to colleagues that "Jess will be retiring from EPA in 5–6 mos and could be useful as we move forward with ongoing glyphosate defense."

The emails were so alarming, appearing to provide evidence of collusion between Monsanto and the EPA and Rowland, that the EPA's Office of Inspector General said it was launching an investigation into the matter.

Just a few weeks after the Rowland emails were made public, Mike and the team got Rowland to sit before a camera and microphone and take questions about the suspicious leak of the glyphosate cancer assessment report he had overseen and about how much "help" he had been providing Monsanto. But after more than a day of questioning, Rowland had said almost nothing of value for the plaintiffs' side. As company scientist William Heydens had done in his deposition, even when confronted with emails and other documents laying out what the plaintiffs' legal team considered damning words and deeds, Rowland refused to acknowledge the story the emails told.

Other unsealed internal Monsanto emails also made headlines. National Public Radio and *USA Today* ran stories about emails that showed Monsanto working to recruit outside scientists they could pay in exchange for coauthoring reports defending the safety of glyphosate. The news outlets also highlighted emails by Heydens, telling readers how he had suggested that the company "ghost-write" scientific information, just as the company had "handled" a scientific paper published in 2000. One email from Heydens stated that Monsanto "would be keeping the cost down by us doing the writing and they would just edit & sign their names so to speak."

Reporters who had largely ignored the Roundup litigation were starting to call and email the plaintiffs' legal team seeking more documents and tips on what more might be coming, and lawmakers in other countries were taking note as well.

Getting the emails out was a win for the plaintiffs' side, for sure. Now people were paying attention. In his office in Los Angeles, Brent was thrilled that Aimee, Mike, and Robin had been able to get some of the discovery documents unsealed and that Monsanto's secrets were starting to come to light. He and Michael Baum did not have a client with a case coming to trial anytime soon, but they still spent a lot of time studying the discovery documents for every thread of evidence that could be pulled. Brent wanted so badly to try one of these cases that he had started drafting opening statements for a future trial he hoped he would get the chance to lead. There was so much to show a jury. So many lies, for so long.

The more he read of the internal files, the less patient Brent became with the process. There was just so much more that should be revealed, now, not a year or two later at trial. Regulators in Europe were currently debating whether or not to relicense glyphosate for another ten to twenty years of use, and they needed to make a decision by the end of 2017, Brent knew.

California regulators were in the midst of a battle with Monsanto over the state's decision to require warning labels on glyphosate-based products, and every day, somewhere, school districts were spraying weed killers around ball fields, city groundskeepers were applying them to parks where kids played, and moms and dads were using them in their own backyards. They all had a right to know what Monsanto was not telling them, Brent thought.

He had to come up with a plan to get more of Monsanto's internal papers into the public spotlight. Attaching them as exhibits to court files as the opportunity presented itself, as Robin, Aimee, and Mike had done, was not going to do the trick. Not if he wanted the world to see what he saw.

Brent read and reread Judge Chhabria's December order laying out the process both sides had to follow before documents could be unsealed. And as he did, a plan started to come together in his head. He was sure if he could pull it off, Judge Chhabria would not like it. And if the judge did not like it, Mike and some of the other co-leaders of the multidistrict litigation would not like it either. Brent knew that if they got on the bad side of Judge Chhabria, it could do lasting damage to their leadership position in the federal litigation, resulting in sanctions or worse. Antagonizing the federal judge would also not sit well with the state judges who would be trying many of the Roundup cases. It was even possible that he could get kicked off the Roundup litigation entirely. But Brent couldn't shake the idea that this was something he needed to do. Monsanto officials had covered up the truth for too long.

As he jotted down an outline for how to put his plan into action, Brent realized the plan would work only if Monsanto's attorneys continued to treat him and the other members of the plaintiffs' legal team with the arrogance and dismissiveness they had shown so far. It was going to be a gamble. But if he was careful, and Monsanto's lawyers were not, Brent just might be able to lead them into a legal trap of their own making.

Time to get to work.

CHAPTER 8

A Risky Plan

The first step in Brent's plan was to rope in some assistance from other members of the Baum Hedlund law firm. If he was going to skip past the court docket and lay out Monsanto's internal files for the world to see, he couldn't do it alone.

Brent knew he could not ask for a lot of help from the firm's senior partner and president, Michael Baum. Though Michael had championed the practice of publicizing sensitive corporate documents that exposed wrongdoing and public health risks, and he was just as eager as Brent to see Monsanto's documents go public, he was far too busy to take on the tedious tasks needed to make it happen. Michael could help him perfect the plan, but first Brent needed someone willing to do the grunt work, someone with time to pore through the vast database of documents Monsanto had designated as confidential. And it had to be someone savvy enough to help make sure that each early step in stripping the confidentiality designation from those documents did not run afoul of court orders.

Importantly, he also needed someone with backbone. If the plan worked and the firm was able to release a trove of what Brent considered damning internal Monsanto documents directly to the public rather than attaching them as piecemeal exhibits to court motions, there would likely be a lot of angry people seeking retribution, US District Judge Vince Chhabria included. The judge had admonished the plaintiffs' attorneys multiple times in the past few months not to use Monsanto's internal documents to conduct a public relations campaign against the company. If the documents were not relevant to the litigation, no matter what secrets they held, they should remain confidential, Chhabria had warned the lawyers.

Brent knew that some of the other lawyers in the Roundup litigation thought he was playing with fire even to contemplate toying with Judge Chhabria. Mike Miller, whose firm had launched the discovery requests of Monsanto and was the first to dig into the document database, was staunchly opposed to the plan to unveil stacks of documents to the public without the judge's express approval. Mike wanted no part of the effort, nor did he want anyone from his firm involved. Mike was a fighter, but he preferred to pick his battles carefully, and he knew that teeing off a federal judge was rarely a good idea.

Most of the other Baum Hedlund lawyers had their own clients and caseloads to handle. But there was a new young lawyer at the firm who seemed to match Brent's zeal for challenging corporate wrongdoing. Pedram Esfandiary was only twenty-five, even younger than Brent. Still, Pedram had a sophisticated worldview honed by a childhood that had included living for stints in Sweden, Iran, Canada, and the United Kingdom, and he had grown up hearing stories of his Iranian mother's work in challenging government power during the Iranian Revolution. By the time he was twelve, Pedram had decided he also needed to be a revolutionary of sorts but would make his mark as a lawyer. He obtained a law degree and a degree in criminology in the United Kingdom before moving to Los Angeles, where he finished his education at the University of Southern California and immediately after signed on with the Baum Hedlund firm.

In appearance, Pedram and Brent were opposites—with his short, well-coiffed hair, Brent looked like just about any other clean-cut white guy in a business suit, while Pedram stood out from the crowd with exotic dark eyes, heavy brows, and a long mane of thick black hair that he wore in waves down his back or sometimes coiled into a bun. He was soft-spoken and had a British accent, evoking a cool calm, in contrast to Brent's almost-frenetic energy. Pedram had passed the bar exam only in December of 2016 and had essentially no real-life litigation experience. But Brent knew he had a sharp mind and a passion for public interest law, which made Pedram the perfect partner for his plan.

The first task at hand was to sift through the hundreds of thousands of documents sitting in the Crivella discovery database that Monsanto had marked as confidential. The system was tricky to navigate, but when tapped by a trained hand it could go far beyond conducting keyword search terms. The Crivella system was designed with algorithms that could quickly identify email conversations that suggested deception or anxiety or anger by the word content.

Using those markers, whenever someone on the legal team found documents they thought would be particularly useful, they flagged them as "hot dox." The hottest of the hot dox were ones that the team thought showed Monsanto plotting to get around worrisome scientific findings about its products, information they hoped would resonate with jurors and members of the public.

Over the several months he had been working at the firm, Pedram spent a lot of hours exploring the database and working with Jeff Travers from The Miller Firm to see what secrets the documents held. Of all the members of the legal team, Jeff was the most adept with the Crivella system, and he sent Pedram file after file of emails and internal Monsanto reports that looked as if they would be helpful to the plaintiffs' cases. Pedram studied each document intensely and practically memorized the Monsanto scientists' words. He read the plans to beat back any public concern that Roundup might be dangerous. He knew which documents best illustrated the company's work to discredit the scientists at the International Agency for Research on Cancer (IARC). He could see, on paper, the company trying to convince regulators to ignore any and all studies that showed evidence of harm.

There were so many revealing documents that it was difficult to decide which ones they should use for their initial confidentiality challenge. It was almost certain that Monsanto would deny their request to unseal the documents, and Pedram and Brent knew that if they planned to keep their careers, they had to follow Judge Chhabria's December 2016 order to a T.

After long days of staring into their computers, Pedram and Brent finally identified eighty-six documents they wanted to push out to the public. Forty-two of them were documents that Aimee Wagstaff had previously tried to unseal with no success. She had emailed Monsanto's attorneys a list of the documents in early May, but the company's attorneys had never responded, even to her follow-up emails.

Pedram organized document summaries in a detailed chart and wrote up arguments for their relevance to the litigation. One set of Monsanto documents from 2008 showed that employees were aware of the publication of a new study in the *International Journal of Cancer* showing that exposure to glyphosate could more than double a person's risk of developing non-Hodgkin lymphoma. The employees expressed concerns, not for Monsanto customers, but for the fact that activists were using the data to promote organic agriculture.

Another set of documents Pedram listed highlighted emails describing "surprising results" in an analysis of the rate at which the company's herbicides were absorbed into skin. In one email, Monsanto scientist William Heydens expressed worry about such "dermal penetration" studies, writing, "My primary concern is with the glyphosate in terms of the potential for this work to blow Roundup risk evaluations (getting a much higher dermal penetration than we've ever seen before)."

The documents were "relevant and reasonably likely to be used in this litigation" because they were related to information that the formulated product was "both absorbed at a higher rate and is more toxic—significant questions for the biological plausibility of glyphosate and Roundup as a carcinogen," Pedram wrote in his chart. "Such information is likely to be considered vital by regulators and researchers when assessing the carcinogenicity of Roundup and glyphosate."

More documents discussed news that French regulators were going to order a withdrawal of glyphosate-based products containing a key Roundup ingredient called tallowamine because the European Food Safety Authority had found evidence of potential human health risks from the combination of chemicals. Company employees were worried—again, not for the health of Monsanto customers but because the move would look bad for Monsanto. "We are expecting the letter of intention from French regulator ANSES very soon, and it might point to 'imminent health risk' regarding the use of tallowamine," a Monsanto executive wrote to colleagues.

The documents showed that the company wanted to make the public think the ban was not related to human health risks, even though the French agency had specifically cited the potential "genotoxicity, long-term toxicity and carcinogenicity, reproductive/developmental toxicity and endocrine disrupting potential" of the Roundup ingredient. Pedram quoted the Monsanto internal discussion—typos and all—in his chart: "We simple would need the argumentation for the ban/withdrawal to not be based on 'human health' but other on considerations like precautionary principle. The consequences of this ban if referring to human health risks have the potential to go beyond France and would potentially have global and trade impact. It is therefore of essence that any intention to ban does not refer to imminent human health risk."

On and on, Pedram added the documents to his chart, careful to explain in as much detail as possible why the documents were relevant to the key question in the case—could Monsanto's Roundup and other formulations cause cancer?

Pedram also threw in several documents showing what he considered the most outrageous of the company's actions. He included documents showing how Monsanto had plotted in 2015 and 2016 to produce an "independent" review of glyphosate as "ghostwriters." The company would use the Intertek consulting group as a conduit for papers that would contradict the IARC scientists and declare glyphosate safe. He added emails showing that Monsanto was secretly directly paying some of the noncompany scientists enlisted as authors on the papers.

And he included emails from early 2015 between Monsanto and an academic named Henry Miller laying out a plan for Miller to appear as the author of an article Monsanto had drafted for publication on the *Forbes* magazine website. The point of the article was to "set the stage" for an attack on IARC's future findings on glyphosate.

There were also pages and pages of emails Pedram added to the chart showing Monsanto's behind-the-scenes efforts to discredit the work of a French scientist who claimed to have found that Monsanto's herbicides were very damaging to human health.

Line after line, Pedram carefully typed out the details he hoped would soon be unsealed and made part of the public record. It took him weeks to pull the whole thing together; the list of documents turned out to be twenty-eight pages long. But Brent was thrilled, and Michael heartily applauded Pedram's work as well.

The time had come to engage Monsanto's attorneys. All three men decided they wanted to sign on to the letter, but Brent's name would go first. It was his plan, after all.

They addressed a two-page letter to Joe Hollingsworth and two of his co-counsels, posting the date of the letter boldly in the middle of the top of the first page—June 30, 2017. The exact date would be critical to the plan, and there should be no mistake about it. They also were careful to include language specifying that their action was made in accordance with Judge Chhabria's December 2016 protection order. That language had been missing from Aimee's May letter seeking to unseal the forty-two documents. This time, everything had to be perfect.

> *Counsel,*
>
> *I write to initiate a meet-and-confer regarding the asserted "confidentiality" of specific documents produced by Monsanto in discovery. I have been appointed by the Plaintiffs' Leadership in the MDL to work on this issue with you. This challenge is made pursuant to Paragraph 16.2 of the December 9, 2016 Protective and Confidentiality Order. We seek to meet-and-confer about documents we believe have been overdesignated as "Confidential" by Monsanto. We have reviewed each document individually and selected only documents, listed out in detail on the attached chart, that do not contain trade secrets, sensitive commercial information, privileged material, or that are otherwise entitled to "confidential" protection under the law. In compliance with the Court's Pre-Trial Order 15 (PTO-15), clear reasons are set forth in the attached chart for why each challenged document is relevant to the general causation stage of this litigation.*

They made sure to be courteous:

> *Recognizing that Monsanto's designation of nearly every document produced in this litigation as "Confidential" was not done in bad-faith, but simply because Monsanto erred on the "side of caution," this letter and the requested meet-and-confer is your chance to address a discrete set of documents, identified in the attached chart, and correct Monsanto's overdesignations. It is my sincere hope that through the meet-and-confer process we can avoid burdening the Court with having to review these documents and this confidentiality dispute can be resolved without Court intervention.*

But they made it clear that the clock was ticking:

I am available to meet-and-confer and ask that you notify us by Thursday, July 6, 2017 of when you will be able to systematically go through each of these documents to see if there is some way we can come to an agreement outside of Court intervention.
    Best,
    BAUM HEDLUND ARISTEI & GOLDMAN, P.C.
    R. Brent Wisner
    Michael L. Baum
    Pedram Esfandiary

The twenty-eight pages of documents laid out in the chart Pedram had carefully prepared was attached to the email, and with a click of the computer mouse, it was sent. Now they just had to wait and see how Monsanto's attorneys responded. Would Hollingsworth and his team actually agree to go over the documents in a good-faith review as the judge had instructed in his December order? Or would they do what they had done in the past—simply swat away the requests and the plaintiffs' attorneys like annoying gnats? Brent generally did not like to be ignored, looked down on, or underestimated. But now, that was all he hoped for.

If Monsanto's lawyers did actually engage and start what could be a long-drawn-out negotiation over the documents, Brent's grand plan would be lost. The judge would be brought in, and chances for a public release would fade away. But if Monsanto's attorneys didn't take the request seriously and failed to follow the protocol the judge had laid out in his December order, well, then, that would leave the gates for a public document release wide open.

Brent thought back to the critical section of the judge's order: The first required step was a notification in writing to Monsanto's attorneys listing the documents they wanted to unseal. That was done. The next step was for the two sides to talk to each other within fourteen days of the date of notification. The judge would get involved *only* if one of the two sides asked him to, and Brent certainly was not about to do that. According to the judge's order, Monsanto would need to file a motion to "retain confidentiality" with the court within thirty days of the date of notification, and—this was the key part—a failure by Monsanto to make such a motion within that thirty-day window "shall automatically waive the confidentiality designation for each challenged designation."

It felt as if they were playing chess with a master and could only hope that the master was not paying attention to their moves. Would Monsanto's lawyers misstep? Brent knew it was unlikely. The Hollingsworth firm was legendary for its litigation skills. Still, Brent thought there was a good chance they would. Michael and Pedram were not so sure.

The team heard back within a week. Hollingsworth law partner Gary Rubin emailed Brent, saying, "We are available to discuss your letter" and that he would be willing to participate in a conference call to address the meet-and-confer requirement set by Judge Chhabria for such document discussions. The two sides agreed to set the call for early on the afternoon of Thursday, July 13, the last day to act within Judge Chhabria's required fourteen-day window for such a meeting following notification of the document challenge.

On the Monday ahead of the meeting, Brent instructed Pedram to email Rubin reminding him of the upcoming document discussion and asking him to note which documents he was not going to agree to unseal, to facilitate the upcoming discussion. But Rubin emailed back only a curt reply: "Thank you for your e-mail. We plan to speak with you on Thursday, 1 p.m. your time."

Brent was in Boston for a hearing in another case that week, but he was able to set aside Thursday afternoon for what he anticipated would be many hours of back-and-forth debate over each of the eighty-six documents. He had the chart and copies of all the emails and other Monsanto documents spread out around his hotel room so he could reference them as they came up in the call. Pedram was not in the Baum Hedlund office in Los Angeles either. He was spending the day in San Jose, California, with his girlfriend and her parents, but he also had planned for hours of negotiations. The girlfriend's father had a quiet study, where Pedram closed the door and dialed in to the call. Along with Pedram and Brent, Aimee also joined the call for the plaintiffs' side. Jim Sullivan, the Hollingsworth firm's discovery specialist, joined Rubin on Monsanto's behalf. Sullivan had played college football and was known for his toughness.

After a brief exchange of greetings, Pedram began to explain Baum Hedlund's basis for seeking to unseal the first document. He didn't get far before a Monsanto attorney cut him off. Sullivan explained that he and Rubin were not going to discuss the de-designation requests for any of the documents laid out in Pedram's chart. Sullivan told them there was no "litigation need" for any of them to be unsealed. Brent was shocked. He had expected to be rebuffed, but he thought Monsanto's attorneys would at least attempt a show of good-faith negotiating. He pushed Sullivan to reconsider but got nowhere. The company's lawyer told him simply that their whole team should just "go away."

They had been on the call only about half an hour by this point, but both sides agreed they were at an impasse. Rubin asked Brent if he would consider filing a joint discovery letter instead of a motion if he wanted to proceed with efforts to try to reverse the company's confidentiality designations on the documents.

Brent was still stunned by the audacity of the Monsanto attorneys. He had been in contentious calls before with opposing counsel but had never simply been told to go away, like a pesky dog at a stranger's foot. He was angry, and insulted, but he also felt a rush of adrenalin. He thought back to the language of the judge's protective order, which he had memorized: "If the parties cannot resolve a challenge without court intervention . . . the Designating Party shall file and serve a motion to retain confidentiality." The language could not be more clear: if Monsanto, which was the designating party, failed to make such a motion within thirty days, the company would "automatically waive the confidentiality for each challenged designation."

But it didn't sound like Monsanto planned to file such a motion. Instead, the company's lawyers were suggesting a joint letter to the judge. There was no way Brent was going to file anything with the court asking for Judge Chhabria's intervention. Hell, no. The burden was on Monsanto's attorneys, and he wasn't about to make that burden any lighter. He didn't tell either Sullivan or Rubin what he was thinking, saying only that he doubted his team would agree to a joint letter to the judge before ending the call.

Thirty days! Monsanto's attorneys had thirty days to file a motion, or the Baum Hedlund firm would blow the documents wide open. Their notification had been delivered on June 30, which meant the thirty-day period for Monsanto to act to protect the documents would expire at midnight on July 30. One week passed with no filing by Monsanto. And then a second week passed. Were they really going to let this thirty-day window expire? Did Monsanto's attorneys understand that the judge's protective order would allow Baum Hedlund to open up the documents once the thirty days had passed unless Monsanto filed a motion to retain confidentiality?

The waiting was wearing on Brent and also on Pedram, who found himself smoking nervously far more than he knew was good for him and easing the stress with a drink—or more—at night. Each day, they expected to get a copy of Monsanto's motion, which would bring Judge Chhabria into the discussion and make a direct document release to the public highly unlikely. But each day passed with no action from Monsanto. Brent started to wonder if he had been clear enough with Monsanto's lawyers about the fact that he was not filing anything with the judge. After consulting with Aimee, Michael, and Pedram, Brent sent an email to Rubin late in the afternoon on July 27.

Following up from the meet-and-confer, we discussed the issue internally, and Plaintiffs have decided that we will not be filing a joint discovery letter with the Court concerning the confidentiality designations challenged in the June 30, 2017 letter.
Best,
R. Brent Wisner, Esq.

Brent said nothing in his email about the fact that Monsanto's thirty-day window was about to close, nor about his plans once the deadline did pass.

Another day passed. And another, and then it was July 30. Monsanto still had not filed the required motion. Were they really this stupid? Brent thought. This arrogant? Did they not believe Baum Hedlund would actually release the documents?

Well, they had made a mistake. A big mistake. Brent would give them one more day, a cushion just in case there was some confusion about timing by Monsanto's attorneys.

The hours on the extra day ticked away slowly, it seemed, but as July 31 edged into evening, it was clear that the company had officially missed the deadline for maintaining document confidentiality. Now Brent wanted the files out as soon as possible. No more waiting. He, Michael, and Pedram determined the release should start just past midnight, when the clock ticked to the start of a new day.

In preparation, the documents from Pedram's chart were loaded onto a law firm web page with a downloadable link for each file. The links would go live with a push of the button by one of the Baum Hedlund staffers Michael had lined up to stay in the office overnight. Brent did not want to pace the law firm's halls all evening, so he decided he would manage the operation from his apartment.

He knew that once Monsanto got wind of what they were doing, the company would more than likely rush to the court and ask Judge Chhabria to force Baum Hedlund to remove the documents from the firm's website. So it was critically important that all of the documents were not only accessible on the law firm's website but also in the hands of journalists and policy makers, people who wouldn't have to answer to Judge Chhabria.

One journalist in particular had been pestering the Baum Hedlund firm for months about the sealed documents, pushing and prodding for details about what secrets the discovery database held. She had spent close to twenty years reporting on Monsanto for a large international news organization and had just finished writing a book about the company and the history of its Roundup business. Monsanto and its allies were working almost as hard to smear her reputation and her book as they had been working to discredit the international cancer scientists who had confirmed links between the weed killer and cancer. Brent first met the reporter when she interviewed one of his clients for her book and knew she could make sense of the documents quickly and write an in-depth story about what the company had been hiding. Best of all, the reporter was more than willing to stay up all night, download the documents, and place them on a public-access website operated by a nonprofit group called, fittingly, U.S. Right to Know.

Brent also wanted to alert California environmental health officials and European lawmakers. Both groups were mired in debate over the safety—or lack of it—of glyphosate-based herbicides, and the documents shed light on important scientific evidence they deserved to know about. Brent put together detailed letters to both groups, including paper copies of all the documents. He took particular care with the letter to California's Office of Environmental Health Hazard Assessment, to which Monsanto had given ghostwritten data presented as independent affirmations of glyphosate safety. He also wanted the California regulators to know that Monsanto had failed to disclose to them data suggesting that the absorption rate of glyphosate was more perilous to human health than had been publicly disclosed.

Finally, he wrote a letter to the Office of Inspector General for the US Environmental Protection Agency, including hard copies of the documents. This oversight arm of the EPA should know how cozy the agency had been with EPA officials. The OIG had already said it was investigating the connection between the EPA's Jess Rowland and Monsanto. These documents could be very helpful, Brent thought. He laid it out as clearly as he could:

> *Regulators must be independent from the companies they regulate. When those lines blur, it raises serious public health concerns and undermines confidence in our regulatory bodies. We would like to bring to your attention a number of documents discovered in the litigation which were declassified today. Please take a moment to review these documents. They tell an alarming story of Monsanto's collusion with EPA officials, manipulation of scientific data and literature, refusal to thoroughly investigate risks of serious adverse health effects associated with glyphosate, and previously undisclosed information about how glyphosate is absorbed by the human body. The documents are particularly pertinent to your investigation into whether a collusive relationship between Monsanto and EPA officials potentially thwarted a robust scientific analysis of glyphosate, thereby resulting in glyphosate being registered without a comprehensive review of the available data by impartial regulators.*

He made sure to copy Monsanto attorney Joe Hollingsworth on all the correspondence.

With the letters completed, Brent watched the clock tick toward midnight. It was almost time to pull the trigger.

CHAPTER 9

Just Past Midnight

It was 12:01 a.m. on August 1, 2017, when Brent gave the go-ahead to the team back at the office, telling them to release the documents as fast as they could get them out. There was nothing more for him to do, so he crawled into bed, exhilarated but exhausted. He knew Monsanto's lawyers would be irate when they learned the documents were public, and he would have to be ready for what would likely be a ferocious countermove. He needed at least a few hours of sleep.

By 2:00 a.m. California time, links to all the documents were displayed on Baum Hedlund's website, and the reporter had posted her story with the *Huffington Post* news outlet. She had also made sure that the Monsanto Papers, as they had been dubbed, were laid out on the U.S. Right to Know website, where anyone could easily read through them.

It didn't take long before news of the document release was racing around the world as reporters from the *New York Times*, Bloomberg, and other news giants scrambled to dig through the unsealed Monsanto records and file stories about their findings.

"Documents released Tuesday in a lawsuit against Monsanto raised new questions about the company's efforts to influence the news media and scientific research and revealed internal debate over the safety of its highest-profile product, the weed killer Roundup," the *New York Times* reported.

The *Huffington Post* headline read, "New 'Monsanto Papers' Add to Questions of Regulatory Collusion, Scientific Mischief." The article quoted Brent: "This is a look behind the curtain. These show that Monsanto has deliberately been stopping studies that look bad for them, ghostwriting literature and engaging in a whole host of corporate malfeasance. They (Monsanto) have been telling everybody that these products are safe because regulators have said they are safe, but it turns out that Monsanto has been in bed with U.S. regulators while misleading European regulators."

As the news spread, calls and emails flooded the Baum Hedlund law firm with reporters and other lawyers clamoring for more information. Oddly, though, Brent heard nothing immediately from Monsanto. Maybe the company's attorneys had realized all along that the documents would be released after the thirty-day window closed, Brent thought. Maybe they weren't upset at all.

By the following morning, Brent knew just how wrong that notion was. A curt email from the Hollingsworth firm instructed Brent and the rest of the team to preserve all email communications regarding the document release. Monsanto's attorneys said they were filing an emergency motion and planned to seek harsh sanctions not only against Brent, Michael Baum, and Pedram Esfandiary but also against Aimee Wagstaff and Mike Miller. And, in a particularly zealous bid for punishment, the Monsanto attorneys said they wanted the group of attorneys removed entirely from the executive committee that formed the plaintiffs' leadership of the nationwide Roundup litigation. Given that they made up the core legal expertise guiding the Roundup litigation, their removal would be a huge blow to the plaintiffs' case.

In the emergency pleading to Judge Vince Chhabria, Monsanto attorneys Joe Hollingsworth and Eric Lasker argued that Brent and the other plaintiffs' lawyers had mocked the judge's instructions for handling confidential documents. They also demanded that the eighty-six documents be removed from the Baum Hedlund website and told the judge they wanted a statement sent to all media outlets that referenced the documents to warn them that the documents should not have been made public and were indeed still held to be confidential by Monsanto.

The pleading also demanded that Baum Hedlund turn over to Monsanto any emails or other correspondence between the plaintiffs' attorneys and the reporter who had uploaded the documents to the nonprofit's website and broken the news of the document release in the *Huffington Post* article.

"Plaintiffs' counsel have blatantly disregarded the Court's Orders, and once again are seeking to try their case in the press through out-of-context disclosures of documents and misleading spin," Monsanto's lawyers wrote.

According to Hollingsworth and Lasker, Brent was wrong to assume that any thirty-day window applied to the document debate, because he and the other plaintiffs' attorneys never had proper grounds to seek to release the eighty-six documents in the first place. Because there was no legitimate litigation need, the provision for a waiver of confidentiality did not apply, they contended. Moreover, they pointed out that Judge Chhabria had previously refused to unseal twenty-four of the eighty-six documents that now were open for public view.

And, according to Hollingsworth and Lasker, during that forty-minute phone call in which their co-counsel essentially told Brent and Pedram to "go away," Monsanto's attorney made it crystal clear that their position was that both sides would need to file a joint letter to the judge to resolve their dispute if Brent and Pedram wanted to continue to press to unseal the documents. The Monsanto attorneys said they were never told by Brent or the other lawyers for the plaintiffs that they planned to release the documents without going to the judge first.

The Monsanto lawyers asked Judge Chhabria to order that the eighty-six documents at issue be barred from use "in any future proceedings in this or any other court." They also asked the judge to bar the plaintiffs' attorneys from making any future challenges seeking to unseal any other Monsanto documents, and they asked that the judge impose monetary fines against Brent and the other lawyers.

"Plaintiffs' counsel made the conscious decision to violate the Court's orders knowing that, by the time Monsanto could object, the damage would be done. Monsanto respectfully suggests that absent a clear and strong message from the Court in the form of meaningful sanctions, plaintiffs' counsel is likely to make the same decision again whenever complying with the Court's Orders proves to be inconvenient or at odds with their desires," Hollingsworth and Lasker wrote in their pleading.

Reading through Monsanto's fourteen-page filing, Brent started to worry. He had followed the judge's orders about document de-designation to the letter, but the company's lawyers were seeking to play on the judge's emotions, trying to get Judge Chhabria to feel personally slighted by the document release. And what if the judge did get angry? He could level monetary fines against the plaintiffs' attorneys, which would hurt, but not much. There was no way the judge could claw back the documents from the media, from European regulators, from the state regulators in California. But what if he agreed to Monsanto's demand that Brent, Michael, Aimee, and the others be removed from the executive committee overseeing the mass Roundup litigation? That sort of thing could etch a big black mark onto a résumé and possibly derail a lawyer's career.

Brent was sure he had the law on his side, and he had anticipated Monsanto's outrage at the document release. But whose side Judge Chhabria would agree with was anybody's guess. In his initial response to Monsanto's emergency motion, the judge merely ordered Brent and his team to file a response to Monsanto by Friday, August 4, and told Monsanto's attorneys to reply to that response by August 7. The judge would then hold a conference call with both sides on the afternoon of August 9.

As the seriousness of the matter settled in, Brent realized he could be in real trouble. If he was sanctioned and his firm was removed from the leadership team, he might never get a shot at taking one of the cases to trial. He had to convince Judge Chhabria that it was laziness, hubris, or just plain bad lawyering by Monsanto's attorneys at the Hollingsworth firm that set up the situation for the document release. If they had just filed a motion to maintain confidentiality, as the judge directed in his protective order, Brent would have been blocked from releasing the documents. It was like a chess game in which Monsanto's attorneys had missed a key move. Now they were crying about how unfair it all was and trying to blame him for their misstep.

It was a good sign that the judge had set the call for August 9, Brent thought. That was a full week away and indicated Chhabria must not see much of an emergency in the document release, despite Monsanto's outcry. In the meantime, Brent was busy handling reporters' inquiries from outlets all over the world. Publications he had never even heard of were writing stories and delving into what the documents showed about Monsanto's forty-year safety pledges surrounding its weed-killing products.

When the following Wednesday rolled around for the conference call with the judge, Brent was feeling confident. He had read over the protective order so many times that he knew it by heart. Everything he had done had been proper, according to that order. He would be fine.

Dialing in that afternoon along with Brent were Aimee, Michael, and Robin Greenwald from New York. Gary Rubin and Hollingsworth joined the call for Monsanto. Almost immediately, Brent's spirits sank as Judge Chhabria wasted no time indicating his displeasure with the young lawyer.

"I think we have a problem, but it doesn't strike me that it's an emergency because the bell can't be unrung," Judge Chhabria intoned over the phone line. "My tentative thinking is Mr. Wisner acted in bad faith."

He went on: "What's clear is that there was a live dispute over whether those documents could be released and whether they could be released without first submitting a joint letter to the court about the release of those documents. And Mr. Wisner, it appears to me, operated in bad faith in releasing the documents without coming to court first."

The judge paused for a moment. "And so what I propose to do is to issue an order to show cause why Mr. Wisner and plaintiffs' counsel generally should not be sanctioned and an order to show cause why Mr. Wisner should not be removed from the executive committee and his law firm be removed from the executive committee, and an order to show cause why we shouldn't start all over in deciding who the lead plaintiffs' counsel should be in this case."

This was bad. Very bad, Brent thought.

"I am strongly inclined to sanction the plaintiffs as I have just indicated, at a minimum by removing Mr. Wisner and his firm from the executive committee and perhaps further sanctioning the plaintiffs' counsel overall," the judge continued.

They would hold a hearing on the issues on the morning of August 24, Judge Chhabria told the group.

Brent hung up the phone. Shit.

Over the next two weeks, Brent, Michael, and Aimee prepared for the hearing with Chhabria as they would for a trial. They decided first and foremost that though they were all under the gun, Brent was the most vulnerable, and he needed his own lawyer to represent him at the hearing. They settled on Richard Zitrin, a seventy-year-old well-regarded law professor who was considered an expert in legal ethics and protective orders and had made a career of fighting corporate secrecy. Zitrin would represent both Brent and Baum Hedlund. The firm could not afford to blow this and get kicked out of the litigation leadership.

In advance of the hearing, Brent filed a fifteen-page response to the accusations, protesting that the document release had been allowed under the judge's own guidelines and that it was Monsanto's fault for failing to follow those guidelines.

"I have personally engaged in numerous meet-and-confers regarding the confidentiality of documents and I have never been told, literally, to 'go away,'" Brent wrote to the judge. "It is unclear how Monsanto's counsel's conduct complied with the Court's requirement that 'the parties shall attempt to resolve each challenge in good faith.'" He reminded Judge Chhabria about the wording of his order: a failure by Monsanto to make a motion to retain document confidentiality within thirty days "shall automatically waive the confidentiality for each challenged designation."

"I contemplated, at that time," Brent wrote, "whether I should advise Mr. Rubin about his impending deadline to file a motion. But after considering the ethical implications of giving such advice, I decided against it, because that would be acting against the interests of my own clients, and thus acting unethically. . . . I knew that as I was responsible for my own competent lawyering, Monsanto's counsel was responsible for their competence, including knowing the deadlines they faced."

He pressed on. "My decision to make these 86 documents public after Monsanto waived confidentiality over them was not done to retaliate against Monsanto or litigate this case in the media. I made these documents public because I felt they needed to be available to regulators, academics, researchers, and other attorneys to help make the world a safer place. . . . The vitriol that Monsanto has spewed about myself, my law firm, and my fellow counsel to this Court and the media, speaks volumes about what is really going on. . . . The Monsanto spin machine is working overtime, spreading speculative and false claims about Plaintiffs' counsel motives and, literally, espousing conspiracy theories. These are the words of someone trying to rationalize their own mistake."

The morning of the hearing was cool, but the sun was breaking through clouds as Brent, Michael, Aimee, and Mike Miller made their way to the federal courthouse downtown. Twenty stories of imposing glass and steel housed federal judges as well as a passport office and a tax assistance center. Across the street sat the Supreme Court of California, and a block over was the San Francisco Superior Court. At night, the sidewalks around the courthouses were lined with homeless people, and the area, known as the Tenderloin, was widely regarded as one of the city's most crime ridden and drug infested. City workers sprayed the sidewalks down each morning, clearing away accumulated human waste and other detritus ahead of the arrival of the armies of busy lawyers and court workers who populated the area by day but scurried back to their homes or San Francisco's upscale hotel district as darkness fell.

Judge Chhabria's courtroom, on the seventeenth floor of the federal court building, evoked a masculine authority with its rich wood-paneled walls and a large raised platform where the judge sat in a wide black leather chair looking down upon the lawyers before him. An American flag stood just behind his shoulder, and the state seal was centered on the wall behind him.

The group of plaintiffs' lawyers took their seats at two long rectangular tables set before the judge's bench. Robin Greenwald joined them. She had flown up that morning from Southern California, where she was visiting her college-age daughter. Zitrin also took a seat. A court reporter and Chhabria's clerk sat between the lawyers and the judge in the "well"—a space where lawyers approached only after being granted permission to approach the bench. Rubin and Hollingsworth took their seats on the opposite side of the room, to Chhabria's far right. They were the only lawyers there for Monsanto, but they didn't need an army on their side for this hearing. The judge had already said he thought Brent had acted in bad faith. This should be a slam dunk for Monsanto.

Brent was worried about Zitrin. The Baum Hedlund partners hoped he could help convince Chhabria that the firm was well within the letter of the law when Brent released the documents. True, Zitrin had an affable air and impeccable credentials. He had chaired the State Bar of California's Committee on Professional Responsibility and Conduct and had authored several books on legal ethics. And Zitrin was dogged about challenging court-sanctioned secrecy that allowed corporations to continue selling dangerous products. He had even helped write legislation promoting transparency for consumers. But while he had been a litigator in his younger years, he had the air of an arrogant professor, and Brent worried that Zitrin might try to lecture Chhabria, which would not work well with the judge's short temper and impatience with long-winded arguments. Brent had given Zitrin specific instructions on what to say to Chhabria, but he did not think Zitrin had paid much attention to the advice.

Brent glanced up at Chhabria. The judge did not look happy, and the hearing had not even started. Brent's spirits sank even lower.

The court clerk called the room to order and instructed the attorneys to introduce themselves for the record. When the formalities were out of the way, Zitrin approached the bench, standing in front of the judge. His bushy mustache and goatee combination contrasted with his cleanly shaved head. This should be easy enough, Zitrin thought. Brent's actions clearly were covered by the protective order. He just had to help the judge see that. And though Zitrin had never met Judge Chhabria before, he had heard through others who had worked with Chhabria that the judge was fair and an overall nice guy.

"Mr. Wisner is available to answer any questions that the Court might want to put to him," Zitrin said in a confident tone. "However, I do have a presentation of several minutes if the Court would indulge me in making that presentation."

Judge Chhabria frowned. "Define 'several minutes' with greater specificity."

"Maybe ten," Zitrin said, a little less confidently.

"No," Chhabria said curtly. "I don't need to hear a ten-minute presentation. I want to have a discussion about this."

Brent's chin dropped. Zitrin was going to blow it. Why did they hire this guy, anyway, he asked himself for the twentieth time. He knew nothing about the case or the judge. This was not going to end well.

"I don't particularly care who answers these questions; it's up to you all," Chhabria continued. He frowned as he looked at Brent. "I think to a large extent the brief filed in response to the Order to Show Cause—Mr. Wisner's brief; Baum Hedlund's brief—misses the point. . . . Regardless of whether self-disclosure of these documents under the circumstances in which they were disclosed violated the Protective Order . . . that's not the issue. The issue is that there was a live dispute about all of that stuff." His voice hardened. "And Mr. Wisner—and apparently, with the knowledge of at least some members of the plaintiffs' leadership group— decided to disregard the fact that there was a live dispute, and go ahead and release the documents. And that is the problem."

All that care, all that attention to detail by Brent, Pedram, and the others, making sure they followed the protective order in every way, and now the judge was saying that didn't matter.

Judge Chhabria continued: "I will say that it seems obvious that these documents are, in fact, relevant to the general causation phase of this litigation. And it seems clear that the position that Monsanto was taking in the meet-and-confer was unreasonable. . . . I mean, it's almost laughable; but again, that's not the point. We had a live dispute about the relevance of the documents. And we had a live dispute about the process by which the relevance of the documents would be adjudicated."

Some of the fault was his own, the judge said. "By the way, that ambiguity—that's my fault. . . . It was I who created the ambiguity that resulted in the dispute between the parties about the appropriate process for resolving the question whether these documents could be released. In the end, I mean, the great irony is that, had you teed this up before me in a joint discovery letter or in a motion, as you told the Monsanto lawyers that you would do, I would have, no doubt, ruled in your favor."

What? Brent's spirits started to lift. Maybe this was not going so badly after all. The judge realized the relevance of the documents and agreed they should not be sealed. And he was saying he shouldered some blame for the circumstances!

But just as quickly as they rose, Brent's hopes sank as the judge spoke again: "But you know, this is about lawyers, you know, conducting themselves, you know, in good faith. And this is about my need to manage this very complex litigation going forward potentially for many years. And I don't see how it would be acceptable to have Mr. Wisner on the Executive Committee going forward, in light of what has happened. I will also say that—and maybe his firm, also."

Brent started to rise, but Zitrin motioned for him to stay seated. "I think you may want to hear from both of us, but let's start out with me, Your Honor, if you don't mind. . . . It's very difficult for me to come in front of a United States District Court Judge for the very first time, someone I have known by reputation, and disagree with him the very first thing I say, but . . . I'd like to take you through it, because there was no violation of the Order, and there was no violation of good faith."

"Okay," Chhabria said. "As I tried to say at the outset, I'm not talking about a violation of the Order here. . . . The point is how counsel conducted themselves when we had a live dispute about the meaning of the Order, and a live dispute about how to resolve the dispute about the meaning of the Order. . . . Mr. Wisner left the impression that they were going to decide—that the plaintiffs were going to decide whether to file a letter, file a motion, or just drop the matter. . . . Then he merely told Monsanto that they were not filing a letter brief and they were not filing a motion, and went ahead and released the documents. . . .

"It was his obligation to get the dispute resolved before going ahead and releasing the documents," Chhabria said. "But the problem is that he was not focused on being a lawyer. He was focused on being a PR man. He was more interested in getting these documents released, and getting them released fast, than he was in being a lawyer, and making sure a live dispute between two parties to the litigation got resolved before he moved forward."

Brent's face grew hot. What the hell. Chhabria was being an ass. He had issued a protective order; Brent had followed it; and now Chhabria was moving the goalpost, saying Brent apparently should have gone beyond the terms of the protective order to make sure Monsanto's lawyers were not caught off guard. Like he should have been helping them do their jobs.

He sat there watching as Zitrin and the judge sparred. He should be speaking for himself, Brent thought again. Zitrin only seemed to be making the judge mad.

"That's not how you lawyer. That might be how you do conduct PR," Judge Chhabria said again.

"Well, Your Honor—" Zitrin tried to interject.

"Don't you agree?" the judge demanded.

"No, I don't," Zitrin said. "I've been teaching legal ethics for 40 years. I've taught trial practice at USF for ten years."

"Neither of those two things is relevant to this," Chhabria said, cutting the professor off. "Could you please just stick to the facts in this case?"

This was going from bad to worse, Brent thought.

"Your Honor—" Brent jumped up.

"No, the story is—" Zitrin interrupted Brent. "The story is that they did not file a declaration. They did not file a motion."

Brent tried again to interject, but Zitrin was having none of it, talking over him and refusing to yield the argument to him.

"Could I please explain?" Brent pleaded. But Zitrin and the judge ignored him. He tried again: "Your Honor, I think there's a confusion on the facts, and I think I can help answer your question."

A visibly frustrated Chhabria glared at the plaintiffs' lawyers. "You guys decide which one of you wants to talk."

"Wait, wait, wait," said Zitrin. His job was to protect Brent, and that meant Brent should stay silent.

But Brent was done with staying silent. "I'd like to talk," he said, taking a step forward. Zitrin needed to just sit down and be quiet.

Chhabria clearly agreed. "Professor Zitrin, sit down," the judge said sternly.

But Zitrin had always liked to think of himself as a fighter. He could not back down now. "Your Honor—"

"Sit down!" Chhabria thundered.

"A record needs to be made on this matter," Zitrin insisted.

"I'm going to have security come to get you removed from the court—" Chhabria replied angrily.

Zitrin couldn't believe his ears. The judge was actually threatening to have him thrown out of the courtroom. He had never been treated this way by a judge before. Chhabria was clearly wrong about the protective order but seemed not to want to admit it.

"I don't want to be removed from the court," Zitrin said.

The judge stared down at the professor. "—if you don't sit down." A defeated Zitrin sank into his chair.

Time to take charge of this shit show, Brent thought. Surely it couldn't get worse. "Your Honor, I'll just answer a couple quick questions, because I think the facts are getting lost here."

Judge Chhabria looked at Brent. "Monsanto said to you that it was disputing the idea that those documents were relevant. And the way you left it with them is that, to get the dispute resolved, you would either file a letter brief, or file a joint discovery letter, or file a motion. You then told them you were going to do neither of those things, and you left it at that. There was still a live dispute."

"That's factually incorrect, Your Honor," Brent said, as respectfully as he could muster. "What happened during the conversation was very simple," Brent continued. "I tried going through the documents. They said, *Go away*. I tried to address the relevancy of them. They said, *We don't have to*. Putting that issue aside, then at the end of it I was unbelievably blown away. I've never been treated so disrespectfully by anybody. . . . And I said to them, *Well, it looks like you're saying I have three options here. I could either file a joint letter, which I doubt we're going to do. We'll file a motion; or I guess if someone talks me into it, we could withdraw. I guess those are our options.* I never once said, *Oh, by the way, Monsanto, you don't have to follow the Protective Order, because the thing says*—and they admit this—we reached an impasse."

Brent paused, but just for a moment. Chhabria didn't interrupt. "And the Order says once you reach an impasse, here is what the obligations are. This is what you're supposed to do. And I looked at it. I studied it closely. I went back and read every transcript; read every Order this Court said. And never at one point did you shift that onus, not even for a second. It's not even ambiguous on that point."

He'd better wrap it up, Brent realized. "So to make sure that they weren't waiting for me to do something, which—I didn't want to run into a situation where they said, *Oh, we are waiting for Mr. Wisner to file a motion.* I made it clear to them I wasn't doing anything."

Brent met Chhabria's eyes and the two men studied each other quietly for a moment. Surely the judge could see the logic of Brent's position. Monsanto's lawyers had not filed the motion they were required to file if they wanted to keep the documents sealed. So Brent had released them. End of story. He waited.

"Release documents first. Ask questions later," the judge said sarcastically. "You were too focused on being a PR man, and not focused enough on being a lawyer. And what we need in this litigation is lawyers."

That was it. Brent had had enough. He knew he needed to rein in his temper, but Chhabria was going off the rails.

"That is preposterous. That is absolutely preposterous," Brent nearly shouted. "The idea that I'm trying to do PR is absurd! . . . I do this because I care about public health. I do this because I live in California, and I grew up here; and my father worked with Cesar Chavez, and helped protect farmworkers from exposures to pesticides. . . . I actually care about people. And there's really important decisions being made right now. . . . And those documents, Your Honor—no matter how you look at them, they tell a really just alarming story of corporate malfeasance. Now, you might not agree with that. That's fine."

Chhabria tried to interject: "I actually tend to agree with you. I mean, I think—"

But Brent barely heard him. He was on a roll: "I barely sleep, because I'm a brief writer. I argue stuff. I appeal stuff. I try cases. The idea that I'm into PR is just preposterous. Ask the person who does the PR at my firm. She can barely get me on the phone. I ignore her. That's not, just not, what this was about. I actually was doing good lawyering. I was following the Protective Order to a T. And they made a mistake. They screwed up. . . . They stonewalled me, stonewalled me, stonewalled me. And in that hubris, they just decided they didn't have to do anything."

As he started to calm down, Brent realized it couldn't hurt to beg just a little: "There is no bad faith here, Your Honor. . . . Please don't take my firm off," he pleaded to Chhabria. "This was my—this was my crusade. This was my attempt to do something. . . . I don't see how sanctioning me is a good idea, or even sends the right message in this litigation. I mean, I literally did everything this Court asked me to do. I worked so many hours to do it. And you're going to sanction me because, at the end of the day, they didn't do their job. I don't think that's right, Your Honor, and so I don't think you should sanction me."

Brent took a deep breath and started to relax. He had laid out the situation as logically as he could.

But now it was Hollingsworth's turn to speak. He had handled many trickier issues than this in the years he'd represented Monsanto, and he sounded cool and confident as he began. He was going to make sure

Brent's dramatic appeal didn't distract the judge from the key offenses Brent and his law firm had committed.

"Your Honor . . . Mr. Wisner knew Monsanto's position that the documents could not be released without involvement of the Court; and that . . . notwithstanding his awareness of Monsanto's position, and notwithstanding that he left the impression that the documents weren't going to be released, he put them out to the world. And he did so in a PR kind of way."

He continued: "There was a live dispute. . . . That's not controverted. . . . The things that are at the crux of the issue of whether or not there was bad faith committed by this committee and by Mr. Wisner here are not in controversy. They haven't controverted those things. . . . Baum Hedlund and Mr. Wisner and others had actively misled Monsanto. And they had left Monsanto with the impression that the documents were not going to be released until this dispute could be decided, which I think were Your Honor's words mostly; not mine. And I think that Your Honor is heading to the right conclusion in that connection. And I don't think that the factual bases that Your Honor needs to get there have been controverted. And that's our position."

Chhabria looked over at Brent and his table full of plaintiffs' attorneys and then over at Monsanto's team at the defense table. They were all trying his patience, and they were still months, if not years, away from a trial in his court.

"There's a lot of discussion of bad faith. . . . Based on everything I've read and everything I've heard today, it strikes me that the record does support, you know, a finding of bad faith," Chhabria said. "One can understand why a lawyer might be very anxious to get these documents released. And, as I've said a number of times, there's absolutely nothing wrong with a lawyer wanting these documents to be released, and communicating them to the press, and, you know, communicating them to government agencies. . . . But in his zeal to get the documents released, he sort of decided to sort of shove aside the fact that there was a live dispute between the parties about whether they could be released. . . . And at a minimum, that's misconduct."

Hollingsworth piped up: "I agree with that, Your Honor." This was going really well for Monsanto.

But then Chhabria's tone shifted. "Okay," the judge addressed Hollingsworth. "How could you have taken the position that these documents are not relevant to the general causation phase?"

Hollingsworth had not seen that one coming, and the turnabout by the judge stunned him for a moment. "Well, I don't see anything—I don't see anything in any one of those documents that has—has any bearing on the issue of whether reliable science is present to support the conclusion that glyphosate can cause non-Hodgkin's lymphoma," he stammered.

Chhabria pushed further: "But the internal e-mails reflect that Monsanto has been ghostwriting reports. And those reports have been portrayed as independent," the judge insisted. "And you—I mean, your whole presentation thus far has been about how all the independent science supports a conclusion that glyphosate doesn't cause non-Hodgkin's lymphoma."

The judge leaned forward as he spoke. "So, you know, I don't understand how you could have taken the position that the issue of Monsanto drafting reports for allegedly independent experts on whether glyphosate causes non-Hodgkin's lymphoma could be irrelevant to the question of whether there's evidence that glyphosate causes non-Hodgkin's lymphoma. I just don't understand how you could take that position."

Brent looked at Michael and tried to suppress a grin. Take that, Monsanto. The judge was calling the company out on its ghostwriting right there in open court. This, at least, was a win.

Hollingsworth seemed flustered, but only for an instant. The scientific reports discussed by Monsanto scientists in the internal corporate documents were not actual scientific studies; they were instead merely "literature surveys," he told the judge. And even though the media and the plaintiffs' attorneys were characterizing the company's involvement with certain papers as ghostwriting, it was not a correct characterization, he insisted.

"I guess your Honor's been influenced by it, —" Hollingsworth said.

Chhabria interrupted him: "Well, wait a minute. It's Monsanto that used the term 'ghostwriting.'"

"Well, yes," Hollingsworth said softly.

Chhabria was incredulous: "So you're saying that Monsanto mischaracterized what it was doing when it was drafting these reports?"

"Yeah," Hollingsworth said. "I think that Monsanto was loosely using the word 'ghostwriting.'"

Brent was not going to let that comment stand without challenge. The company's internal documents showed clearly that Monsanto had been submitting ghostwritten papers to regulators to show the safety of its herbicides, and the regulators had been citing those papers as reasons for confirming the product safety.

"It is our position and will be argued to the jury that this is conduct that manipulates science," Brent interjected. "And that's really a problem, particularly since our regulatory agencies are actually relying on that science."

Chhabria sighed. These lawyers never made it easy. This entire dispute was annoying him. It was time to wrap this up.

"One question I do want answered by somebody is," he said, "if there is going to be a removal from the . . . Executive Committee, should it be Mr. Wisner, or should it be the firm of Baum Hedlund, or should it be broader than just Mr. Wisner and Baum Hedlund?"

Brent squared his shoulders. He had hoped the judge might stay focused on Monsanto's misdeeds a little longer. "The short answer to the question you just asked is if there should be any punishment, it should be at me," he told Chhabria. "The leadership here appointed me to take on this task because I asked them to let me do it."

He wasn't going to win this, Brent realized. It was time to play his final card. If the judge was determined to kick him off the litigation leadership team, maybe he could at least convince him to delay the ouster. There was a big hearing coming up in December in which both sides would present their expert witnesses to the judge and each witness would testify and be cross-examined about the scientific evidence pertaining to the key question of the litigation—whether or not Monsanto's Roundup really caused non-Hodgkin lymphoma. Brent and Baum Hedlund had to be at that hearing.

These types of pretrial evidentiary hearings were commonly referred to simply as "Daubert" hearings, taking the name from a 1993 US Supreme Court case that set the standards for admissibility of the testimony of expert witnesses—people who have scientific, technical, or other specialized knowledge about specific issues of relevance to a case.

The general public may believe that each side is allowed to present any expert witness it wants to at trial, leaving it to a jury to determine the credibility of the witnesses. But in reality, the experts often first have to convince a judge they have the credibility even to be part of a trial.

Chhabria had set the Roundup multidistrict litigation's Daubert hearing for the week of December 11, and it would be, without a doubt, the most critical courtroom event in the case to date. If the judge determined that any or all of the plaintiffs' six expert witnesses lacked solid scientific positions tying Roundup to cancer, he would ban their testimony at trial, which could seriously derail the litigation. Monsanto wanted badly to win Daubert and get some or all of the plaintiffs' experts excluded. If the plaintiffs had no expert witnesses, they could not possibly win a trial. The company could likely get the judge to issue a summary judgment in its favor if it could convince Chhabria that the plaintiffs' expert witnesses were relying on junk science in trying to show ties between Roundup and cancer.

Daubert was a big deal. If the judge wanted to bar him and Baum Hedlund from the litigation leadership, at least he should wait until after Daubert, Brent said.

"Our firm has provided considerable resources to this project, and we are heavily involved in all aspects of Daubert right now," he said. "If any order to remove us was to be issued, it should at the very least not take effect until after December, when we've got these things briefed, because there's too much work right now. We're literally in the middle of the expert depositions. . . . You could maybe mix it up at some later point, if you want to, if you're concerned that we're not doing a good-enough job. But right now it would be very dangerous and really bad."

Brent figured one more mea culpa couldn't hurt: "And I apologize to the Court if you believe I acted with misconduct. That was never my intent. I do respect this Court deeply."

Aimee had kept quiet for the past hour, but she knew time was running out, and she wanted the judge to hear what she had to say. Monsanto's argument was such bullshit. The company's lawyers had acted like assholes, and now they were whining to the judge that Brent and the other plaintiffs' lawyers had not played fair. And Hollingsworth's attempt to downplay the ghostwriting was ridiculous. He and other members of Monsanto's legal team had repeatedly cited the ghostwritten articles proclaiming glyphosate's safety in seeking to get the lawsuits dismissed. "F" these liars, she thought.

"I am a target in Monsanto's sanctions motions, myself," Aimee said to Chhabria. It was only fair, she said, that if Monsanto wanted to see the emails between the plaintiffs' attorneys, then Monsanto's lawyers should also have to turn over their emails.

"I would request that we also look at the internal correspondence between Monsanto and the Hollingsworth firm, to decide really what they were thinking, and if they really thought there was a live dispute . . . before we just take that at face value," she said.

She pushed on. A key paper published in the scientific literature showing Roundup's safety, the Williams, Kroes & Munro paper—the paper Monsanto's scientists had described as ghostwritten—was cited by both Monsanto's attorneys and the company's expert witnesses in efforts to get the lawsuits dismissed. For Hollingsworth to try to tell the judge the ghostwriting was not consequential, not relevant, was absurd, she said.

"They've been relying on that article throughout the entirety of the litigation, contrary to what Mr. Hollingsworth just said," Aimee said, trying to keep the anger out of her voice.

Chhabria needed a break. It was *really* time to wrap this up. Maybe he could handle some of this better if he brought the lawyers into his chambers for an off-the-record settlement talk. Both sides had acted badly, and this extended argument was giving him a headache.

"I think what we'll do right now is give the court reporter a little break," Chhabria said. The lawyers should meet with him in his chambers to talk things over off the record, he said.

When he called court back into session, they had a deal worked out. His anger over Brent's release of the Monsanto Papers had cooled. He was not going to sanction Brent or the Baum Hedlund firm, nor was he going to order the lawyers to provide copies of their email discussions about the documents to each other. Brent and Baum Hedlund had agreed to voluntarily resign after Daubert was concluded.

The only really productive thing that had come out of this hearing, as far as Chhabria was concerned, was the realization that he needed to clarify the protective order to make sure that no one on the plaintiffs' side could release any more of the Monsanto discovery documents without first notifying the court. And Monsanto's attorneys needed to know they could not just ignore document de-designation requests as they had done here, starting this whole mess.

Daubert was coming up. The focus needed to be on making sure that hearing, which would require several days to complete, was properly set. Daubert would determine if this freight train of a case continued on track or derailed.

Chhabria was ready to call the hearing to a close. He looked at the lawyers standing before him. Their conservative suits and polite and proper mannerisms belied the vitriol boiling between them. It was starting to become clear that this litigation was going to be a long and brutal battle—and both sides were out for blood.

"Court is adjourned."

CHAPTER 10

Lizard Man

Across San Francisco Bay, lying in a narrow bed in the darkness of his apartment, Lee knew nothing about the courtroom drama surrounding the release of Monsanto's secret documents. His daily focus now was on surviving another day of pain.

The doctors had warned Lee about the side effects of chemotherapy, the mouth sores, the nausea, hair loss, and fatigue. But the pain—no one had prepared him for the unrelenting agony that enveloped his body as the chemotherapy effects combined with the burning sensations that emanated from each of the cancerous lesions lining his limbs and torso. Every movement was nearly unbearable. Open sores on the back of Lee's head oozed onto his pillow each night, and his sheets were scattered with shredded skin each morning. Infection was a constant threat; he had already had more than one serious bout of infection settle into his wounds.

Lee looked over at the clock and saw it was midmorning. His bladder was about to burst, but rising and walking just the few feet to the cold linoleum-lined floor of the bathroom promised a torment Lee dreaded. It seemed a lifetime ago when he had bounded out of bed before dawn to get dressed for work and wake his boys for what had been joyously normal days.

"I'm going to strive, I'm going to survive," Lee repeated to himself. The mantra had become a self-directed pep talk that he invoked frequently. Everyone was so certain he was going to die from this disease, and he wanted badly to prove them all wrong.

These days, when he awoke, Lee usually had the apartment to himself. Araceli and the boys would be long gone for work and school when Lee emerged from a sleep that was aided by painkillers and marijuana joints he rolled. Lee had often smoked weed in his youth. He could not count the number of times he and his friend Daryl Waters had loaded filter papers with heaps of cannabis that they then rolled inside large tobacco leaves. They'd pass the thick joints between them when writing raps or when headed out to party at a club. But those days were gone, and smoking weed was no longer for fun. Now, in Lee's view, it was the only thing that allowed him to make it through the days. The pain medicine prescribed by his doctors left him foggy and lethargic, but smoking both eased the pain and actually seemed to help him focus on something other than the torment of being trapped inside his diseased body.

Today was going to be a good day, Lee told himself. He could open his eyes, for one thing, so that was a good sign. Sometimes when he awoke his eyelids would be so swollen and so filled with pus leaking from the marred skin on his face that his eyes would be stuck shut and he'd have to pry them open.

He shuffled into the bathroom and relieved himself. Before he got sick, Lee had enjoyed long, hot showers and the fresh feeling of slick, clean skin. But now a shower only meant more pain, so Lee limited himself to one every two to three days. Instead of washing, the morning routine now consisted largely of spreading thick coatings of lotions, ointments, and oils onto every inch of his skin. Without what he called "the grease," Lee could hardly bear to move. When he was fully greased up, Lee felt more flexible, like he could stand and walk and sit and turn without his flesh cracking.

Daryl, who had known Lee long enough to be able to say such things, had recently told Lee that he resembled the "lizard man" character in a 1985 movie called *Enemy Mine*. Daryl loved the science fiction film, but now every time he saw Lee he was reminded of the film's alien soldier, a reptilian humanoid who becomes close friends with a human before dying tragically.

It was an apt description, Lee supposed, draping a long gold and black scarf over his head and wrapping himself in a fluffy white robe, avoiding looking at himself in the mirror. He would put off getting dressed as long as possible, at least until after his morning smoke. Clothing irritated his skin, and he could tolerate only attire that was loose fitting, lightweight, and as soft as possible. Getting dressed also meant swapping his velvety oversize slippers for thick socks and—if he had to go somewhere—shoes. Shoes. Cursed shoes. Both feet were marked by so many weeping or scabbed sores that shoes had become almost like a torture device for Lee.

One of the worst parts of each day was tending to his right foot. An opening on the outer edge about midway between his little toe and his heel had refused to heal, and the flesh had been eaten away so aggressively that Lee could see bone and sinew within the quarter-size lesion. By day's end, the bandages he kept over the site would be soaked through with a pinkish ooze that sometimes adhered threads from the sock to the wound. Just changing his socks had become a grisly undertaking. Often friends would ask why he did not let Araceli help him dress or apply the lotions and ointments that coated his body. What they didn't understand was that he didn't trust her, or anyone, for that matter, to understand just how painful the process was. He knew just how much pressure each inch of skin could withstand without tearing.

Some days he never left the apartment. For a man who had been so athletic, so filled with vitality, hiding away in the tiny Vallejo apartment was carving an emotional wound that Lee feared would become just as devastating as his physical decline. But at least staying in meant he could find a spot on the orange sofa and just try to keep still.

This was not a day to stay home, though. With the trial date set for June of 2018, only six months away, Tim Litzenburg and Monsanto's attorneys had agreed that it was time to take Lee's deposition. As is customary, the deposition would be video-recorded and transcribed by a court reporter. Lee would get his first real chance to tell his story under oath. For Monsanto's legal team, it was part of the discovery process, an opportunity to see how well Lee held up under questioning and whether or not the story of his accidental exposures would hang together.

For Tim, getting Lee's sworn testimony on video was crucial. The doctors were not sure how long he would live; they feared he might not even survive until the summer trial. Tim knew Lee had recently completed a round of chemotherapy and was in bad shape. But the deposition could not wait. If Lee died before the trial, Tim would need to show jurors the video so they could see for themselves the horrendous impacts of the Roundup exposure.

Tim had been prepping Lee for days for the deposition. Monsanto's lawyers were sharp, and they would be probing every detail of Lee's life and health in search of inconsistencies or statements they might be able to use to undermine his case. All of the cancer treatments had left Lee with memory trouble; he sometimes told Tim he felt like his brain was shrouded in a thick fog. To help Lee prepare, Tim put together a set of note cards for him to study. Key dates and events, such as when he had started work for the school district, when he had started spraying Monsanto's herbicides, when the sprayer accident had occurred, and when he had been diagnosed. The time line was important. Study these cards, he told Lee. This is a test you can't afford to fail.

After Lee had looked over a few of the note cards, Tim would quiz him, throwing questions at him in no logical order—"When did you start spraying Roundup at work, Lee?" "When?" Lee did his best to study the cards and commit the dates to memory, but it was hard. He was so sick he could barely keep any food down, and the little sleep he was able to get was tormented by strange hallucinations. One night he spent hours imagining he was making sandwiches.

Tim and Monsanto's attorneys had agreed that there would be two days of depositions so they'd have plenty of time, both for discovery-oriented questions aimed at gathering information that could potentially lead to additional evidence for trial and for eliciting testimony that itself might be used at trial. The depositions were initially set to take place in downtown San Francisco but then were moved to a hotel in Vallejo near Lee's apartment. Monsanto was sending three lawyers, while Tim was handling the assignment solo; no other lawyers from The Miller Firm were attending.

It was a sunny, though cool, morning that Thursday, December 7, as Tim made his way to the hotel. He had offered to pick Lee up, but Lee wanted to drive himself. It was one of his remaining pleasures, driving fast and choosing his own route, simple things that made him feel slightly—and temporarily—in charge of the direction of his life.

Tim waited just outside the hotel's front entrance. He wanted to grab a few minutes to prep Lee again before they sat down for what would be several hours of questioning. He hoped today would not be a repeat of yesterday's fiasco, when Lee had failed to show up.

He thought back to the day before. What a shit show that had been. He and Lee had agreed to meet at 9:00 a.m., but when it neared 9:15 and Lee was nowhere to be seen, Tim had dialed Lee's cell number. No answer. He texted and called repeatedly, with no reply. He called Lee's mother and Araceli, but no one knew where Lee was. He knew Lee had gone for a chemotherapy treatment just the day before and was likely very sick. How sick? Had he died? Tim finally grew so worried that he drove to

Lee's apartment. As usually was the case, the blinds were closed across the lone front window that sat just to the left of the front door. Tim knocked, then pounded his fist on the door, calling out for Lee. Nothing. He dialed Lee's cell phone again. Ringing could be heard inside the apartment. So Lee *was* home. Why wasn't he answering? The lump grew in Tim's throat. He beat on the door with an urgency that rattled the frame.

It wasn't until nearly 3:00 p.m. that Tim finally got a call from Lee, saying he'd just been in too much pain to make it to the deposition.

Tim shook his head at the memory and glanced at his watch. He hoped Lee would make it today. Monsanto's lawyers would not be happy at all if Lee was a no-show again.

But today Lee was feeling stronger, and he was only a little late arriving at the hotel, where Monsanto's legal team was waiting in a reserved conference room. Two of the Monsanto lawyers were from the Washington, DC–based Hollingsworth firm—senior partner Bill Cople and a young associate attorney named Stephanie Salek. Joining them for Monsanto's defense was Sandra Edwards, a partner and head of the environmental law department in San Francisco for the law firm Farella Braun & Martel.

Tim was not too worried about Stephanie. But Bill had been a lawyer longer than Tim had been alive, and even though Sandra had a quiet and pleasant demeanor, Tim knew that prior to joining the Farella firm twenty-one years earlier she had worked as San Francisco's assistant district attorney, and she was known for being both whip-smart and successful at winning tough cases, particularly cases like this. She had a competitive streak honed as a nationally ranked college tennis player and could not stand to lose—at anything. It was going to be a long day. He hoped Lee had the stamina.

Lee sat down at the table and stared at the camera across the room. Everything he said would be recorded on video and by a court reporter, who would prepare a transcript of the questioning. His stomach churned nervously.

It was almost 9:30 a.m. when the court reporter formally swore Lee in, marking into the record that Lee had pledged to tell the truth. With that out of the way, Cople began.

"Good morning, Mr. Johnson."

"Good morning," Lee replied.

"I'll be asking you questions for the rest of the day while you're under oath, and we certainly appreciate you joining us here today to answer our questions under oath," Cople said, adopting a formal tone. "You do understand, however, that you are under a legal obligation to be here and give testimony, right?"

"Yeah," Lee answered, trying to hide his embarrassment. "I'm sorry about yesterday. I'm going through a lot right now."

"Well, we can talk about that, not about apologies. That's not what we're looking for," Cople responded crisply. "We'll talk about some of the facts about your treatment and so forth, but we won't get into that just yet. All right. Mr. Johnson, you were diagnosed with a form of non-Hodgkin's lymphoma called mycosis fungoides; is that correct?"

"That's correct."

"And you received that diagnosis of mycosis fungoides in August of 2014; am I right about that?" Cople asked.

Tim cringed. Lee had such a hard time with dates.

"I'm not really super clear about the dates because they're so far away, but that sounds about right," Lee replied.

As Tim had expected, Cople proceeded to ask Lee about several specific dates—when did he start work for the school district, when did his employment end, when did he apply for workers' compensation, and more. Lee was handling it well, making clear that while he could not recall certain specific time frames, his work and medical records held the sought-after information.

"All right. Now, you claim that you were exposed to Ranger Pro manufactured by Monsanto as part of your job responsibilities working for the Benicia School District; is that right?" Cople asked.

"That's right," Lee said.

"All right," Monsanto's lawyer repeated. "Was there an incident that you claim that occurred involving your work at the Mary Farmar school?"

"Yes." Lee nodded. "I don't recall the year or the month, but I do recall that incident happening."

"What incident? Describe it," Cople probed.

Tim relaxed slightly. He knew that while Lee might have trouble re-membering specific dates, the accident with the truck-mounted sprayer was locked firmly into his memory.

Lee sat up a little straighter as he began to describe the spraying event at the elementary school that he was convinced had triggered his disease. "An incident happened where I was spraying a hillside where you came up the parkway, where you get into like a little driveway where you get into Mary Farmar, there's one big long driveway. It goes uphill. I went up-hill, turned the truck around and start to go downhill. So I went enough to where I could spread my hose out. It's like 250 feet. I went as long as I could up, and my truck is down. You understand? Can you see how this is happening now?" Lee paused and looked at the lawyer.

"So my tank and my truck is down lower towards the bottom of the hill. I'm up here at the top of the hill. So I'm spraying the hill. Everything is fine. I'm spraying the hill, spraying the cracks, everything is fine. And I get down to another move. I'm going to move the truck down another 250 feet. I'm coming down with my hose. For some reason the hose came disattached from the back of the truck, disattached, and it was just juice everywhere, flying out the back of the truck. So that's when I had to hop in because the switches are in the back."

Lee's voice slowed. He could see the hillside again and the chemical spewing into the air. "I had to reach in the back there and turn it off, and that's when I got it on the back of my neck and the back of my head and everywhere. And on my face." He looked over at Monsanto's lawyer.

"How long did this exposure last? Was it instantaneous?" Cople asked.

"I would say the rest of the day," Lee answered. "I'm saying when I got ahold of that liquid on my skin that day, it got red, it got irritated. . . . I just waited until after work and went home and showered and changed clothes like nothing ever happened."

Cople appeared unmoved. "You understand that you're supposed to wash immediately if you are exposed to . . ."

"We didn't have—we didn't have an eye wash or shower station," Lee said helplessly.

"The second time I was exposed, I went home at that time. You know, I got exposed from the backpack. I said I'm leaving right now. I left, went home and showered and even came back."

"I'll ask about the second time in a moment," Cople said. "Whose responsibility was it to correctly attach the hose?"

"Oh, me, all day," Lee said.

"You were required to wear personal protective equipment, correct?"

"Yes, PPE all the time," said Lee.

"Tyvek suit?" Cople asked.

"Tyvek," Lee confirmed.

"Which is not permeable to liquid like Ranger Pro, correct?" the lawyer insisted.

"It's supposed to be not permeable to drift, you know what I mean? Light drift," Lee said. "So if you were spraying out of that water bottle, and it was just dripping a little bit, it's okay, it will stop that. If I poured the water bottle on the Tyvek suit, it just went straight through to your skin. It's just the way that suit worked."

"You were wearing the Tyvek suit?" Cople asked again.

"Yes."

"And the boots?"

"Oh, yeah."

"And the goggles?"

"Yes."

"There was a faucet available at Mary Farmar that you could have used to wash immediately, correct?" Cople asked.

"No."

"There was no faucet available?" Cople asked disbelievingly.

"You mean like a water faucet?" Lee asked.

"Yes."

"Oh, maybe, but not for what I had over me," Lee said.

"Did you check?"

"No, no." Lee was stunned. Why was this lawyer for Monsanto spending so much time focused on when and how he washed up? Monsanto marketed the stuff as so safe you could practically drink it, and now this slick lawyer was implying Lee should have rushed to get it off his skin.

Lee explained that it took him about twenty minutes to get back to the district's maintenance offices after dealing with the spray accident. He tried to rinse himself as best he could using the small sink in a mobile trailer that sat in the yard.

"At the time that all of this occurred, did you hold the qualified application certificate, QAC?" Cople asked.

Of course he would ask that, Lee thought. "On my first exposure, no. No, I didn't," he answered. "I hadn't got the license yet."

"So you were applying Ranger Pro at the time of your first exposure, and you did not yet have a QAC certificate?" Cople asked again.

"No, sir," Lee said. So they were trying to blame him. Well, screw them.

Cople's questions continued. He wanted to know if anyone else had witnessed the sprayer hose pop off and the chemical spray Lee had described. He wanted to know who had mixed the Ranger Pro that day before the spraying, and he wanted to know if Lee had reported the exposure to his superiors and coworkers.

Lee said he had reported it, but no one had been too worried. "Nobody was really amazed or shocked about it because we had been trained that the glyphosate . . . was okay enough for us to drink. So we didn't really worry like oh, my God, you got it on your skin, you're going to die tomorrow."

Cople continued to press Lee about whether a formal record of the accident had been created, or whether there was any corroboration for the events Lee described.

"Did you ever create a record about that incident?" the lawyer asked.

"No, not at all," Lee replied.

The questioning had been underway for only about twenty minutes, but Lee already felt drained. Tim had told him this would likely go all day, seven to eight hours. The examination dragged on. Cople asked Lee about the fact that he had failed the test for his pesticide applicator's license three times before finally passing. At times, the court reporter had trouble understanding what Lee was saying and would ask him to repeat himself. The damn mouth sores made it so hard to talk. He tried to explain, but no one seemed to care. The questions continued. Monsanto's lawyer appeared fixated on whether or not Lee had been "splashed" across the head with Ranger Pro or whether the herbicide had "drifted" onto his face. Cople also wanted to know about the second accident—the one with the backpack sprayer—and about Lee's discovery of the first suspicious spot on his leg.

"All right. That backpack incident . . . that you indicate happened to you, did the backpack itself leak?" Cople asked.

"You know that day I did not inspect that backpack because they'd just been spraying with it this morning," Lee replied. "So they usually don't leak. They usually don't have problems. . . . So yeah, I was just going along spraying. I thought it was okay that my back was getting wet. I thought it was just sweat. Usually you get a little sweaty out there. . . . So I figure I was just getting wet from that. And I kept on tripping like: Man, if this is Ranger Pro getting on your skin, you're already messed up. This is all bad.

"So then when I got back to the yard," Lee continued, "I asked them, I said, 'Is this actually getting through to my clothes? Is this Ranger Pro? Is the Tyvek suit wet and my clothes wet?' And after everybody looked, and they said, 'Oh, yeah, you definitely got it.'"

The memory haunted him. How had he been so stupid? He was already sick by that point, but his doctors thought that the disease was manageable. Why had he kept spraying? he asked himself for the thousandth time. Maybe if he had refused, maybe if he'd never had that backpack leak all down his back, maybe he could have kept the cancer at bay.

But the damn stuff was supposed to be safe. Hell, he had even called Monsanto to ask if he should be worried about the exposures, about the company's chemicals getting on his skin. No one had ever called him back.

The questions continued. More probing about his training, about who else knew about the accidental exposures Lee had described. And then, Monsanto's lawyer seemed to sense Lee's discomfort.

"All right. Now, before we continue, I want to be sure that if you need a break at any time, just ask us, and we'll be happy to accommodate that. There's—there's no reason that you or any of us should have to struggle if we need a break, so just ask us and we'll take care of that, and we'll break for however long you need."

Lee nodded. He would push on as long as he could. He just wanted this day over.

"The other thing I need to ask you about," Cople added, "because it can be important in a deposition, is sometimes when folks are taking medications, anybody, including me, it can cause some confusion or fuzziness . . . or the reduced ability to say what you want to say, so I need to ask you, have you taken any medications in the last 48 hours?"

Was he kidding? I have *cancer*, Lee thought.

Out loud, he just said, "Oh, yeah." Lee listed the medications he was taking. "I'm in serious, very chronic pain right now," he said.

"All right. Is it affecting your ability to concentrate?" Cople asked.

"Sitting down like this, I'm good. When I start to move, that's when it's really bad," Lee answered.

"Okay. Well, again, reminder, if you need a break, let us know."

"I'm good right now," Lee said.

For the next several hours, Cople kept poking and prodding. He asked Lee questions about how many times per year he had sprayed and if he had read the Ranger Pro label each time. He asked about Lee's personal habits: when had he last smoked a cigar, what type of cigars did he used to smoke, and how many a day for how long?

Lee answered them all as best he could. He had sprayed dozens of times per year, mainly in the months of June, July, and August. He had read the label every time he sprayed, at least the part about mixing. He had known it was important he get the ratio of water to the chemical mixture exactly right. As for the cigars? He probably smoked one a day for two years but stopped in 2006. He never stopped enjoying the smell of a good cigar, however.

Cople seemed to be jumping all around with the questions. Now he was asking why Lee had not shown up for yesterday's scheduled deposition.

"Tuesday night you—you got ready, you prepared for this deposition, right?" Cople asked.

"Sorta kinda," Lee said. "I just had a really long night. I don't know if I was anxious or whatever. I just couldn't get sleep. And by the time I was ready to go, I was in so much pain, I was just dragging around. It was a mess."

"And you didn't have chemotherapy yesterday?" Cople asked.

"No."

"It was just the day before?"

"Right."

"All right. Now, yesterday you were supposed to be here for the deposition in time to start at 9 o'clock. You're aware of that, right?"

"Yeah, I talked to Tim about that," Lee said quietly.

"Okay. And you did not show up. Can you tell us why?" Cople pushed.

Lee was annoyed. Was this guy an idiot? Did he not just hear what Lee had said about the pain?

"I just—I thought I explained. I was in a lot of pain, and it was very hard for me to walk. It just was a really bad morning for me."

"All right. Had—had you anticipated this on Tuesday night?" Cople asked.

"No, not as bad, because, you know, I have some good nights and some bad nights. Like today was way better than yesterday, but I think I started preparing the night before," Lee said. "I started finding—I went and bought some different clothes that was a lot smoother . . . different stuff like that that didn't chaff up against my skin. I have too many open wounds, too many open wounds to really even have clothes on. It's like really hard to put on clothes."

"Could you have told the doctor you have a deposition so you need to put it off?" Cople asked.

"Definitely," Lee said.

"But you didn't do that?"

"No."

"Is there a reason why you didn't do that?"

"I thought I would be okay," Lee said simply. He wanted to scream at the lawyer, I have *cancer!* Chemo was more important than a deposition any day, every day. He didn't understand why Monsanto's lawyer was so interested in the details of the missed deposition.

He got the answer a minute later, when Cople told Tim that the company's legal team was reserving the right to make Tim's law firm pay for their wasted time the day before. They would most certainly now have to return at a later date for more questioning, which would involve more costs, the Monsanto lawyer said.

Great, Lee thought. He was not about to feel sorry for inconveniencing Monsanto's expensive lawyers. How many more questions could they possibly want to ask?

Cople pivoted again, asking Lee to discuss an aggravated assault charge from the 1990s. A misdemeanor, Lee explained. He had been given probation. Cople pressed for more details, and Lee grew angry.

"And who did you assault, or who were you accused of assaulting?" Cople asked.

"I refuse to answer that. That's not important."

"What's that?" Cople seemed incredulous at Lee's response.

"It's not important. I refuse to answer that," Lee said firmly.

"You refuse to answer who you were accused of assaulting?"

"Whoever I was in a situation with or combatant with, it doesn't matter."

Eventually Lee acknowledged that the mother of his oldest son had filed a domestic abuse complaint against him, and he had spent a night in jail because of it. It was a period in his life he had tried to forget. He had moved beyond the chaos of his youth and now was a solid family man who held down a good job until this cancer came for him. Why wasn't this Monsanto lawyer focusing on that?

On and on it went. Questions about his family life, jobs he had held at restaurants, a job he once had waterproofing windows, another as a school janitor. One of the jobs drew particular interest from the Monsanto attorney.

Lee had been working as a maintenance man and was trying to patch a leak in a school classroom when he kneeled down into a patch of waterproofing roofing cement. The product had soaked through his jeans in the area where Lee's lesions had first sprouted.

Cople asked why Lee decided to sue Monsanto. "Did anybody tell you to sue Monsanto?"

"Nobody told me but myself," Lee answered.

Under Cople's questioning, Lee admitted that none of his doctors had told him that his disease was caused by Ranger Pro, and in fact one of the physicians who examined him wrote in his chart that his medical condition was not likely caused by "factors of employment." His doctors all talked to him about treatments, not causes, Lee said.

Cople had Lee list other chemicals he had been exposed to, such as the insecticides he sometimes used at work at the school district. He also got Lee to admit he had not followed the first aid instructions on the Ranger Pro label calling for anyone who had skin contact with the pesticide to "take off contaminated clothing" and "rinse skin immediately with plenty of water for 15–20 minutes."

There were questions about the health history of his relatives, how much alcohol he used to drink, a car crash he had been involved in years before, different treatments he'd tried, and how non-Hodgkin lymphoma had affected his interactions with his extended family, with his children, and with Araceli.

"Has your cancer affected your relationship with your wife?" Cople asked.

"We just not all affectionate like we used to be. I don't want her squeezing me, I don't want her touching me," Lee said. "I can't take that right now, all over my skin."

Cople asked him to describe the pain.

"It feels like fire," Lee answered. "Especially from the kneecaps to the ankles, it feels like fire when I walk. I have open lesions on the back of these legs from the hip up in the front and in the back so every time I take a step the clothes are rubbing . . . and it's bad."

As the afternoon wore on, Lee became increasingly irritated. How many more hours was this supposed to take, he wondered. Cople asked

Lee to answer questions about a vicious staph infection in one of the wounds on his scalp, about learning that he had cancer, and about the call he received one day from his doctor telling him the cancer had invaded his blood.

It was nearly 5:30 p.m. when Cople seemed to take note of Lee's fatigue. "You okay, Mr. Johnson?" he asked.

"No, I'm struggling," Lee replied. "We'll get through it though."

"All right. We'll get it done," said Cople. "No more breaks unless you tell us you need it."

Cople moved to a line of questioning about why Lee had skipped some treatments and doctor appointments, both during the period before the cancer took its deadly turn and after. Why, he wanted to know, why would Lee choose to go to work sometimes rather than go for medical treatment?

Clearly this lawyer had no idea what it was like to be tight on money, Lee thought.

"If I left a day, I would lose a hundred and something dollars per day. I had no sick leave. My sick leave was burnt out from this cancer," he answered. Sometimes he was just too sick to go anywhere at all. And then there had been a period when he lost his health insurance. Damn lawyers. Didn't they get it? He was exhausted.

Just before 6:00 p.m., Cople seemed to have run out of questions.

"Thank you for your patience today, Mr. Johnson," he said. "We reserve the right to continue the deposition of Mr. Johnson based on additional records being made available about his employment and about his medical condition and diagnosis and treatment and based on information that may be obtained from any of his treating physicians."

So they were done? Lee started to rise, but then Tim spoke up.

"I've got some questions," Tim said. He wanted to be sure he got certain statements from Lee on the record. "How do you feel today, just generally?"

"I feel pretty bad and under right now just from the pain. I have a lot of pain going on right now," Lee said, grimacing.

"How do you feel today versus how you felt four years ago?" Tim asked.

"I was able to exercise; I was able to work out with my kids; I was able to go outside and shoot the hoops; I was able to do different things that I could do all the time," Lee replied. He knew Tim wanted his words recorded, in case he didn't make it to trial. But the memory of his lost health inflicted its own kind of pain.

Tim moved on, asking about his use of Monsanto's herbicide. "You said somebody made a statement about its safety during your training, is that right?"

"I was told more than one time it was safe enough to drink," Lee answered.

Tim asked Lee about his call to Monsanto after the first accident doused him and he started to show signs of disease. "Did the lady on the phone tell you that the World Health Organization had classified glyphosate as probably carcinogenic to humans?"

"Not at all," Lee said.

"And in this phone call, you let—you let the telephone operator know at Monsanto that you were continuing to use the product after being diagnosed with cancer, right?" Tim continued.

"Yes."

"Now, if . . . the lady at Monsanto had told you yes, in fact, this can cause non-Hodgkin lymphoma, would you have kept using it after that?"

"Objection!" Cople interrupted. "Calls for speculation. Incomplete hypothetical."

"Absolutely not," Lee replied coldly.

"And if Monsanto had known, going back to the '80s or the '90s, that this is something that could cause cancer, would you have wanted them to share that information with you in the label or in some other way?"

"Objection," Cople said again.

Lee ignored him. "Definitely."

Tim was pleased. "Okay. I know it's been a long day. Thank you for coming in. And no further questions."

Cople was not about to let the testimony end with that. "I have some redirect, Mr. Johnson," he began.

Oh hell no, Tim thought. Monsanto's lawyer had used up his allotted time. He was not entitled to any additional time.

"We're going to walk," Tim said defiantly, motioning for Lee to exit the room with him.

"This is our deposition," Cople said angrily. "If you walk from the deposition we're going to call the judge."

"That's fine." Tim gathered his things. "You've used up your time. I was shocked that you weren't reserving any time."

Cople repeated his warning. "If you're walking out, then we'll take this up with the judge."

"That's fine," Tim said again. He and Lee walked as quickly as Lee could muster out of the room. Tim knew that in the weeks to come, Monsanto's attorneys would require Lee to sit through many more hours of deposition questions after they reviewed additional medical and personal records.

But for today, at least, they were done with these assholes. Done.

CHAPTER 11

A Question of Science

While Tim was focused on Lee's upcoming trial, Brent, Aimee, and the other members of the litigation leadership team had a very different focus. They were battling to keep hundreds of their cases alive.

Judge Vince Chhabria had ordered what he referred to as "science week," several daylong sessions in which the lawyers for both sides would put the best experts they could find on the stand in Chhabria's courtroom to testify about how scientific studies did or did not show links between Monsanto's products and cancer. If Chhabria found any of the expert opinions to be flimsy, he could ban their testimony at trial. Because the burden of proof would rest with the plaintiffs, expert testimony was especially critical for their side. The plaintiffs' lawyers knew they would have virtually no chance of winning if jurors didn't hear from multiple experts who could explain the scientific studies showing that Roundup exposure caused non-Hodgkin lymphoma.

These Daubert hearings, as the legal community called them, were named after a precedent-setting case from 1993. *Daubert v. Merrell Dow Pharmaceuticals, Inc.* was brought by parents whose baby suffered severe birth defects after the mother took an anti-nausea medication called

Bendectin, made by Merrell Dow and prescribed for pregnant women. Hundreds of lawsuits were filed against the company, which eventually pulled the drug off the market. But it was the Dauberts' case that led to a US Supreme Court ruling declaring that when scientific testimony is offered, it must first be assessed by a judge to determine whether or not the testimony is based on valid scientific methodology. The ruling called for judges to be gatekeepers, protecting jurors from shady lawyers who might use disreputable witnesses to try to present unvalidated junk science as evidence. But having a judge, who specialized in law and not science, determine what is or is not scientifically valid, could be dicey, the lawyers knew.

There were more than three hundred lawsuits consolidated in Chhabria's court by that time, and although some plaintiffs were in remission, others were suffering and dying from their cancers. It was up to Aimee, Mike Miller, and the rest of the team to make sure their cases stayed alive. The experts they had hired would be relied on not only for the cases going through federal court but also for most of the cases pending in state courts around the country.

It had not been easy finding scientists with both the expertise and the gumption needed to go up against Monsanto. But Aimee, Mike, and the others were thrilled with the experts they had managed to secure. One of their most important experts was Beate Ritz, chair of the epidemiology department at the University of California, Los Angeles, whose work focused on studying pesticide exposures and disease. Another key expert for their case was Dennis Weisenburger, chair of the pathology department of the City of Hope Medical Center in Omaha, Nebraska. Weisenburger specialized in the study of non-Hodgkin lymphoma, which made his testimony about links between the disease and Roundup essential.

Also on their side was Chadi Nabhan, the board-certified clinical medical oncologist whose evaluation of Lee's medical condition had been important in getting Lee's expedited trial date; Alfred Neugut, an expert in epidemiology, a practicing medical oncologist, and professor of cancer research at Columbia University; and Charles "Bill" Jameson, who had been a member of the working group of the International Agency for Research on Cancer that classified glyphosate as a probable carcinogen. Jameson was a member of the American Chemical Society and the Society of Toxicology.

Two others would also be heavily relied upon: retired toxicologist Christopher Portier, who led a US government environmental health and toxic substances research department within the Centers for Disease Control and Prevention; and Charles Benbrook, a former research professor who had served as executive director of the board on agriculture of the National Academies of Sciences.

The experts would each be paid handsomely for their time and treated to first-class airline tickets and upscale hotel rooms for the travel involved. Portier lived in Switzerland, so his travel was especially pricey, but the costs were all part of the process. Collectively, the lead law firms in the litigation were already spending well into the millions of dollars gathering the experts and evidence for a roster of plaintiffs that seemed to be expanding weekly. They were not about to nickel-and-dime on plane fare. The lawyers saw their experts much like superstars on a professional basketball team; they needed to pamper them, prep them, and make sure they were unbeatable when they were called to the court.

For the Roundup litigation, Chhabria had originally set the Daubert hearings to be held in December of 2017, but Monsanto's lawyers had convinced him to order a delay. A postponement was necessary, according to Monsanto, because in early November twelve scientists from various health institutions, including the National Cancer Institute, had published an update to an ongoing study of farmers' health and pesticide exposures known as the Agricultural Health Study. The findings of that study, which included more than fifty thousand farmers, supported

Monsanto's position that there was no association between non-Hodgkin lymphoma (NHL) and glyphosate-based herbicides. The authors concluded that "no association was apparent between glyphosate and any solid tumors or lymphoid malignancies overall, including NHL and its subtypes."

The news of the study proved to be a dramatic shift in Monsanto's favor. The study was published the morning of November 9, 2017, the very same morning that a key hearing was scheduled before Judge Chhabria to help the two sides prepare for Daubert. It also was the same day that European Commission officials met in Brussels, Belgium, to vote on whether or not to relicense glyphosate for continued use in the European Union. The Europeans were deadlocked over the matter at the time, though after the study was published they eventually did permit the relicensing of glyphosate for five years, not the ten years or more Monsanto had sought.

The study also came down as the chemical industry attacks on the International Agency for Research on Cancer (IARC) were intensifying. The American Chemistry Council had formed a group early in 2017 called the Campaign for Accuracy in Public Health Research, or CAPHR for short. CAPHR's main objective was to promote "reform" of IARC and to draw attention to the cancer research agency's "deficiencies, misinformation and troubling practice of producing questionable scientific evaluations."

CAPHR was backed financially by CropLife America, a lobbying organization for Monsanto and other companies selling agricultural chemicals. CropLife and others from the chemical industry were working with Monsanto not just to discredit the IARC scientists but also to convince Republicans controlling the US Congress to strip funding from IARC because of the classification of glyphosate as a probable carcinogen. CAPHR called the update to the Agricultural Health Study a "landmark report," and it quickly became a key talking point for the defenders of Monsanto and its herbicides.

Aimee and the rest of the team found the timing and the nature of the release of the study highly suspect. Embargoed copies had been sent out in advance to journalists, and the London health reporter for Reuters was one of the first to publish, authoring a splashy story that sent the study findings racing around the globe. "Large U.S. farm study finds no cancer link to Monsanto weedkiller," the Reuters headline blared. The reporter was the same Reuters correspondent who earlier that year had published multiple stories critical of IARC. The lawyers could see from the discovery documents they obtained from Monsanto that the company and its consultants had fed multiple story angles to the Reuters reporter as part of its secret strategy to discredit the IARC cancer scientists.

Those stories had bolstered Monsanto's arguments that the international cancer scientists were wrong about glyphosate being a probable cause of cancer and that the plaintiffs suing the company had no valid case. The new study gave Monsanto another boost, and the company proclaimed it to be the largest and best epidemiological study of the carcinogenic potential of glyphosate-based herbicides.

On that November day in court, Monsanto lawyer Eric Lasker told Judge Chhabria that the study was a "significant development in the science" and would "obviously be a key focus in the Daubert hearing." There was no way they could proceed with the hearing in December because Monsanto needed additional time to develop supplemental expert reports that incorporated the new study results. The new study shattered the plaintiffs' allegations, and Monsanto's lawyers should have the time needed to make that point clear, Lasker argued.

Mike protested any delay, arguing the "new" study was actually just an update to an earlier version of a flawed study that had found the same faulty lack of association between glyphosate and NHL. And there were still plenty of more valid studies that found there was an association. The request for a delay was merely more Monsanto posturing as the company sought to delay progress in the litigation, Mike asserted.

"Science is evolving," Mike told Judge Chhabria. "If the defendants are going to get a continuance every time a new piece of science comes out we will never have a Daubert hearing."

Despite the protests, Chhabria sided with Monsanto, pushing the hearing to March of 2018. That would be a mere three months before the start of Lee's trial, and though Lee's case was being heard in state court in San Francisco, not in Chhabria's court, if the expert testimony was barred by a federal judge, the state judges would likely take the same position, the plaintiffs' lawyers feared. In fact, one of the California state judges, the Honorable Ioana Petrou of Alameda County Superior Court in Oakland, was planning to sit next to Chhabria on the bench for the Daubert hearing so she could observe the expert witnesses in preparation for Roundup trials in her court.

The delay in Daubert was not a big blow to the plaintiffs, but it was a disappointment. Public interest in the litigation had surged following Brent's August release of the internal Monsanto documents, and the legal team was eager to show the world the science that Monsanto had worked for decades to suppress.

Reporters from Europe, Australia, Canada, and South America had joined journalists from the United States in publishing story after story about the scandalous revelations found within the company files that Brent had unsealed. Brent had also become a bit of a media darling. Television, radio stations, and newspapers around the world sought him out for interviews, casting Brent as the youthful avenger seeking to take down an evil corporate behemoth.

In fact, just the day before the hearing in front of Chhabria and the release of the new Agricultural Health Study, an episode of a popular daytime television talk show called *The Doctors* aired a segment focused on the concerns about Roundup. Brent was a featured guest on the show, and with the cameras rolling in front of a live studio audience he drew loud applause as he proclaimed that Monsanto's defense of

Roundup mirrored the lies told for years by the tobacco industry about cigarettes.

"For years, they generated studies saying it didn't cause cancer, saying 'We need more science, we need more science, we need more science.' It took lawyers, a coalition of activists, and people who really cared to expose the fraud for what it was, and we are in the middle of that right now," he said.

The show displayed for viewers images of some of the emails showing Monsanto's efforts to ghostwrite studies and to convince regulators not to look deeper into toxicity concerns about the company's herbicides.

"They not only talk about ghostwriting in the documents, they brag about it," Brent told the television audience, his voice growing louder as he hammered the air with a raised fist. "There are dozens of epidemiological studies that show without a question that there is a risk. And I don't think it is time to wait and see. It's time to take action."

The release of the Monsanto Papers not only had drawn attention to the litigation but also had generated such public outrage that groups across the United States and in many other countries were calling for bans or sharp restrictions on glyphosate-based herbicides and demanding more research on just how pervasive and dangerous these herbicides might be.

In Indiana, a group of doctors decided to track pregnant women exposed to Monsanto's pesticides and the potential impacts on their babies, while a separate child-focused wellness group started a program to test for glyphosate in foods served to kids in school lunch programs.

A cancer research organization in Arizona began collecting urine from people around the United States for a long-term biomonitoring project to track disease incidence against indicators of Roundup in bodily fluids. And some of North America's largest grain-handling companies told farmers they should no longer spray their crops with glyphosate shortly before harvest—a common farming practice to dry out the mature crop—because of concerns about glyphosate residues in food.

Across the Atlantic, the European Parliament held a "Monsanto Papers" hearing to discuss the public health implications of the disclosures in the company's unsealed documents. Parliament leaders invited Monsanto's chief executive officer, Hugh Grant, to speak at the hearing in Brussels, Belgium, but the company refused to send any representative. Parliament members were so outraged at the snub that they banned the company's lobbyists from access to lawmakers on Parliament premises.

Brent and Michael Baum had traveled to Brussels just before the hearing, taking two plaintiffs with them to talk to European media and members of the European Commission about what the lawyers were finding in Monsanto's internal documents about the company's efforts to try to control the scientific record and regulatory assessments. The lawyers' visit was covered widely by the press in Europe.

Monsanto continued to complain that the lawyers were conducting public relations, not law. The Roundup litigation was a sham, the company insisted, pushed by greedy lawyers who cared little for their clients with cancer and were focused instead on twisting evidence in ways that would enrich their own bank accounts. Monsanto maintained it had done nothing wrong and was simply the latest target of the unscrupulous industry of plaintiffs' attorneys.

But Brent and Michael were unapologetic. This was not just about winning money for their clients and rich fees for themselves; this was about alerting the world to a broken regulatory system, a corrupt company, and the health dangers resulting from it all, they insisted. European regulators were just as bad as US regulators when it came to ignoring studies showing concerns about Monsanto's herbicides, they said.

"This is deeply disturbing in the US, for these are the people that are supposed to be protecting us. It should be disturbing in the EU as well. . . . This is the tip of a very large iceberg," Brent told reporters at a gathering in Brussels. Calls for bans on glyphosate grew across Europe following the visit from the two lawyers.

Yes, the plaintiffs' team definitely had the public's attention. But this new farmers' health study showing no link between glyphosate-based herbicides and cancer was problematic for the plaintiffs' case, at least in the court of public opinion. Even though it was just one update to one study and didn't negate the others that did show cancer linkages, Monsanto was working hard to make the world believe the Agricultural Health Study was definitive proof of the safety of its products.

With Daubert delayed until March, Monsanto and chemical industry lobbyist CropLife America made a hard push for Congress to step into the public debate. They succeeded in convincing the Republican leadership in Washington to schedule a hearing through the US House of Representatives Committee on Science, Space, and Technology focused on the credibility of IARC. The goal was not just to undermine IARC but also to push for a measure to strip about $2 million in annual US funding from the cancer research group, moves intended to teach IARC a lesson about daring to classify a highly profitable corporate product as a potential carcinogen.

The hearing took place on February 6, 2018, a month before the delayed Daubert hearing. Led by Representative Lamar Smith, a Texas Republican, the event turned out to be little more than an assault on the IARC scientists. In his opening remarks, Smith wasted no time ripping into the integrity of the work of the international scientists: "There are serious repercussions to IARC's unsubstantiated claims, which are not backed by reliable data," Smith told his fellow lawmakers. "IARC's irresponsible handling of data does real harm to job creators and the public's view of the scientific process."

Appearing to take a talking point straight from Monsanto, Smith went on: the IARC scientists "failed to consider the most significant study on human exposure to glyphosate," the Agricultural Health Study, he said.

Smith did not mention that the Agricultural Health Study had been published only three months prior, while the IARC review of glyphosate took place three years prior. The Republican representative put up three witnesses to testify against IARC and allowed just one who testified in support of IARC.

Democrats on the committee sought to counter the Republican message, but with minority status there was little they could do other than protest. The leading committee Democrat, Eddie Bernice Johnson, called for protecting the cancer researchers rather than Monsanto.

"Chemicals have the potential to greatly improve our quality of life when developed and produced in a responsible manner," she said. "However, when produced or proliferated irresponsibly or without sufficient understanding of their potential impacts, chemicals can pose a grave and significant risk to every one of us. Unfortunately, by the time we realize the harm being caused by unsafe exposure to such toxic chemicals, the damage has often already been done. . . . If we knew then what we know now, would we have filled our homes, schools, businesses, hospitals with asbestos? Would we have supported the widespread installation of lead pipes to provide us with our daily drinking water?

"Mr. Chairman, chemical companies will continue to innovate and manufacture chemicals that seek to improve human life, and I support their initiatives in doing so. But such innovations should not come at the cost of human health," Johnson implored. "That is why the work of independent organizations like IARC is so important and why we in Congress should be supporting that work rather than attempting to undercut it."

The hearing amounted to more political theater than an actual policy change. But it generated positive press for Monsanto and negative publicity for IARC and for the Roundup litigation.

Before the hearing, the Democratic House staffers had reached out to Michael for guidance on how to prepare for the hearing, and he had been happy to oblige. He made the cross-country trip from his Los Angeles law firm to Washington, DC, in late January. Armed with two oversize black binders containing indexed copies of the internal Monsanto papers obtained through discovery, Michael met with staff members for the Democrats on the Science, Space, and Technology Committee. He laid out for them the case he and the other plaintiffs' attorneys would be making when they went to trial.

Not only did the plaintiffs' law firms have a number of scientific studies showing cancer risks with glyphosate-based herbicides, he told them, but they also had company communications showing how Monsanto tried to control what the science said about its products—the third-party payouts, the ghostwriting of scientific literature, the coziness with the US Environmental Protection Agency and other regulators. If Monsanto's herbicide was truly not carcinogenic, there should be no reason for the company to have engaged in decades of covert tactics to promote its safety. The staffers should include the information in the Democrats' presentation at the hearing, Michael urged.

He also got an audience with Senator Sheldon Whitehouse, a Democrat from Rhode Island, who in early 2017 had published a book titled *Captured: The Corporate Infiltration of American Democracy*. Whitehouse didn't have much time for the California lawyer with his big black binders, but he sympathized with Michael's task.

It was a long day on Capitol Hill and not an especially productive one in terms of advancing the Roundup litigation. His time would probably have been better spent strategizing with the other Roundup plaintiffs' lawyers for the Daubert hearing in March, Michael thought as he made his way back to his boutique hotel in the city's Dupont Circle neighborhood, pulling his scuffed rolling briefcase behind him.

After a simple dinner and a glass of red wine, Michael retired to his room for the night, but he wasn't ready to go to sleep yet. Was all this work actually going to achieve reforms that helped people? His profession came under sharp criticism so often, and here in the nation's capital there was a near-constant push for tort reforms to rein in lawyers like him, to restrict litigation just like the Roundup lawsuits, and to curtail monetary damage awards such as the ones his plaintiffs were seeking.

Michael's father had been a biochemist for the pharmaceutical industry and had hoped Michael would also take an interest in science, encouraging him to read the scientific magazines that came to the house. When he was still a young boy, his father had subscribed to a weekly science kit so Michael could run simple experiments. But while he grew to have great regard for the power of science, Michael felt that the kind of law he practiced allowed him to use scientific research to help people more directly.

He knew there were sleazy attorneys out there pushing lawsuits that probably never should be taken seriously. He knew case backlogs existed at courthouses around the country due to a deluge of litigation, some of it frivolous. But he also knew, all too well, that without the work he and Brent and Aimee and so many other plaintiffs' attorneys did, consumers who were really hurt by dangerous products would have no way to recover damages or curtail continued corporate wrongdoing. It frustrated him to no end when he thought about it all too much.

Enough career contemplation. What Michael needed after a long day was a battle—a virtual reality duel, he decided. When traveling, he often carried with him a headset, speaker, and other gaming equipment that could turn a dull hotel room into a 3-D virtual reality scene from *Star Wars*. Some of his colleagues found the virtual reality habit to be odd, another quirk to Michael's multifaceted personality. But Michael didn't care what others thought. When he slid on the helmet, the stresses of the day fell away.

On that night in Washington, in a cramped hotel room, careful not to trip over the edge of the bed, Michael straightened his shoulders and took a deep breath as a dark and foreboding figure appeared in the barren virtual reality landscape, lightsaber in hand. Michael drew his own saber; he relished a good fight. And though the virtual combatant lacked any identity, in Michael's mind there was no doubt. The enemy was Monsanto.

CHAPTER 12

San Francisco Showdown

When the "science week" showdown in San Francisco got underway on March 5, 2018, both sides of the legal battle were there in force. The opposing teams of dark-suited attorneys filled Judge Vince Chhabria's courtroom, six lawyers for each side crowded at two rectangular tables situated in front of the judge's bench, their laptop computers, lined yellow legal pads, and plastic water bottles competing for space. Additional members of the legal teams sat among the spectators on the hard wooden benches.

Aimee, Mike, Brent, and Robin took their seats at the table to Chhabria's left, while Joe Hollingsworth, Eric Lasker, and Kirby Griffis were in place for Monsanto to his right. The two tables were squeezed so closely together that the backs of the opposing attorneys' chairs nearly touched.

Each side would have eleven hours to present its scientific case to Judge Chhabria. The objective for the plaintiffs was to convince Chhabria that their experts were using valid scientific methodology in their analysis of multiple studies and their conclusions that Monsanto's herbicides caused non-Hodgkin lymphoma. If the judge determined the experts were reliable and could testify at the trials yet to come, it would then be up to juries to decide how believable the experts were and how the evidence applied to individual plaintiffs' claims.

Monsanto's job was both to undermine the credibility of the plaintiffs' scientists and to convince Judge Chhabria that the expert witnesses testifying on Monsanto's behalf were credible enough for the company to use at trial.

One of many points of contention for the week was the importance of the mouse study known as Knezevich and Hogan that Monsanto had submitted to the US Environmental Protection Agency in the 1980s. As the plaintiffs' lawyers had seen in the EPA's archived documents, US government scientists who looked at the study initially concluded the tumors that developed in the laboratory mice exposed to glyphosate indicated the chemical was a potential cause of cancer. The agency decided the study did not show carcinogenicity concerns only after Monsanto argued that the tumors were not related to glyphosate and refused to accept the findings of the EPA scientists. Discussions between Monsanto and the EPA about how to interpret the study dragged on for several years, and at one point the EPA asked Monsanto to redo the study, but the company declined to do so.

Now, during the critical science week in San Francisco, the plaintiffs planned to introduce hundreds of pages of data from the mouse study into the court record, a prospect Monsanto was adamantly opposed to. The data were "confidential" and "proprietary" and should not be made public, Monsanto's lawyers argued.

Chhabria made short work of Monsanto's request. "It is difficult to understand how Monsanto's mouse study from 35 years ago could justifiably remain confidential in this litigation," he wrote in a pre-hearing order. "The plaintiffs will be permitted to elicit testimony about the study without restriction."

To oversee the hearing, Chhabria was joined by Alameda County judge Ioana Petrou. The two judges sat together at a raised oval table, both wearing black robes, hers set off with two strands of fat white pearls. Each judge faced a computer screen that would show the exhibits the lawyers would introduce. Brass water pitchers and drinking glasses were set at their elbows. A wrinkled American flag stood against the wall just behind Judge Petrou's chair.

For other state court judges who had Roundup trials on their calendars, Chhabria had provided an open phone line to allow them to listen in on the proceedings. He also was having the hearings video-recorded, but Monsanto had requested the videos not be made available to anyone until after the hearings were concluded.

The first to take the stand was plaintiffs' expert Beate Ritz. Attorney Kathryn Forgie, a partner in Aimee's firm who was considered an expert in preparing witnesses, would conduct the direct examination for the plaintiffs' legal team. Though she was two decades older than Aimee, the two women were good friends, and Aimee admired Kathryn's quiet but determined courtroom demeanor. Kathryn had worked as a criminal prosecutor and as a corporate defense lawyer before crossing over to join the plaintiffs' side of the litigation business. She knew how hard Monsanto's lawyers would try to undercut the expertise of her witnesses; it was her job to make sure that didn't happen.

Clad all in black with her long chestnut hair knotted into a loose bun, Kathryn took her place at the podium facing the witness stand, arranging her notes in careful order. A black microphone angled atop the podium amplified her words throughout the high-ceilinged courtroom.

"We'd like to call Dr. Beate Ritz to the stand, please," Kathryn began. The scientist was quickly sworn in by the court clerk.

"Can you state exactly what it is you do, please?" Kathryn asked Ritz.

"I'm an occupational and environmental epidemiologist. I actually am tasked by the state of California in the Center for Occupational and Environmental Health at UCLA to investigate occupational and environmental causes of disease," Ritz answered steadily. "And my specialty has been pesticide-exposure assessment. Over the last 25 years I've done very large studies in the Central Valley, using the California registries; the pesticide use report registries. And I've worked on many different diseases, including cancer. I'm also currently the President—the sitting President of the International Society for Environmental Epidemiology. . . . And I have published more than 260 peer-reviewed papers in the area that I study; and pesticides are a big proportion of it."

The weight of Ritz's résumé alone should be enough to deem her credible for trial, Aimee thought as she watched the questioning unfold. Ritz also very much looked the part of a serious scientist, with her graying bob of dark hair and black-rimmed glasses. A narrow striped scarf was casually looped around her neck. She appeared confident but not as if she were trying to impress anyone.

Kathryn asked Ritz to define "epidemiology," to explain the difference between "cohort" and "case-control" studies, and to explain how experts in the field used information drawn from studies of real people and their exposures to figure out what level of risk a chemical might pose. Gleaning conclusions from epidemiology was a particularly challenging task because unlike laboratory rats, people can be exposed to myriad toxins every day, from the chemicals coating the frying pan they use to cook breakfast to the air pollution they might breathe in as they commute to work. To conclusively show that one substance caused one specific type of disease in one individual was a very difficult task, but not impossible, Ritz explained.

Kathryn asked Ritz to address the concept of "confounding" factors, such as the other contaminants a person could be exposed to, and how those complications were handled in assessing epidemiology.

"Right," Ritz responded. "It comes from this concept of—that we would want to know what would have happened to those who are exposed if we could take the exposure away from them. So, would they have had the same disease risk if there hadn't been the exposure? That's, of course, a counterfactual. We can never know that for a group of people who has been exposed, or for one individual. So what we do is we construct these comparison groups. So the comparison groups are supposed to give us this counterfactual rate; the rate when you have disease when you're not exposed," she continued.

"But how do we know whether these unexposed are actually the right comparison group? Well, we know it by trying to judge whether there's potential confounding. And potential confounding comes in when really there are other underlying risk factors for the disease that the unexposed have, but not the exposed at the same degree, so that really, the unexposed either are at higher risk of the disease due to other factors, or lower risk. Right?"

Aimee could sense a collective frustration in the crowd of journalists and other onlookers watching the testimony from behind her. Ritz's explanations were far too technical for a general audience. They would have work to do before she went live before a jury.

The questioning continued, with Ritz explaining the findings of various epidemiology studies conducted over the years that showed links between glyphosate formulations and cancer. Some of the literature showed that individuals who used glyphosate-based herbicides more than two days per year, "routine users," had a significant risk of developing non-Hodgkin lymphoma, Ritz testified.

She explained the imperfections and occasional contradictions found within the scientific literature and how drawing conclusions from the data was like putting together the pieces of a puzzle. When enough puzzle pieces come together, a picture emerges, even if it is incomplete.

"All of these studies add up," she said.

Under Kathryn's direction, Ritz laid out the various ways scientists evaluate whether or not a substance has the potential to cause cancer, including using laboratory tests to see if a substance is genotoxic, a term used to refer to something that causes chromosome breaks, changes in DNA.

"And is there any peer-reviewed publications that showed genotoxicity with regard to non-Hodgkin's lymphoma and glyphosate-based formulations?" Kathryn asked the scientist.

"Absolutely," Ritz answered. "There are—there's animal data; but more importantly, there is even human data and human lymphocytes. . . . DNA breaks have been shown to occur when individuals are exposed."

What about the study Monsanto had pointed to as critical evidence proving there was no non-Hodgkin lymphoma link to glyphosate? Kathryn asked. Ritz explained that, in her view, the Agricultural Health Study had several shortcomings. The study, which began following farmers in the 1990s, was quite a large study, with more than sixty thousand people tracked. But among the problems, Ritz testified, was that the researchers were unable to find and follow up with 37 percent of the study participants as the years went on. A bigger problem was that the researchers relied on the memories of farmers they could find to recall if they had used glyphosate-based herbicides in past years and, if so, how often and how much—not an especially reliable strategy for accurately calculating exposure.

Some "misclassification of exposure undoubtedly occurred," Ritz told the court.

Making the whole study even less reliable was the fact that the researchers had essentially tried to guess at the exposures of those farmers who dropped out of the study—the 37 percent of the original study participants who were not found for any follow-up. In making those estimates, the researchers failed to take into account the roughly hundredfold surge in use of glyphosate-based herbicides that occurred during the 1990s and 2000s, according to Ritz.

"I just cannot take this study seriously, in terms of the science that it produced," she said.

Kathryn's questioning of Ritz went on for more than three hours, covering the scientist's analysis of years of scientific literature about the health effects of glyphosate formulations.

"I'm a scientist because I want to get to facts," Ritz said, clasping her hands together and banging them down onto the witness stand for emphasis. "I want to get to the truth. I want to protect the public interest. And I don't want to do this in a way that is biased."

"Okay. And have you reached some conclusions and opinions in this case?" Kathryn prompted.

"Yes. After reviewing all of the scientific literature at hand, I really concluded that, to a reasonable scientific degree of certainty, glyphosate and glyphosate-based compounds, including Roundup, do indeed cause NHL."

Perfect. The scientist's testimony came across just as Kathryn had hoped. "Dr. Ritz, I know this is the first time that you've ever testified. In fact, I think it's the first time you've ever been in a courtroom, so I hope it wasn't too bad an experience," she said with a small smile, gathering her notes. "I thank you very much. And I pass the witness."

It was Monsanto's turn to question Ritz, but as Eric Lasker started to rise from the defense table, Chhabria swiveled in his chair to face Ritz directly. He had questions of his own.

"You talk a little bit about toxicity, and you talk a little bit about the mechanistic data. I take it your opinion is based on the totality of the evidence, not just the epidemiology. Is that right?" Chhabria asked.

"That's very right. Yes," Ritz replied. "This story has gone on for, like, 30, 40, years. There's a lot of information out there."

"And your opinion that Roundup causes NHL—is it—is it that Roundup is currently causing NHL in the exposure levels that human beings are experiencing today, or is it that Roundup is carcinogenic, and therefore it's *capable* of causing NHL in the abstract, or somewhere in between?" the judge asked.

Ritz appeared uncertain about what the judge was asking. "It's probably the second, because I base my opinion on the farmer studies. And we know that farmers are really at the front line. Right? They're the ones who have the highest exposure. And that's what I'm basing my opinion on, because that's the studies we have at hand; the human studies that we have."

"Okay," Judge Chhabria said. "So is that to say, then, that your opinion is not that it is currently causing NHL? It's that it's capable of causing NHL?"

"Currently, it's—yeah, it's capable of causing NHL," Ritz replied.

What? Kathryn looked bewildered. So did the other lawyers at her table. What had their expert just said? That Roundup was *not* currently causing non-Hodgkin lymphoma? Kathryn had already started to take her seat as Lasker walked to the podium to start his cross-examination of Ritz, but Aimee motioned for her to step back up there. They could not let that confusing answer from Ritz stand.

Kathryn eased up beside Lasker, lightly tapping his shoulder as she moved in front of him to face the judge. "Your Honor, he's graciously letting me come back for one second." She turned to Ritz. "I want to make sure you understood the Judge's question," Kathryn said to the scientist.

"Are you saying that currently—is it your opinion that glyphosate-based formulations can and *are* causing non-Hodgkin's lymphoma in the community today?" Kathryn made sure to emphasize the word "are."

Ritz took a long pause. "It depends on what 'the community' is," Ritz answered carefully. "And it's a dose question. Right? We—we know that the toxicology is in the dose. So definitely it can cause NHL. What the dose is, I wouldn't venture."

"You'd have to look at the individual to determine that," Kathryn said.

"Right. Yes." Ritz nodded.

"But in other words, your opinion is that non-Hodgkin's lymphoma can and is being caused by glyphosate-based formulations. Correct?"

Ritz continued nodding. "As long as there are farmers who have been using it in the way that we have studied it, definitely."

"Or landscapers?" Kathryn pressed.

"Landscapers, yes." Ritz agreed.

"Other people that have been exposed to it in some way?" Kathryn asked.

"Yes, yes, yes." Ritz nodded.

"Okay. Thank you." Kathryn took her seat, still unsettled by the judge's twisting of the testimony.

It was Monsanto's turn. Lasker took his position at the podium and opened a thick black binder. His objective was to discredit Ritz and her opinions, to show that her methodology was too flawed to be taken seriously. If he was successful, Chhabria would block her from testifying at upcoming trials, or at least sharply limit her testimony.

For the next hour and a half, Lasker grilled Ritz about study after study, challenging her conclusion about glyphosate formulations causing NHL. He questioned her methodology and statements about odds ratios and whether or not she had properly adjusted her analyses to account for risks presented by other pesticides that study subjects had been exposed to. The back-and-forth between the two sometimes turned prickly as Ritz grew irritated with the lawyer's scrutiny of her scientific analyses. More than once, Ritz brushed off the lawyer's questions, telling him they made no sense or were not relevant.

At one point, the sparring prompted Judge Chhabria to interject: "Hold on a second. So you do need to answer the questions that he asks you," he told Ritz. "And then if you need to say something to give it context you're perfectly free to do so."

Again and again, Monsanto's lawyer asked Ritz about the Agricultural Health Study that had been released in November and showed no connection between glyphosate and NHL. How could she possibly discount the fact that this large study of farmers that tracked usage over so many years found no association between glyphosate and non-Hodgkin lymphoma?

Ritz explained, as she had under questioning from Kathryn, that it was her opinion that the study was fraught with problems, including the fact that glyphosate use had seen a dramatic surge between the start of the study and the latest data collection, and that surge in use had not been accurately accounted for.

"It's useless for glyphosate," she said. "It's a beautiful study otherwise, for every other pesticide in the world that didn't change in the way that glyphosate changed, but it's useless to assess the effect of glyphosate currently."

Lasker also devoted a lot of time to asking Ritz about a large epidemiology study called the North American Pooled Project, which he referred to as NAPP for short. The NAPP researchers had gathered data on glyphosate use and incidences of non-Hodgkin lymphoma in groups of farmers from four US states as well as farmers from six provinces in Canada.

The NAPP researchers had concluded that farmers who used glyphosate "had elevated odds ratios for NHL overall" and that "significant or nearly significant risks of NHL overall were observed" in farmers using the chemical more than two days per year. They stated the data showed that glyphosate use "may be associated with elevated NHL risk."

But when questioning Ritz, Lasker focused on another finding of the researchers—that while there were "suggestive increases in NHL risk overall with more lifetime days of use," the "trend was *not statistically significant*." It is a bedrock of scientific methodology that when findings are not statistically significant, they may be explainable purely by chance.

Didn't Ritz agree with that finding? Lasker asked.

"This was under the exposure model that I didn't like, where they are mixing in routine and nonroutine users," the scientist answered. "I think things are very different when you look at the routine users." In fact, Ritz testified, for routine glyphosate users, the NAPP data showed a *doubling* of the risk of developing NHL. That study, like so many others, was an important piece of the puzzle, but it could not be relied on by itself to answer the question of whether or not glyphosate weed killers caused cancer, Ritz explained.

Finally, Lasker concluded his examination. It was time to move to the next expert.

But before Judge Chhabria excused Ritz, he asked her again about her position on current exposures and cancer. "Is it your opinion that in the exposures some people are getting right now—farmers—glyphosate is causing, has caused or is causing non-Hodgkin's lymphoma for them?" he pressed.

"If the dose is high enough, yes," Ritz affirmed.

It had been a long day for both sides, and they were only getting started. Next up was Dennis Weisenburger. Just as Ritz had done, Weisenburger laid out for the judge his analysis of multiple studies that he said lent support to the allegations that glyphosate-based herbicides cause non-Hodgkin lymphoma. He talked specifically about studies that found that both glyphosate and glyphosate-based formulations caused genetic damage, the type that leads to NHL. "The body of evidence is strong evidence," Weisenburger testified.

The scientist became flustered at times under pointed questioning by Monsanto lawyer Kirby Griffis and seemed to lose points with Chhabria when Griffis pushed him to explain a wave of NHL cases in the 1950s, well before glyphosate was introduced to the marketplace in the 1970s. Chhabria added his skepticism, asking Weisenburger to confirm that glyphosate would not be the cause of NHL in people diagnosed in the early 1980s. After all, Weisenburger had previously testified that the disease could take decades to develop after exposure.

"Well," Weisenburger started, "that—that's obviously what the defense is trying to say, but—"

Chhabria interrupted. "I'm not really paying that much attention to the defense, but I'm paying attention to what you're saying."

"So we've known for a long time that farmers have an increase in non-Hodgkin's lymphoma. And that's what prompted these studies of pesticides," the scientist tried to explain. "Glyphosate isn't the only thing that causes non-Hodgkin's lymphoma. We know other pesticides do. . . . So I think it could have been the other pesticides, or it could have been other exposures that the farmers had. We don't really know."

When Weisenburger finally was dismissed, he left the witness stand with a grim look. "It's like going to hell and back," he mumbled.

For the next several days, one scientist after another took their turn on the stand to spend hours explaining what they believed different scientific studies showed about a causal connection between Monsanto's herbicides and cancer. The plaintiffs' experts, not surprisingly, all saw clear evidence of a connection, while Monsanto's scientists found the opposite.

One of the experts Monsanto brought to the stand was cancer epidemiologist Lorelei Mucci, a professor at Harvard T.H. Chan School of Public Health and leader of the cancer epidemiology program at the Dana-Farber/Harvard Cancer Center. She testified that of multiple publications that had evaluated glyphosate and the risk of non-Hodgkin lymphoma, there were four main studies that best summarized the overall findings. She said the newly released Agricultural Health Study was the most "powerful" of all the studies.

"When you look at the body of epidemiological literature on this topic, there's no evidence of a positive association between glyphosate and NHL risk," she testified. "Based on following a standard methodology and evaluating all of the studies, there's no way to come to a causal conclusion about glyphosate and NHL risk."

In his cross-examination of Mucci, Mike Miller pressed her about how she could contradict the International Agency for Research on Cancer scientists, given she had looked only at epidemiology, while the IARC scientists who concluded glyphosate was a probable carcinogen had looked at animal studies and cell studies as well.

Wearing a stern expression, Mike leaned both hands on the podium and peered intently at Mucci.

"You said to counsel just before he sat down that you looked at the totality of the evidence. Do you remember that?"

"Yes," Mucci said, with a slight hesitation.

"To be clear, you did not look at the mechanistic evidence, the toxicology, or the animal data. Fair?" Mike said, shaking his head and growing more stern.

"What I was commenting on specifically was regarding the epidemiology studies, which—I did look at all of the available epidemiology studies on glyphosate and NHL risk," Mucci answered, nodding her head.

"Yes, ma'am, but you did not look at the toxic data. Right?" Mike said, leaning over the podium to stare at the scientist.

"I was evaluating the validity of the epidemiological findings specifically. And that's what I commented on in my discussion," she said.

"Okay, you're entitled to explain, but I just want to be clear." Mike would not let it go.

"No, I did not look at the toxicological data," Mucci said quietly.

"Yeah. All right. And, Dr. Mucci, you looked at—you did not look at the animal data. True?"

"I did not look at the animal data," Mucci said somberly.

"All right. Yes, ma'am. Thank you," Mike said.

It was exhausting and stressful work for all involved. Even the attorneys who were not handling the direct examinations and cross-examinations had to be on their toes every minute, ready to help right the ship if the questioning started going off course into areas that could hurt their case.

Each evening, Aimee, Brent, Kathryn, Mike, and the other team members spent hours preparing for the next day as if cramming for a final test. But they also made sure to take some time to gather in the hotel bar first, chasing down hot wings with margaritas and beers as they analyzed the wins and losses of the days.

They worried about Chhabria. He seemed unconvinced of the science and unimpressed with the experts the plaintiffs' team had presented. He clearly was not convinced that the human studies, the epidemiology, showed a clear causal connection between glyphosate and cancer. And he had made clear his displeasure with Dr. Ritz. He seemed to agree with Monsanto's lawyers that she had not properly accounted for risks from other pesticides in the odds ratios she cited. If he decided to limit or bar her testimony and that of the other plaintiffs' experts, the plaintiffs would have virtually no chance of winning any trial. He could even grant summary judgment in favor of Monsanto, stopping the litigation in its tracks.

When the hearings concluded, Chhabria ordered the opposing legal teams to appear before him to hear his thoughts on the scientific testimony. For Monsanto, only Lasker and Hollingsworth showed up, but Aimee was flanked by Robin, Brent, Kathryn, Michael Baum, Pedram Esfandiary, and another lawyer from Aimee's firm, David Wool. They knew their chances for success in the litigation would swing on what Chhabria said next.

"I think that the plaintiffs' experts' opinions are shaky," Chhabria said without hesitation.

"I think that the evidence that glyphosate is currently causing non-Hodgkin's lymphoma in human beings at the levels of exposure they are currently experiencing is pretty sparse. I also question whether anybody could legitimately conclude that glyphosate is not currently causing non-Hodgkin's lymphoma in human beings. I mean, it seems to me that, you know, there's at least a strong argument that the only reasonable conclusion one could draw right now is that we don't yet know," Chhabria said.

He took issue with the plaintiffs' heavy citations of the IARC classification, saying the IARC assessment was a hazard classification, not a confirmation that glyphosate was actually causing cancer in people who used it. He also was concerned that the plaintiffs' experts were presenting the science in a way that ignored the fact that while some studies showed an elevated risk, the odds were not strong enough to be considered statistically significant.

And yet—had the judge just used the word "shaky"? He had! And that was certainly no accident. Aimee tried to suppress her glee as the judge continued to talk. The other lawyers also caught the significance. Under the Daubert standard, concerns about evidence considered to be "shaky" are not sufficient to ban the evidence. A trial is the proper place to sort out those issues, according to the standard.

Judge Chhabria looked at Monsanto's lawyers. "The potential problem for you is that my role is not to decide whether glyphosate causes cancer. My role is to decide whether the opinions offered by the plaintiffs' experts are, you know, for lack of a better term, within the range of reasonableness."

"Right," Lasker said, nodding. It was clear; the plaintiffs were going to win this one.

The judge later summarized his decision in writing:

> Some epidemiological studies suggest that glyphosate exposure is slightly or moderately associated with increased odds of developing NHL. Other studies, including the largest and most recent, suggest there is no link at all. All the studies leave certain questions unanswered, and every study has its flaws. The evidence, viewed in its totality, seems too equivocal to support any firm conclusion that glyphosate causes NHL. This calls into question the credibility of some of the plaintiffs' experts, who have confidently identified a causal link. However, the question at this phase is not whether the plaintiffs' experts are right. The question is whether they have offered opinions that would be admissible at a jury trial. And the case law—particularly Ninth Circuit case law—emphasizes that a trial judge should not exclude an expert opinion merely because he

thinks it's shaky, or because he thinks the jury will have cause to question the expert's credibility. Given how close the question is at the general causation phase, the plaintiffs appear to face a daunting challenge at the next phase. But it is a challenge they are entitled to undertake.

They had made it through Daubert. Barely. The cases would go forward.

CHAPTER 13

The Cavalry

The month of April is considered one of the best times to visit the desert city of Las Vegas, Nevada. With waving palm trees, balmy temperatures, and lines of luxury hotels and casinos offering glitzy, round-the-clock entertainment, the city that never sleeps is a favored destination for many travelers. Especially lawyers.

Twice a year, more than a thousand members of the plaintiffs' bar descend on Vegas for a three-day conference focused on how to make the big business of mass tort litigation even bigger. The 2018 spring meeting of the aptly named Mass Torts Made Perfect conference was being held at Wynn Las Vegas, a sprawling five-star resort complex with more than four thousand guest rooms and more than two hundred thousand square feet of convention space.

The conference is largely the creation of litigation legend Mike Papantonio, a sixty-four-year-old multimillionaire who leads a nation-wide mass torts firm out of Pensacola, Florida. "Pap," as associates call him, has made a name for himself as one of the most successful litigators in the land, inducted in 2015 into the Trial Lawyer Hall of Fame by the National Trial Lawyers association. With his suntanned good looks and folksy Southern drawl, Pap stars in his own weekly television show called *America's Lawyer*, which he records in a studio built out of one wing of his law firm. He uses the show to explain high-profile cases and to excoriate companies and individuals caught in wrongdoing. He has particular disdain for regulatory agencies, which—in his view—have failed consumers over and over again.

"The cavalry is not coming," he often says in explaining his line of work. "We are the cavalry."

Pap was among a group of lawyers who secured a $670 million settlement with the industrial chemical giant DuPont in 2017 for the company's release of toxins in the Ohio River Valley that sickened thousands of people. By early 2018, he had published two novels and was working on a third. Pap liked to use his real-life cases as inspiration for his books, in which a handsome young attorney would prevail against ruthless corporate villains.

With the first Roundup trial approaching in June, Pap was one of scores of personal injury lawyers around the country who were securing clients and jostling for positions on court calendars. The Vegas conference was the perfect opportunity to highlight the Roundup litigation potential and to encourage more lawyers to join in, because when it came to mass tort litigation, the bigger the better. Although personal injury firms compete against each other for clients and leadership in litigation, they also realize that the larger the number of injured parties suing—no matter whose firm signs them—the more pressure can be brought to bear on corporations to settle.

The sessions over the course of the three days ran the gamut—young attorneys just getting their feet wet in the business could attend the Nuts & Bolts of Mass Torts session on Wednesday morning and then catch an afternoon session on marketing and financing strategies. It was not uncommon to spend $500,000 to $1 million to try just one case, so finding financing was often critical. Firms that didn't have millions of dollars in the bank to burn trying multiple cases in yearslong mass tort litigation could connect with companies advertising loan packages to help cover the costs of putting together cases. One such company, called Advocate Capital, offered not only case financing but also strategies to help law firms recoup the borrowing costs from their cases.

"You owe your clients the best possible legal representation . . . but you do not owe them interest free loans," Advocate Capital advised.

Those who did not want to go into debt to cover litigation costs also could explore what the plaintiffs' attorneys called third-party litigation funding, a practice in which hedge funds or other financiers put up money as an investment in the outcome of the litigation. The investor would then take a percentage of the winnings if the court cases were successful.

The Wynn's ornate ballrooms also held breakout sessions on how to advertise and secure mass tort clients, the pros and cons of agreeing to try a bellwether case, and the art of "scaling your intake department for growth." One Thursday afternoon session offered attendees a "deep dive" into strategies for "acquiring mass tort cases," including the use of demographics and "heat maps" to target areas for finding prospective plaintiffs. Another Thursday offering was focused on "creating the science when the defense refuses to."

There were many sessions on specific cases, including updates on litigation against the makers of a diabetes drug for allegedly failing to warn patients of the risk of kidney failure and other dire side effects, and work by a consortium of law firms suing distributors and manufacturers of opioid painkillers for creating an epidemic of drug addiction through deceptive marketing and other tactics.

Veteran litigators compared strategies, discussing the value of compiling a large "inventory" of plaintiffs and the steps needed to bring a corporate defendant to the settlement table. Senior lawyers shared tips on how to select jurors likely to favor a plaintiff. Tip number one: ask prospective jurors what they think of the jury system. If they say they believe in the right to a jury trial, you want them. If they say they don't know, or equivocate, you want them off your jury.

Training witnesses how to behave on the stand when giving testimony was also key, according to presenters. They should be taught never to look over at the plaintiffs' lawyers when answering questions from the defense, for instance.

The lawyers also found time for distraction, including an opening night gala at the XS nightclub and a raunchy performance by celebrity comedian Whoopi Goldberg.

The Roundup litigation was not favored by many of the lawyers in attendance. It seemed a risky undertaking, especially considering that Monsanto had solid backing on the safety of its herbicides from the US Environmental Protection Agency. But others were eager for a piece of the action. With that in mind, the agenda offered an informational session about the Roundup litigation that Robin Greenwald had agreed to help lead. As was the case for the conference overall, corporate defense attorneys were not welcome to attend.

One of the highlights of the conference was Thursday's luncheon and the 2018 Trial Lawyer Hall of Fame Induction Ceremony. A museum had been established in 2014 at Temple University in Philadelphia as a place to honor lawyers who had left "an indelible mark" through service to the "American public, the Constitution and the American trial bar." And the mass torts conference was the perfect place to make the designations.

While attendees munched on caprese salad, chicken breast, and risotto, Pap held court on the raised stage at the front of the hotel ballroom. He warned the group of an "onslaught" of legislative efforts underway in Washington aimed at reining in products liability litigation, and he blamed the actions on rich contributions that powerful corporations were handing out to lawmakers.

"You have corporations that put that little rat trail down and congress-people and senators follow that trail," Pap said. Those lawmakers were the "real bottom feeders, the real rats," he said. The Vegas conference was the opportunity for the plaintiffs' attorneys to arm themselves with tools to "fight back" against this threat to their livelihoods, according to Pap. He noted the wealth in the room and praised the accomplishments of the industry so far.

"As I look around the room, there are dozens of you who have changed things, making sure that we have airbags in cars to making sure that cars are safe when they roll over, making sure there is not some pill killing somebody, or some river being contaminated by a corporate polluter," he said.

Seated at a table just in front of the stage, Pap's pretty blonde wife, Terri, snapped pictures of her husband with a cell phone.

"With that energy is a big responsibility," Pap continued. "The responsibility is we have to continue doing that. I've told you so many times . . . It is on your shoulders. You are the cavalry."

Glasses and silverware clinking, lawyers around the room nodded in agreement.

~

Far from the gathering in Las Vegas, where Pap, Robin, and others were spreading the word about the Roundup litigation, Monsanto's top executives were planning their exit strategy.

After two years of wooing investor, consumer, and regulatory approval, Germany's Bayer AG was about to purchase Monsanto for $63 billion. European regulators had approved the sale in March on the condition that Bayer agree to dispose of more than $7 billion of its own assets to a rival chemical company. The US Department of Justice also gave its conditional approval after Monsanto's chief executive officer, Hugh Grant, and Bayer's chief executive, Werner Baumann, made a joint trip to Washington, DC, to meet in person with Justice Department officials.

Not everyone was on board with the sale. Advocates for farmers feared that after acquiring Monsanto, Bayer would be able to unfairly dominate the agricultural seeds and chemical business, a market worth roughly $100 billion. The company was already a heavyweight in health care and agriculture, with more than 99,000 employees around the world and annual revenues of more than 35 billion euros. And buying Monsanto would double the size of Bayer's agriculture business. Monsanto was both the world's largest seed company and a key maker of glyphosate, the world's most widely used herbicide. Monsanto brought in more than $2 billion per year from its herbicides, such as Roundup, and more than $10 billion more per year from its seed business, including the lines of genetically engineered seeds designed to tolerate being sprayed with Roundup as farmers fought weeds in their fields.

But while critics said that combining Bayer with Monsanto was going to create a behemoth that could crush competition, raise prices, and leave farmers vulnerable to price hikes and fewer product options, Bayer and Monsanto executives contended such worries were groundless. By combining their strengths in technology and research, the companies would be able to bring better products to market more quickly than in the past, they asserted.

"Together with Monsanto, we want to help farmers across the world grow more nutritious food in a more sustainable way that benefits both consumers and the environment," the company said in a press release after obtaining the European Commission's approval.

The Monsanto name would disappear after the deal was done, and several of the company's top executives would also take their leave, including Grant, who spent more than thirty-five years at the company and was named CEO in 2003. Grant, who was paid $19.5 million for 2017, would get an exit package of roughly $32 million following the

Bayer deal. Also walking away with hefty payouts would be Monsanto's chief financial officer, chief technology officer, chief strategy officer, and general counsel, among others.

Some Bayer investors were wary of taking on Monsanto. The company's checkered reputation with environmental and health advocates was worrisome, and the acquisition was expensive. Bayer was securing $57 billion in financing to pay for the acquisition, paying a premium of more than $17 billion over Monsanto's share price. Investors were also worried about the rising number of lawsuits filed over the Roundup cancer concerns.

But Baumann had no qualms about the acquisition. The deal was his dream—his first big move after becoming Bayer's "chairman of the board of management," in May of 2016. Baumann had been with Bayer since 1988 and was not afraid of litigation; it came with the territory for a major pharmaceutical player. Bayer had been able to settle four thousand lawsuits filed against the company over a contraceptive device for only $12 million and was also successfully fending off court cases filed over its top-selling blood-thinner drug, Xarelto. The Roundup litigation might be a nuisance, but it certainly was not a reason to scuttle Bayer's purchase of Monsanto.

At the company's 2018 shareholders' meeting in Bonn, Germany, Baumann reassured doubters, enthusiastically telling shareholders that the future was bright. "We anticipate being able to close the acquisition of Monsanto in the near future. I've been involved in a lot of transactions during my career," he said. "Viewed from various aspects and overall, I'm convinced that this acquisition has very great potential for creating value for our company, our stockholders and our customers."

As for Monsanto's image issues, Bayer would easily overcome them because its own reputation "for the highest ethical, environmental and social standards" would prevail, Baumann told those gathered at the meeting.

The deal was going to be the biggest acquisition in Bayer's history. It was expected to deliver more than $1 billion a year in new income. There was nothing to worry about, Baumann told the company's investors. Acquiring Monsanto was something to celebrate.

With necessary regulatory approvals in hand, the German company would officially become the sole shareholder of Monsanto on June 7.

That same month, in a California courthouse, the very first Roundup trial would begin.

CHAPTER 14
Staying Alive

Lee was trying not to think about the upcoming trial too much. After multiple rounds of cancer treatments, he was actually starting to feel better, strong enough to paint a little and work on his music. He knew many of his friends and family members didn't consider him an artist, but Lee had always harbored a creative streak.

Without a job to get up for each morning, Lee often slept until late in the morning and then spent the afternoon sketching and painting. Years earlier, when his grandmother was dying and Lee took time off work to be her caregiver, he had used the spare hours in his days to write essays he hoped one day would make for a popular book. He liked writing, but sketching was easier, he'd found. And working with his hands helped take his mind off the weakness in his legs and back that made it almost impossible for him to throw a football with his boys anymore or take long bike rides as the family had when Lee was healthy.

The scuffed white wall over the orange sofa in the family's apartment was filling up with Lee's art—a black-and-white drawing of a thickly lashed eye hung just to the right of a canvas depicting a catlike creature with pointed ears. The animal's face and tail were covered with blister-like lesions bubbling out of the skin. A third piece of art presented a slim dark-skinned man carrying an enormous unknown burden, a weight that appeared ready to overwhelm the frail figure.

When Lee was not drawing, he worked on his music. He had hung a large dry-erase board in the hallway between the apartment's bedrooms and living room. He and Araceli would jot down grocery lists and upcoming appointments on one half of the board. On the other half, Lee kept a running tally of the songs he was writing. "Survive" was one title. Another was called "Better Times," and a third he had dubbed "Can I Live?" At the top of the list was his favorite, a piece he was calling "Not My Time." Lee was structuring the tune as a slow and easy rap with a refrain that repeated simply: "Gotta keep holding on, holding on . . ."

Lee knew that his lawyer was excited about the start of the trial in June. Tim had explained to Lee that, much like the studying and memory work they had done before the depositions, he would prep Lee for his testimony at trial. Lee's testimony would likely take only one or two hours, but Lee should plan to be in the courtroom every day that he felt up to it, Tim told him. The trial would be long, five or six weeks in all, probably, and Lee wasn't sure he would have the stamina. But he knew Tim and the other lawyers thought it was important for the jurors to see him every day, to see what the disease had done to him.

As Lee worked on his music and art, across the country in The Miller Firm's Virginia office Tim, Mike Miller, Jeff Travers, and the other lawyers were spending long hours memorizing what would be the meat of the trial—the scientific studies that showed associations between Monsanto's herbicide and cancer, and the internal company documents that contained discussions about how to suppress and discredit such science while promoting Monsanto's studies that identified no cancer risk. They felt certain the jury would be outraged at the overt references to ghostwriting scientific papers.

Mike had spent weeks crafting the opening statement and closing argument he would make to the jury. Though Mike had never met Lee in person and it was Tim who had handled each interaction with Lee up to this point, Mike was the head of the firm, the captain of the ship. The openings and closings were critical elements of any trial: opportunities for attorneys to lay out the entire case for the jury, to highlight the strongest evidence, and to implore the jury to find for their client. In a case this complicated, an opening statement could take an hour or more, and it was imperative that the delivery not bore the jury, but rather pull them in and make them eager to hear more. There was no way Mike would let Tim or anyone else take that role.

Not only did Tim lack the experience and charisma Mike thought the trial demanded, but the young lawyer had also been behaving increasingly erratically over the past few months. He had recently gone through a bitter divorce, and the anger and anxiety over the breakup, along with battles over custody of his two young children, appeared to be wearing on Tim. He was missing meetings and deadlines, and sometimes the emails he sent to his colleagues made no sense. Some of the lawyers at The Miller Firm suspected Tim was abusing drugs, and they were deeply worried about his ability to perform at Lee's trial. Tim had always been considered the eccentric one at the firm, though, and they were all far too busy to dig into Tim's personal life with the trial looming. They would just hope for the best and handle problems as they happened, if they happened.

While Mike prepared, Tim and several other Miller Firm lawyers were filing pretrial motions and responding to motions brought by Monsanto. In law firm lingo, these motions "in limine" are aimed at getting the judge's agreement to exclude certain evidence from being introduced at trial. No matter how critical one side might think a piece of evidence is to their case—or how damaging it might be—the judge has sole discretion to determine which evidence can or cannot be presented to the jury.

Miller Firm lawyers filed one motion in limine seeking to have Lee's arrest record and other "bad acts" excluded. Another they filed sought to block evidence of Lee's "drug usage." Monsanto had "put forward no evidence that smoking marijuana is a risk factor for NHL. Thus, there is no relevance to marijuana usage and all references to marijuana should be excluded," the lawyers argued. Similarly, Lee's former habit of occasionally smoking cigars should be excluded from mention at trial because he had stopped smoking six years before first using Roundup, and any relevance was "outweighed by the prejudicial nature" with which Monsanto planned to introduce the information, the Miller Firm lawyers argued.

Monsanto's attorneys filed several of their own—on one day in late May alone, the company's lawyers filed more than two dozen motions asking the judge to block everything from any reference likening Monsanto's actions to those of the tobacco industry to any "evidence, argument or reference to 'ghostwriting.'" The company lawyers sought to block evidence about the fraudulent studies at Industrial Bio-Test Laboratories and Craven Laboratories; the 2009 email from Monsanto scientist Donna Farmer saying the company had "not done carcinogenicity studies with Roundup"; and the 2013 document that appeared to be a letter from EPA scientist Marion Copley to the EPA's Jess Rowland stating that glyphosate was a probable carcinogen and hinting at corruption in the agency.

The company also pressed the court to block media requests to record and broadcast the trial. "Publicity in this case, and the glyphosate litigation generally, has already led to multiple threats and disturbing communications directed to Monsanto employees and lawyers," the company's attorneys argued in a brief. "Televising this trial would make that worse."

According to the lawyers, one Monsanto employee had received harassing phone calls, including a voice mail saying, "I want to see you in jail." They told the judge of another call that said, "I'm just calling to let you know what a piece of shit I think you are."

Some employees had received postcards mailed to their homes with an image of a skull and crossbones, according to the company attorneys. One read "Stop poisoning us."

The judge would rule on many of the motions in the opening days of the trial, before the jury was seated and testimony started.

As the trial neared, Mike and Nancy Miller started packing up their office along with several weeks' worth of clothes and other personal items they would need while they lived in California over the course of the trial. Aside from a weekend trip home here and there, they would likely not be spending much time in Virginia again until August. They were used to this; it was part of the job. When they tried cases out of town, they typically rented a house or large apartment for the duration, somewhere close to the courthouse that was comfortable and clean.

There had been a hope—a slight one—that Monsanto might agree to a settlement before the trial. Mike had extended a written offer to the company in April. For $6 million, The Miller Firm would call off the trial and send Lee his share, and they could all stay home. But the company's lawyers had not even bothered to make a counteroffer. Monsanto was not going to settle.

～

With a long summer of work ahead, Mike wanted to make sure he enjoyed the three-day holiday offered by Memorial Day weekend. It was his turn to have custody of his two teenage sons from his prior marriage, and he was craving some time on the beach, so he and Nancy loaded up the kids and took off for Cape Hatteras, North Carolina. Mike was a water sports fanatic, a bit of a daredevil, and he thought few hobbies were more thrilling than kiteboarding. Considered an extreme sport, kiteboarding involves harnessing yourself to a sixteen-foot kite, strapping your feet onto small surfboards, and using the power of the wind to race across the water at speeds of twenty-five miles per hour or faster while making jumps ten, twenty, or thirty feet into the air.

Mike loved kiteboarding so much that he had bought his own rigging to use when the family stayed in their second home in Hawaii. North Carolina wasn't Hawaii by a long shot, but it would do for a quick weekend getaway. Mike checked the family into a resort that doubled as a kiteboarding and surfing destination on an otherwise quiet stretch of the Cape Hatteras seashore. The property featured a lodge, a surf shop, and a rustic bar and grill and was bordered by the Atlantic Ocean to the east and Pamlico Sound to the west. A long wooden pier extended from a grassy lawn into the teal-green water, where kiteboarders glided from surf to sky and back again. Nancy, who preferred non-extreme sports, could sit on the outdoor deck and sip a cold drink while she watched her husband soar into the sun.

It was just after lunch on Saturday, and Mike and the boys were headed back to the water. Nancy had hoped Mike would have had his fill with the morning run, and she tried to convince him to spend the afternoon with her on dry land. But in the end, he had decided to go back out.

Planning to relax with some quiet time on the balcony of their room, Nancy saw the commotion coming from the waterfront before she heard it. Suddenly people were running frantically to the pier. She scrambled downstairs, running through the lobby and out toward the crowd. One of the kiteboarders had lost control and slammed hard out of the sky into the pier. She could see a crumpled and bloody body lying facedown, and she heard someone say they were calling for an ambulance. It couldn't be Mike, she thought. But she knew as she ran— somehow she just knew—that it was.

"Mike!" Tears blurred her eyes as she bent over her husband's still form. A man from the property's surf shop was there too, and gently they rolled Mike over. His face was covered in blood, but he stirred and tried to speak. "I can't breathe," Nancy heard him whisper.

Medics were on the scene quickly and loaded Mike into an ambulance, which took him to a helicopter for transport to a hospital a couple hours away in Norfolk, Virginia. Nancy quickly gathered the two boys and their belongings and drove the 130 miles to Norfolk as fast as she felt she safely could. On the way she called other family members, doing her best to assure them Mike would be fine. He had to be fine.

But when she made it to the hospital and met with the doctors, she learned Mike was in the trauma unit and it was not at all clear that he would be fine. Both lungs were collapsed, his sternum and several ribs were broken, and his nose was shattered. He should recover, the doctors told her. But they would need to closely monitor him for several days to make sure of it.

Under the pull of pain medication, Mike slipped in and out of consciousness the first couple of days. But he was gaining strength, getting better, not worse, thank God.

In addition to calling family members, one of the first people Nancy notified was Miller Firm law partner Dave Dickens. Dave was thirty-seven and had been working for the firm for twelve years, proving himself to be a critical player in its pharmaceutical litigation. Dave had been helping out as needed with some of the Roundup casework and was considered a trusted advisor as well as a friend. Apart from Mike's recovery, the most pressing issue for the firm to figure out was what to do about Lee's trial.

They could ask the judge for a delay and most assuredly would get it. Monsanto's lawyers would no doubt prefer it that way; after all, they had argued against holding an early trial for Lee. But delay seemed like a bad idea. As hard as Lee was working to hold on, to stay alive, the firm had an obligation to keep his trial date intact.

From his hospital bed, a groggy Mike insisted he was still capable of trying the case. Lee was dying of cancer, and all Mike had were a few broken bones. Lee could not miss his chance in court because of Mike's misfortune, he insisted each time he woke from a medication-induced sleep. Her husband's stubborn streak was one of the reasons Nancy loved him, but she knew it would be impossible for Mike to be well enough to travel in time for the trial, let alone spend long days battling Monsanto's lawyers in court.

Tim was practically begging to take over the case as lead counsel, and ever since learning of Mike's accident, he had proclaimed himself the obvious replacement. While Mike and Nancy thought Tim could be helpful, they did not trust him to carry the case.

The most obvious choice, the only real choice, to replace Mike was Dave. Dave not only was a skilled litigator of complex cases but also was known for his stalwart nature and ability to keep a cool head amid chaos. It was not the best time to tap Dave for such a stressful undertaking, to be sure. His mother had been diagnosed with cancer shortly before Christmas and then had died in January, leaving Dave reeling with grief. But if they were going to get justice for Lee, personal pain had to be pushed aside.

Even with Dave taking charge and Tim assisting, they were going to need more help. After some deliberations, a call was made to the Baum Hedlund Aristei & Goldman firm to see whether Brent Wisner was available to join the trial team. Mike had disagreed with Brent's brash actions to release and promote the internal Monsanto documents, but Brent had been very impressive at the Daubert hearings in March. He was younger and less experienced than Dave but had a dynamic court-room presence that would play well with a jury, the Miller Firm lawyers believed. Even better, Brent knew the science inside and out, and the Miller team believed Brent would take Monsanto's experts apart if given the chance.

And so it was decided—though Dave and Brent had never met Lee, they would be lead co-counsels for the upcoming trial that was to start in less than three weeks. Tim would assist by handling the direct testimony of Lee and Araceli.

Tim was not happy about the arrangement, and his angst was on display when, nine days after Mike's accident, Dave called him into his office for a conference call with Michael Baum and Brent. As Dave sat at his desk and dialed the phone, Tim took a chair and waited for the Los Angeles attorneys to come on the line. Just as Dave heard Brent's hello, he noticed Tim shaking his head oddly. No, it wasn't his head; it was his whole body. Tim started to straighten out of the chair, and Dave watched, first in confusion and then in alarm, as Tim tilted forward, slowly at first. Then he was falling, his head thudding hard against the corner of Dave's desk before he slumped to the floor, where his body seized and shook uncontrollably. Blood seeped from a split in Tim's head, soaking into the carpet.

"Gotta call you back!" Dave yelled into the phone, hanging up quickly and calling for help. Though most people did not know it, Dave had dealt with epilepsy his whole life and recognized immediately that Tim was having a seizure. He needed medical treatment right away.

As the doctors would later confirm, Tim had suffered a grand mal seizure, perhaps brought on by anti-anxiety medications he was taking. He would be fine, but clearly he could not handle highly stressful trial duties right away.

I can't believe it. We've lost another one, Dave said to himself. What is going on?

The case had been challenging enough before Mike's accident, but now the odds seemed solidly against them. Monsanto had dozens of lawyers at its disposal from among the biggest and most respected firms in the nation. And Dave and Brent had only about two weeks to prepare for what was likely to be the most high-profile trial of their careers.

Dave flew to California on June 15, sad to be leaving his wife and seven- and five-year-old children behind but unable to delay his departure any longer. With the trial due to start on the 18th, he and Brent had much to do, including meeting for the first time with Lee and moving into apartments they had rented near downtown San Francisco. Tim was joining them to help as he could, as were Jeff Travers and several other lawyers from The Miller Firm and the Baum Hedlund firm who would help from the sidelines.

One of the most critical elements of the trial would be the opening statement. Initially, Dave and Brent had discussed splitting that up, but Brent convinced Dave he had been practicing an opening for nearly a year, running lines through his head as he showered or drifted off to sleep at night. He had not known until the emergency assignment to Lee's case when he might get a chance to use the monologue he had crafted. But he convinced Dave he was more than ready. Mike was not so sure, but Dave brought him around.

It was time to meet Lee. With Tim along to make the introductions, Brent and Dave made the forty-minute drive from San Francisco to Vallejo to visit with Lee in his apartment. As expected, Lee was not happy to learn that two guys he had never spoken to were now in charge of the case, though he wasn't sure it mattered. He didn't expect them to actually beat Monsanto. In his experience, the little guys never beat the big guys.

Araceli was also not happy to have strangers show up on her doorstep. Lee had not even told her he had filed a lawsuit, let alone that a trial was about to start. Now here were two unfamiliar men talking about testimony and trial preparations and how her family's lives could be forever changed, depending on the outcome in court.

She pressed the lawyers: how much would they get if they won— $50,000, $100,000? Why would Monsanto pay them anything? she asked. Lee was sick. Was it worth their time to pursue this?

Dave was stunned that Araceli did not know what was happening. How could Lee leave her in the dark? "It's definitely worth pursuing, even though it will be hard on the family," he assured Araceli. "We can't guarantee anything, but we'll be asking for more than $100,000."

Brent chimed in: "We're asking for a lot more," he said. "We're asking for hundreds of millions of dollars."

Araceli started to cry.

"Yeah. It's all going to be worth it," Brent told her with a grin. "Because we're going to kick their ass."

CHAPTER 15

The Trial Begins

The sixth-floor hallway of the San Francisco County Superior Court is laid with large square tiles of marbled gray and cream, accented with veins of charcoal and pink. Hard wooden benches with no backs sit against taupe walls, and arched windows offer views of the glistening gold-etched dome atop San Francisco's historic City Hall that soars more than three hundred feet into the sky.

Prospective jurors, lawyers, and journalists wait out courtroom breaks in this hall. Many sit silently; others speak with heads close together in hushed, almost-reverent murmurs. The quiet is intermittently disrupted by the staccato of hard-heeled shoes clacking against cool tile as people stride busily up and down the hall.

Jury selection for the trial of *Dewayne Johnson v. Monsanto Company* was scheduled to be held in Department 602/604, a jumbo-size courtroom with ample seating for the legions of reporters and spectators eager to attend what many expected to be the first of several trials that would pit cancer patients against the chemical company. Among the spectators was famed environmental activist and attorney Robert F. Kennedy Jr., who had offered to lend a hand in the Roundup litigation. Kennedy had brought his teenage son Aidan to observe.

Importantly, the high-ceiled space had plenty of room for the more than one hundred prospective jurors called to show up and sit through voir dire—the often-tedious examination process in which lawyers for both sides question each juror candidate to haggle over the final makeup of the jury.

Some lawyers believe the voir dire process is the most critical part of the case. Trial lawyers often hire jury consultants to advise them as they scrutinize a juror's background and beliefs. Plaintiffs' attorneys are looking for individuals most likely to be sympathetic to their clients, while defense attorneys are looking for the opposite. An individual's age, race, level of education, occupation, income, and existing knowledge of the issues involved in the case are all potentially critical indications of how a juror will evaluate evidence and vote on a verdict.

Overseeing it all for the Johnson case was Judge Suzanne Bolanos, a fifty-four-year-old Yale Law School alumna and former prosecutor who had the distinction of being the first Hispanic woman on the San Francisco bench. Her appointment in 2003 by California governor Gray Davis came at the recommendation of former vice president Al Gore, and she was recognized by peers as generally soft-spoken and convivial but stern if the situation demanded a firm hand. The judge wore her dark brown hair in a sophisticated bob that fell just below her chin, and she often dressed up her judge's robe with a pearl necklace.

So far, Judge Bolanos had been somewhat sympathetic to Monsanto's many requests to exclude evidence. But she was worried about the company's bid to block broadcasting of the trial. Public interest in the case was high, not just in the United States but around the world—one request to broadcast the trial came from the French news outlet Agence France-Presse, for instance. So she provided a compromise of sorts. To meet the demand for information, Judge Bolanos said she would allow media to record and broadcast the opening statements as well as the closing arguments and the reading of the verdict. The days of testimony in between would not be broadcast, she ruled.

Before the cameras rolled, there was the matter of jury selection. Twenty prospective jurors were asked to move from the gallery, where they and other spectators could watch the proceedings, to take seats in "the box" for questioning. Each time one of the twenty was dismissed, another person from the pool would be called to come and sit in the jury box. Twelve would ultimately be selected, along with several alternate jurors who could step in if at any point during the trial a core juror had to be replaced.

Handling the juror questioning on behalf of Monsanto, Sandra Edwards offered a warm smile to the juror prospects and asked each of them to "please be very honest" as she probed for their views of the company and its weed-killing products. "You are the most important part of this trial," she told the jurors. "We need to find out who you are."

Her first question was for a show of hands of those who had weeds to deal with, followed by a question about who avoided using chemicals when dealing with weeds. Juror after juror told Edwards they were concerned about unknown effects tied to weed killers and chemicals generally.

One man, sitting in the number 11 jury spot, said he held very negative views of chemical companies, including Monsanto. "There is that taint," he told Edwards. Other jurors admitted that they would be worried to see a neighbor spraying Roundup.

She asked one juror to describe in detail his affiliation with, and feelings about, the Sierra Club, and asked another about how the woman's job as a social worker informed her ability to analyze facts and context. Edwards also wanted to know what the prospective jurors thought of the US Environmental Protection Agency and its regulatory prowess.

One of the men in the jury box sparked chuckles in the courtroom when he said he believed the EPA to be "solid" and doing a "good job," though under Administrator Scott Pruitt the agency was "a little suspect." Another prospective juror told the court: "I trust the EPA. If EPA says it's alright to use a product then I agree."

Edwards wanted to know if cancer had impacted family members or otherwise hit too close to home for jurors to be objective in hearing the Johnson case. She also asked them if they looked "carefully" at labels when buying groceries.

A number of the prospective jurors admitted that they had negative feelings about Monsanto and tried to eat only organically grown food, or, as one juror prospect put it—to eat "clean." One man, the son of vineyard operators who was in the wine business, said he worked only with organic vineyards and was part of an organization that encouraged farmers to convert to organic production. He said it would be "extremely hard" to set aside his bias against Monsanto.

Another potential juror said his knowledge of Monsanto was only "casual," but he did know that the company had invented genetically engineered seeds designed to be used with its Roundup herbicide. That is "either a very sick business plan or a very clever one," the man said. He told Monsanto's attorney he was an ethical man and could judge the case fairly.

One prospective juror told the court that both of his parents had died from lung cancer. Another said she held a bias against big corporations in general after working at Wells Fargo, a disgraced bank that had been caught defrauding customers. Corporations did not always act ethically, in her view. "They're in it to make a buck; that is the bottom line," she said.

In response to Edwards's probing, one of the prospects said that he had grown up in a rural community, learning to drive a tractor before he learned how to drive a car. A friend of his had died from cancer, and he said he believed chemicals can be carcinogenic. Nevertheless, he used Roundup. He said he wore gloves and washed his hands after using the product, taking care not to get the weed killer on his skin. "I definitely take precautions when using a chemical like that," he said.

As Lee's attorney, Dave Dickens asked one potential juror after another whether or not they would be comfortable awarding large damages if they found in favor of Johnson, telling the group his client would be seeking "tens, hundreds of millions" of dollars. Some jurors said they were uncomfortable with that prospect, but many others expressed being open to the idea, saying it might take large amounts to punish a company for wrongdoing.

As the first day of questioning dragged into a second day and then a third, the lawyers for both sides periodically broke to meet with Judge Bolanos in her chambers to discuss who they wanted removed and replaced among the juror prospects. When they emerged, the judge would excuse and thank those who were being dismissed and ask for their seats to be filled with other members of the jury pool.

Among those dismissed was a social media manager for natural products businesses; a woman who had declared a strong dislike and distrust for Monsanto; the man who said he worked to convince farmers to convert to organic practices; and the woman who distrusted corporations after working for Wells Fargo. The man whose parents had died of cancer was also excused, as was a woman who brought her knitting to court and remarked that she thought big damage awards were sometimes needed to punish a company that does wrong.

Finally, after two and a half days of intense questioning, a jury of seven men and five women was locked in. One was a product manager at a software company, another worked as an advisor to municipalities, and yet another was a molecular biologist who worked for a genetic research company. And even though it was only June, Judge Bolanos told them to prepare to serve well into August. To win the case, under California law Lee's lawyers would need to convince at least nine of the twelve that Lee's cancer was caused by Monsanto's herbicides.

The jury selection process had taken a lot out of the lawyers and the jurors alike. With the Independence Day holiday coming up the following week, Judge Bolanos determined it made sense to give everyone involved a bit of a breather before opening statements and the presentation of evidence. All parties should return on July 9 at 9:30 a.m. for what promised to be a long and bitter contest, she told the jurors and lawyers.

While all lawsuits are by definition contentious, the Roundup litigation felt personal, especially for Brent Wisner. Monsanto's attorneys had made it clear that they were not happy that Brent had been brought into Lee's case after Mike Miller's accident. The company's executives and lawyers were still furious over Brent's release of the company's internal documents the previous August and the fact that the Baum Hedlund firm was still helping lead the litigation. They were most outraged by the many media appearances Brent had made over the past year to tout what he claimed was evidence of ghostwriting and other corporate misconduct.

Before the jury selection started, Monsanto's attorneys had filed a brief with the court complaining that Brent had been acting as a lobbyist rather than a lawyer. Those actions violated a California rule prohibiting an attorney from acting as both an advocate and a witness in the same proceeding, according to Monsanto.

Brent had been acting as "PR man" and had "personally embarked on an extraordinary lobbying effort," including seeking to convince European regulators "to classify glyphosate as carcinogenic," Monsanto's lawyers argued. Because his lobbying involved efforts to allege that Monsanto had engaged in ghostwriting scientific papers, conduct Monsanto firmly denied, Brent and the rest of Lee's trial team should be barred from presenting any evidence or arguments about Monsanto and ghostwriting, the company's lawyers pleaded.

It was a desperate effort that went nowhere, and both Brent and Dave believed it underscored how worried Monsanto's attorneys were about the trial. To be honest, though, Dave was also having his concerns. It was a big hill to climb to prove that one company's chemical caused one man's cancer, especially given the fact that regulators denied any carcinogenicity concerns. Sure, there were several scientific studies that showed links between cancer and Monsanto's glyphosate herbicides, but there were also studies that disputed that connection. And though the documents showed Monsanto's scientists and executives had engaged in some pretty slimy conduct, that did not prove their products were killers.

It was going to be a battle.

~

A crowd of journalists and spectators filled the courthouse hallway on the morning of Monday, July 9, as Brent and Dave made their way to Judge Bolanos's courtroom. Dave had managed to sneak away for three days during the break to visit his wife and children back in Virginia, but Brent had spent a lot of the week off practicing his opening statement. Brent firmly believed that while the facts were the foundation of a good case, a lawyer couldn't win on facts alone. A good litigator knew how to connect with a jury, how to win them over on an emotional level. Jurors should never be bored; they should get caught up in the story, the shame, the scandal, the wrongdoing. They should feel the injustice that had been done. That was how to win.

Appearances were also important. For delivery of his opening statement, Brent chose a simple dark suit set off with one of his favorite ties—butter yellow with slashes of crisp blue and white. The scruff of goatee was gone, and with his clean-shaven face and closely cropped wave of auburn hair, Brent looked every bit an earnest Boy Scout as he stepped before the jury. Exactly as intended.

Brent and Dave took seats at the plaintiffs' table facing the judge, while Sandra Edwards, Kirby Griffis, and a lawyer named George Lombardi sat at the defense table facing the jury.

Lee and Araceli walked in together, but Araceli sat down in the first row of the spectators' area while Lee made his way to a chair next to Brent and Dave. He had dressed up for the occasion, choosing a periwinkle button-down shirt under a dark blue jacket. In his left ear, a tiny earring sparkled. He and Araceli had spent the prior night in a downtown San Francisco hotel to avoid a long rush hour morning drive and be fresh for court. But neither had gotten much sleep.

After a few introductory remarks from Judge Bolanos, it was time for opening statements. A lawyer from each side would outline the evidence and the experts they planned to present. A large screen sat angled in front of the jury box where the opposing lawyers could project PowerPoint slides to augment their commentaries.

Brent was up first.

"Good morning. My name is Brent Wisner. I'm an attorney for Mr. Johnson," Brent said, directing the jury to where Lee sat, next to Dave. His arm swept the air as a ringmaster's might, orchestrating the attention of his audience. "And for this special occasion, I decided to shave. So you might not recognize me from last time." Brent smiled. Some of the jurors smiled back.

"This case really is about choice. It's about the right of every single person in this room to make a choice about what chemicals they expose themselves, their family or their children to. . . . Some people are willing to take greater risks. After all, people still smoke, and we all know smoking causes cancer. But at the end of the day, it's our choice. And really nobody has a right to take that choice away from us. . . . That's why in California it's pretty simple. If a chemical company sells a product and they know or suspect that that product can cause cancer, they have to warn. They have to give us a choice."

As he spoke, Brent took short steps to his right and then his left, angling his body toward the jury and then slightly away. His voice rose as he emphasized certain points but then softened into a sigh on others. The courtroom was Brent's stage, and he never missed a line.

"This case is about a chemical company, Monsanto, and its multibillion dollar product Roundup," he said. "You are going to learn that for at least the last 40 years, since the 1980s, Monsanto has known that the primary ingredient in Roundup can induce tumors in laboratory animals. And starting in 1998 and moving forward, there have been study after study showing that, in fact, the use of Roundup is associated with a specific type of cancer."

It was but a slight change in tone and cadence, but a hint of anger crept into Brent's voice as he went on. "That cancer is called non-Hodgkin's lymphoma. And you're going to learn it's not just one study. It's been study after study after study that continuously finds an association with this specific type of cancer. The evidence will show that Monsanto has known this for over 20 years, but instead of just warning and telling consumers, 'Hey, these studies show this stuff can cause cancer,' Monsanto has refused. They have fought science. . . . And the consequences of that conduct are why we're here today."

Photos of Lee and his family appeared on the screen in front of the jury box.

"Because of what Monsanto has done, Mr. Johnson was not given a choice."

Brent looked from juror to juror as he spoke, hoping to meet the eyes of each. "They have to warn. And if you don't warn, if you don't give someone a choice and somebody gets hurt because of that or God forbid somebody actually gets cancer, then I personally believe, and I think you will as well, that you should be responsible for the consequences of that."

Brent could tell he had them intrigued. Now he had to lay out the facts. And he had to do it in a way that was compelling but as concise as possible. Practice run-throughs of the opening had taken three to three and a half hours, and he and Dave had held many detailed discussions about a need to simplify it all. The PowerPoint deck for Brent's opening contained 234 slides, for crying out loud, Dave had argued. Just that weekend, Brent had presented a mock opening to the entire trial team, both those in California and the lawyers in Virginia listening by phone. The consensus of the group was that Brent's opening was far too long and too argumentative. He must cut it down to two hours, the trial team decided.

Brent started off by detailing Lee's story—his job, his routine use of Monsanto's herbicides, how the accident with the hose and the later leak from the backpack sprayer had both soaked his skin in Monsanto's chemicals.

"You're going to learn that on multiple occasions he was literally drenched through his clothes for multiple hours, and that over two years, at the end of the second spraying season, he discovered a lesion on his knee," Brent told the jury somberly. "The evidence will show that that lesion started to spread. . . . It covered his entire body."

Brent flashed more photos onto the screen in front of the jury box. These photos were close-ups of Lee's hands and torso, showing the skin eaten away by disease. Lee sat silently next to Dave.

"I have a really hard time talking about this with Mr. Johnson in the room," Brent said, looking down at his hands and pausing. "But you're going to learn that he's not supposed to be alive today. He's actually on borrowed time. And every doctor agrees that it's just a matter of time. Maybe two years at best."

Brent drew in a deep breath and shoved his left hand deep into his pocket, letting his words hang in the air.

Then he shifted gears again. "You're going to learn, ladies and gentlemen, that this is not the first lawsuit," he said. Lee's was only one of many lawsuits against Monsanto over allegations that its weed killers cause cancer. But, he said, Lee's was the first case to go to trial.

"And so I want to be very, very clear. You members, as part of this jury, are actually part of something really important." Brent's tone grew more serious. "Because this product has been on the market for 40 years, and without a question, each one of you, whether . . . you want to be or not, are actually part of history. And the world's watching because what you do here has really important consequences."

The jury members would see "stuff that nobody has ever seen." Internal Monsanto records that had been hidden away for decades would be a big part of the trial, he promised.

Brent was pacing back and forth now. Time to move into the next phase of his presentation. He explained to the jury the basics of how the evidence would be presented and the steps to verdict. He told them they had a lot of complicated scientific concepts to learn. Some of it would be "boring and dry," but it all was important, he said.

"The first question is what is Roundup? We've talked about it a lot. We've all seen commercials for it, but actually what is it?" he asked rhetorically.

The jury would have to decide specifically whether or not Roundup had caused Lee's cancer, and if they found that it had, the jurors would need to consider what amount of monetary damages he should receive as compensation. The last question they would have to answer, Brent said, was whether or not Monsanto should be punished.

Next came the tricky part. Because so much of the evidence involved scientific research, Brent had to give the jurors a crash course in a range of arcane terminology and research findings, and he had to do it without losing their attention and interest. It was not an easy task, teaching jurors about chemistry, but it was essential if Lee was going to win.

Brent told the jurors how Monsanto combined glyphosate with chemicals called surfactants to help the weed killer adhere to and be absorbed into the tissue of a plant. "Roundup is both glyphosate and surfactant. . . . And this is something that's going to come out a lot throughout the trial, particularly when it comes to regulatory agencies because they look at glyphosate. They don't look at Roundup."

One surfactant used by Monsanto in its herbicides was called polyethoxylated tallow amine, Brent said, apologizing for the complex terminology.

"I will never say that word again because we just call it POEA. And that's the surfactant that's used in both Roundup and Ranger Pro," he explained. "You're going to hear testimony that, in fact, this substance is banned in Europe for safety reasons. But it is used here in the United States. It was used in the product that Mr. Johnson used."

Onto the PowerPoint screen Brent flashed a slide of a 2015 email written by Monsanto scientist William Heydens acknowledging that "the surfactant in the formulation will come up in the tumor promotion skin study because we think it played a role there."

Brent looked pointedly at the jury. "That's really important because the plaintiffs believe, and we intend to prove through the evidence, that it's not just glyphosate that's the problem," he told them. "It's part of the problem. But it's glyphosate plus the surfactant, that when you put them together, they have a synergistic effect. . . . I like to think of it as like baking soda, pretty benign, vinegar, pretty benign. You put them together and you get that volcano eruption that you did in your science project in the seventh grade."

Dave was quiet as he watched Brent at work. He was doing a great job. The jury seemed interested, engaged. Pens scratched across notepads in the jury box as several jurors recorded the points Brent was making.

Brent could see it too. Thank God, he said to himself. They were still paying attention. He pressed on, describing to the jury the importance of mechanistic data, which he described as research from studies about how Roundup affects the DNA in human cells; epidemiology, the study of disease in groups of people; and toxicology, or animal carcinogenicity studies. He explained the progression of cancer, how cells can become damaged and mutate, leading to the formation of tumors; how certain things can promote the growth of mutated cells. One key word jurors needed to know, Brent said, was "genotoxicity," the property of chemical agents to damage genetic information in cells in ways that can lead to mutations.

Jurors continued to take notes. This was going well, Brent thought.

He told the jury that Monsanto had not conducted any long-term studies to determine if its products could cause cancer since at least 1991. But many other people had, and many of these independent studies showed Monsanto's products could be carcinogenic. He showed a series of slides charting the findings of studies done on mice and rats from 1981 to 2009. In study after study, the animals exposed to glyphosate in their diet developed tumors, including kidney and thyroid tumors as well as "a lot of skin cancer," Brent said.

"We see in three of the studies we have elevated rates of kidney cancers," he said, pointing to the slide. "We also see in the last four studies not done by Monsanto every single study shows malignant lymphoma. Now, we're talking about non-Hodgkin's lymphoma. You're going to hear testimony that seeing such a consistent result in these mice studies related to a specific type of lymphoma is really strong evidence about whether or not it actually can cause lymphoma in humans."

He told the jurors about a different type of study from 2010 in which scientists had applied the chemical to the skin of twenty mice multiple times a week for thirty-two weeks and found that 40 percent of the animals exposed developed tumors, while none of the animals in the control group—those not exposed—developed tumors.

"You're going to hear evidence that this study provides strong evidence that it's a tumor promoter," Brent said. "So of the 13 mice and rat studies, there's only one study that has it clean across the board."

Brent had been talking for forty-five minutes and was not yet close to being halfway finished with his presentation. There were many more studies the jurors would need to become familiar with, but before they heard about those, Brent wanted to make sure they knew about what he thought of as the Parry incident.

"I'm going to tell you a little story," he said to the jury. "In the 1990s, there was four independently-published studies specifically related to genotoxicity. . . . It spurred a lot of concern within Monsanto. I want to show you how Monsanto dealt with it and what they learned back in the '90s."

The use of Roundup was increasing around the world back then, increasing dramatically, Brent said. So more and more independent scientists wanted to know if there were health risks with the product. In South America, Roundup was being sprayed from the air over swaths of cocoa fields to try to wipe out the production of cocaine, and researchers wondered how people living near these sprayed areas were impacted, if at all. They started taking blood samples from people living in areas where Roundup had been sprayed aerially and found a significant increase in DNA damage in exposed individuals.

"We'll go over this study later with an expert," Brent said. "They're saying that there's serious damage occurring with the formulator product." Additional studies coming out around the same time in the late 1990s also showed evidence of DNA damage following exposure to Roundup, he continued.

"In response, Monsanto gets together, and it decides that they need to research the issue," Brent said, advancing his presentation to a new slide. "So they're recognizing a problem, and they say, 'Hey, let's hire an expert to look into this.' Sounds pretty reasonable. So they hire Dr. Parry. Now, Dr. Parry, unfortunately, he passed away in 2001, but in this time he was really a prolific and well-respected genotoxicity expert."

Monsanto was hoping that James Parry, after examining the genotoxicity concerns, would refute the genotoxicity studies and vouch for Roundup's safety with regulators, Brent explained. But at the same time, before Parry had even weighed in with his view, Brent said, Monsanto was making statements to the public and issuing press releases denying and attempting to discredit the genotoxicity concerns raised by the studies.

Then, much to Monsanto's disappointment, Parry raised his own concerns, Brent said.

"So he looks through all the data, and he says, 'Guys, it causes genotoxic effects.' He cautions Monsanto." Brent clicked his presentation to a slide showing part of Parry's report to Monsanto. One sentence of the report was enlarged to make it easy for jurors to see from several feet away.

Brent read Parry's words to the jury: "If the genotoxic activity of glyphosate in its formulation is confirmed, it would be advisable to determine whether there are exposed individuals in the group within the human population. If such individuals can be identified, then the extent of exposure should be determinant and their lymphocytes analyzed in the presence of chromosome operations."

Brent looked back at the jury members. "So he's saying, . . . 'Let's go out and look at humans who are being exposed and see what's happening to their chromosomes.'"

Holding the slim black PowerPoint remote aloft as though it were a baton, Brent advanced his presentation to a slide showing an email written by Heydens, the Monsanto scientist, to his colleagues about Parry's concerns. Brent read aloud: "We want to find/develop someone who is comfortable with the genotox profile of glyphosate/Roundup and who could be influential with regulators and scientific outreach operations when genotox issues arise. My read is that Parry is not currently such a person, and it would take quite some time and money/studies to get him there. We simply aren't going to do the studies Parry suggests." The last line was outlined with a blood-red box on the slide.

Brent flashed a new slide onto the screen and read more from Heydens's emails to his Monsanto colleagues. "Mark, do you think Parry could become a strong advocate without doing this work? If not, we should seriously start looking for one or more other individuals to work with."

Continuing, Brent stressed the next part as he read: "We have not made much progress and are currently very vulnerable in this area. We have time to fix that, but only if we make this a high priority now." The email was signed simply "Bill."

Monsanto was worried, Brent explained. But not about people using Roundup.

"This is an important admission. Monsanto admits that it never sent the—Dr. Parry's reports to the EPA," he told the jury solemnly. "The evidence will show that Monsanto didn't share it with anybody. Instead, you're going to learn that Monsanto sponsored the publication of something called the Williams paper."

Brent quickly checked the time; he was more than an hour into the presentation. He was in his element, getting to the meat of what he considered the juiciest evidence.

"And I'm going to teach you a new word right now. It's called ghost-writing," Brent said to the jury. "This is when a company writes a favorable publication that pays a prestigious author to put their name on it. This is the idea of, you know, writing something and having someone sign it, and so it looks authoritative even though the person wasn't really involved in putting it together."

He advanced the presentation to a slide with a picture of Heydens next to a 2015 email in which the Monsanto scientist suggested to his colleagues that they "ghostwrite" a scientific paper just as they had, according to Heydens's email, in the year 2000. Monsanto had presented the EPA with the 2000 paper, titled "A Safety Evaluation and Risk Assessment of the Herbicide Roundup and Its Active Ingredient, Glyphosate, for Humans," and had touted the fact that the paper concluded Roundup posed no health risk. It hoped to do the same with the new paper Heydens was proposing in his email, Brent said.

"So just to get the timeline of events, Monsanto gets a report from Dr. Parry saying it's genotoxic. They give him more data. He says, 'Yes, it's genotoxic. You need to study the formulated product.' And instead of submitting that report to the EPA or even giving it to anybody, they ghostwrite an article saying that it's not genotoxic." Brent's outrage was clear and he hoped the jury was also starting to feel a sense of outrage, but he couldn't tell.

It was nearing noon and the jurors could use a break, but Brent was not even close to being done. He pressed on.

There was a "mountain of data," Brent said, and experts testifying for Lee would share it all with the jury, including several epidemiology studies that connected Roundup to non-Hodgkin lymphoma (NHL), a cancer that starts in the white blood cells. He outlined six "core studies" as well as a 2014 meta-analysis of those six studies and the updated Agricultural Health Study published in 2018. Did the jury know what a meta-analysis was? Just to be sure, Brent flipped to a slide with the definition: "A statistical approach that combines the results of multiple studies into a single summary estimate."

Jurors would hear expert testimony on all of it in the coming weeks, he said. They would hear that in some studies, people using glyphosate-based herbicides for more than two days a year had a doubling of the risk of developing cancer than did people exposed fewer than two days per year.

Advancing his PowerPoint presentation, Brent clicked to a slide summarizing a 1999 study as showing a "230% increased risk of NHL for glyphosate formulation." He clicked to another slide highlighting a study from 2001 that showed a 212 percent increased risk of NHL when using Roundup more than two days a year.

Click. Another slide, another study. This one showed a 306 percent increased risk of NHL from Roundup use.

Click. This slide showed an internal Monsanto memo in which company scientists discussed the various studies and one wrote, "It looks like NHL and other lymphopoietic cancers continue to be the main cancer epidemiology issues. . . ."

Click. Another internal Monsanto email appeared on the screen in front of jurors. This one was written by Monsanto scientist Donna Farmer to colleagues about the studies showing an increased risk of NHL from use of Roundup, and activists' calls for support for organic agriculture in response. "How do we combat this?" she wrote.

"I show you this so you can see that Dr. Farmer's instinct when she sees this is to combat it. That's, I think, a philosophical thing that you'll see a lot on these documents from Monsanto," Brent told the jury.

Okay, it was really time to take a break. The jurors and the lawyers alike were hungry for lunch after Brent's nearly two-hour presentation. He still had more to show the jurors but welcomed the judge's call for an hour-and-a-half recess.

"Am I going too long; did I go into too much detail?" Brent asked Dave quietly as the jurors filed out of the room. "They're not looking bored, right?"

"This jury just got more information in two hours than most juries do over an entire trial. But it's going great," Dave reassured him. "With this jury, detail is a good thing."

One change they should make, both lawyers agreed, was to have Araceli join Lee at the plaintiffs' table. The jury needed to see both of them, and Lee could use the support, they felt.

When the trial resumed, Brent was recharged. It was time to tell the jury about the International Agency for Research on Cancer (IARC) and Monsanto's fear of the cancer group's scrutiny of glyphosate.

"In the 1960s, countries around the world got together and said, 'You know what? Studying cancer risks is actually really difficult. It's hard to get the data,'" Brent told the jury. "'It's expensive. You don't always get cooperation from the manufacturers.' And so they formed the International Agency for Research on Cancer. And its sole mission is to convene independent experts to evaluate and assess chemicals to see if they cause cancer. That's literally its entire job."

He clicked to a slide showing the agency's headquarters outlined by flags from multiple nations. "So in 2014, IARC announced that it would be investigating glyphosate. . . . The reason why IARC did that is because they had seen all the signs and stuff I have shown you, and they were really concerned. . . . What they do is they get all these scientists together, they read all the data, they peer-review it, they critique it, they discuss it, they study all the science that's available, for well over six months. And then they get together for a week in France, hash it out face-to-face."

Once they have thoroughly reviewed the scientific literature, the protocol called for the cancer scientists to classify a substance as to the likelihood—or not—that it was carcinogenic. For glyphosate, the classification would come down in March of 2015.

When Monsanto learned in 2014 that IARC was going to review the carcinogenicity science on glyphosate, the company's internal records showed the Monsanto scientists were very, very alarmed, Brent told the jury.

He clicked to a slide showing yet another internal Monsanto email. "This is from Dr. Heydens. The subject is 'IARC Evaluation of Glyphosate,'" Brent said. "You see it's dated in October of 2014. And if you read down here, he goes, 'While we have vulnerability in the area of epidemiology, we also have potential vulnerabilities in the other areas that IARC will consider, namely exposure, genotox and mode of action.'

"So what this shows is that even before IARC met, their own internal scientists have recognized that they have particular vulnerabilities streaming together the evidence," Brent said.

The IARC scientists were among the top in the world, Brent continued, flipping to a slide listing several of the scientists by name and title. The chairman of the IARC group on glyphosate was the leader of the United States' National Cancer Institute, Brent pointed out, and other members of the group had equally impressive areas of expertise.

These experts, after reviewing the scientific evidence, determined that glyphosate was a probable human carcinogen, Brent explained. And, importantly, they observed a positive association with NHL, he said to the jury. This group had announced their findings just as they had for hundreds of other substances. But the reaction to the glyphosate classification was "an unprecedented attack," Brent said, with at least one scientist—Dr. Christopher Portier—coming under vicious assault on his reputation and credibility. The jury would hear from Portier during the trial, Brent promised.

He then flipped to a slide showing an internal Monsanto strategic plan aimed at countering IARC. Tagged as Plaintiff Exhibit 0292, the paper listed "strategies and tactics" for responding to IARC's classification of glyphosate. One of the tactics was dubbed "Orchestrate Outcry with IARC Decision." Several bullet points detailed exactly how the outcry would be engineered through social media and other channels.

"So it looks like Monsanto's, you know, ready to respond to IARC's classification," Brent said with a smirk. "The problem is this document is actually dated February 23rd," which was three weeks before the IARC scientists even concluded their review of glyphosate, he explained. "What you can infer from that is up to you. But it is interesting to note that Monsanto was already planning to orchestrate outcry . . . when they haven't even seen the statement."

Brent hoped the jury got the point. Monsanto knew what IARC would find; the company was so certain its weed killer would be deemed a probable cancer hazard that it outlined *in advance* a plan to discredit the international scientists.

Brent looked from juror to juror, checking for signs of fatigue. Happily, he thought they all appeared to be following his narrative intently. He laid out more scientific data and explained to them that when evaluating the safety of a chemical, the Environmental Protection Agency does no testing of its own but instead relies heavily on information provided by the companies that want to sell the chemicals. In finding no cancer concern with glyphosate, the EPA had been guided by Monsanto. Testimony would show the EPA violated its own guidelines for evaluating studies in its handling of glyphosate, Brent said.

"All right." Brent recognized he needed to start to wrap up. "So the question that I've been answering for, like, two hours is: Can Roundup cause cancer? And the question is: Is it more likely than not that it does? That's really the threshold issue here. I believe we're going to present evidence and testimony and a lot of science that really supports that it does."

He paused to allow the jurors to absorb his words. "Before I move on to Mr. Johnson's cancer, I want to point out something that's really important. . . . I just want to make it really clear. Nobody here is saying—and we're not going to present evidence—that glyphosate or Roundup should be banned. Nobody is saying that. Okay? . . . We are saying, however—and we plan to prove with evidence, that you should just warn; right? Cigarettes are still on the market, but people know, because it says right there on the label. And that's all this case is about. It's about giving choice."

It was well after 2:00 p.m. now, and he had started just after 10:00 a.m., Brent realized. Dave was going to kill him. Even deducting the lunch break, he was way over the time limit they had agreed to. But there was still more he had to tell the jurors.

He had laid out the evidence that Monsanto's products could cause cancer and that the company had known that but did nothing to warn people. Now he had to tell jurors about the evidence that showed Lee's cancer had been caused by the company's herbicides. He started by taking them through the work Lee did for the school district, the spray accident, and the backpack leak.

He told the jurors that Lee would never have agreed to spray the herbicides if he had known they could cause cancer.

"Monsanto has admitted that it had never warned any consumer that Roundup could cause cancer. They have also admitted that it has never warned Mr. Johnson that Roundup could cause cancer. So this is actually an element of our case. We don't have to prove it. They admit they never warned," Brent said.

"The only question now is: Should they have warned?" He let the question hang in the air.

Then it was back to the slide presentation, where Brent pointed to photos of Lee's lesion-covered body. Blown-up photos of Lee's hand, his calf, a close-up of his stomach. The pictures were stomach-turning. One hand looked as though a hot poker had been drilled into the skin over and over.

"Eighty percent of his body is covered in these lesions," Brent said. "The last treatment he did almost killed him."

What about other possible causes for Lee's cancer? There were none, Brent told the jury. "He doesn't have other chemical exposures. You're going to hear testimony that we've gone through all the possibilities. There's nothing there. And what's really interesting, you'll hear science about this, data about this, but this type of cutaneous T-cell lymphoma is essentially unheard of in African men. It just doesn't happen. The only reasonable explanation—you'll hear testimony—is that it was exposure to a chemical."

Brent clicked to a slide with photos of Lee and his family, including one from a snowboarding outing.

The jury should consider all that Lee has lost and still has to lose in calculating damages for Monsanto to pay, Brent told them. The loss of his health, the loss of time with his family.

"And the mental suffering that he has to live with knowing that he's going to die. Not seeing his kids go to college or get married." Brent sighed heavily. "Disfigurement, physical impairment. You can see from Mr. Johnson's face he's scarred. Not just emotionally, but physically. What is the value of being disfigured? . . . These are all very difficult things. . . . How do you put a number on that?"

Brent, Dave, Mike, and the other members of the trial team had discussed what sort of monetary award they should ask for, but Brent was not going to go there yet, not in the opening statement.

"Before I let off for the day, I just want to finish off on a couple of things," Brent said, again eyeing the clock. "And this is something—it's a document that I find really important for this case."

Onto the screen flashed the image of another Monsanto internal email, this one written by toxicologist Donna Farmer in 2009.

Brent read the words from the email aloud: "'You cannot say that Roundup does not cause cancer. We have not done the carcinogenicity study with Roundup.'"

He looked pointedly at the jury. "I want you to think about what that sentence really means. . . . Why didn't they study?"

So, with all that he had just told them, the ultimate question, Brent said, was this: "Should Monsanto be punished for its conduct? We believe, when the evidence is fully in, you'll be believing that they should."

Brent put up his last slide. Jurors saw a photo of Lee's wife and two sons standing together on a sunny California hillside. Lee was nowhere to be seen, as though he didn't exist.

Silence sat over the courtroom for a moment.

"This was a long opening," Brent told the jury with a hint of self-consciousness in his voice. "It was supposed to be, like, an hour and a half. Clearly I have no concept of time."

He smiled sheepishly. "I apologize for that. There's a lot of science and a lot of data to discuss. And, quite frankly, we've only scratched the surface of it. . . . I really do appreciate you guys listening carefully, taking notes. . . . And I appreciate having you guys for the next month or so."

Judge Bolanos straightened in her chair. It had indeed been a long opening, and the jury no doubt needed at least a short break. A fifteen-minute recess should do it. Court would resume again at 2:55 p.m., the judge announced.

It was time for Monsanto to lay out its defense.

CHAPTER 16
For the Defense

If Brent's impassioned opening statement was supposed to intimidate Monsanto's attorneys, he had failed miserably.

As George Lombardi rose from the defense table to address the jury, he didn't actually swagger, but the Chicago lawyer's confidence and comfort in the courtroom was palpable. Unlike Brent, Lombardi had decades of experience successfully litigating cases for some of the world's biggest companies. He was a partner in a 160-year-old law firm whose one thousand lawyers were spread throughout offices in the United States, Europe, Asia, and the Middle East, aligned with numerous powerful and prestigious clients.

He had already proven to be skilled at helping Monsanto win big cases. Lombardi had been named Litigator of the Year in 2014 by the *American Lawyer* publication for his representation of Monsanto in a bitter courtroom battle with rival DuPont over a seed-licensing arrangement. Lombardi's lawyering helped secure a $1 billion verdict for Monsanto in that case, endearing him to the company.

Importantly, Lombardi had experience representing other companies with less-than-virtuous reputations, including securing numerous litigation victories for the Philip Morris tobacco company.

This Roundup cancer case would not be a slam dunk for Monsanto, but close to it, in the view of the company's lawyers. Sure, some of Monsanto's executives had made comments in emails that didn't reflect well on the company's intentions, but there was no clear-cut proof that glyphosate or the company's glyphosate-based products caused anyone's cancer. And the company had the US Environmental Protection Agency firmly on its side. Monsanto's lawyers just needed to make sure the jury focused on facts, not emotion.

With a slow but deliberate stride, Lombardi walked to the podium placed just a few feet from the jury box and laid down a sheaf of note paper along with the PowerPoint clicker he would use later to show slides to the jury. Co-counsels Sandra Edwards and Kirby Griffis sat ready to assist at the defense table, stacks of evidence files at their elbows.

"Ladies and gentlemen of the jury. Once again, my name is George Lombardi. I was introduced to you during jury selection."

Lombardi clasped his hands together as if ready to lead the group in a prayer.

"Now, I have to confess to you that it was not my foremost desire to be the guy that stands up at 3 o'clock to start talking to you, but that's where we are. And I appreciate in advance your attention. I know you've had long sits through the jury selection process and a long sit today, but I appreciate your attention."

Similarly to Brent, Lombardi made slight steps to the right and then the left as he addressed the jury. Always in motion.

"Cancer is a terrible disease. Mr. Johnson's cancer is a terrible disease. We all do, and we all should, have great sympathy for what he's going through and what his family is going through."

But, Lombardi said in a serious tone as he looked from juror to juror, Lee Johnson and his lawyers would not be able to prove that Monsanto's products caused his suffering.

"The scientific evidence is overwhelming that glyphosate-based products do not cause cancer and did not cause Mr. Johnson's cancer,"

Lombardi said, subtly shaking his head back and forth. "It's the science that's going to answer that question for you. And it's the science that has guided the scientists at Monsanto."

Lombardi covered much of the same ground that Brent had—telling the jury there was a long history of relevant scientific research, including animal and cell studies as well as studies analyzing disease incidence in farmers exposed to glyphosate. But in Lombardi's telling, the studies agreed with Monsanto's determinations of safety with the weed-killing chemical. The "single most relevant study," Lombardi told them, was the Agricultural Health Study, which had found no association between glyphosate and non-Hodgkin lymphoma.

"That is the most up-to-date science. It's the biggest study. It's the most sophisticated study," he assured the jury.

It was up to Johnson's attorneys to connect his cancer to his exposure to Monsanto herbicides, Lombardi said. "And they're not going to be able to do that. They don't have the science to do it. It's just not true."

Because of Brent's lengthy opening and the lateness of the day, the jurors were visibly fatigued and starting to show signs of restlessness. They were also not warming to Lombardi as they had to Brent. The Monsanto attorney came across as affable enough, smiling and addressing the jury in a friendly, matter-of-fact manner. With his lean frame, receding gray hairline, and slightly crumpled dark suit, Lombardi could have been mistaken for a college professor as he explained slides showing flowcharts that detailed how glyphosate impacted the amino acids within plants. But even at this early stage of the trial, it was evident that the Chicago lawyer was not connecting with these jurors as Brent had.

Pressing ahead, Lombardi told the jurors that there was no way Johnson's cancer was related to his use of Monsanto's herbicides at the school district.

"Mr. Johnson's cancer began years before he took on this job at the school district," Lombardi argued. "Cancers like non-Hodgkin's lymphoma take years to develop."

The jury should not take the bait Brent threw at them and misinterpret company emails, he warned. "We've seen the Monsanto emails, little snippets from them. . . . And we'll talk about that. Because you're entitled to the context for those things. And the context provides you with the whole story."

Lombardi told the jury they should understand how important glyphosate was to farming, how effective it was in killing weeds, and how it helped farmers avoid tilling their soils. And, he assured the jury, how safe it was for people. It wasn't just Monsanto that sold glyphosate-based herbicides, he pointed out. The company had patented the chemical as a weed killer many years ago, but now several companies sold glyphosate-based herbicides all over the world.

One very important thing for the jurors to know was that well before glyphosate-based herbicides were ever introduced to agriculture, in the 1950s and 1960s, farmers were developing non-Hodgkin lymphoma much more often than nonfarmers. "Something was causing farmers to get non-Hodgkin's lymphoma, and it wasn't glyphosate," Lombardi said.

As for the studies that Brent had made such a big deal of—studies Brent said showed 200 percent or even 400 percent increased risks for people who were exposed to glyphosate to develop cancer—the truth was something far different, Monsanto's lawyer told the jury. The truth was that there were lots of problems with the studies Brent cited. The number of study subjects was small, only fifty-one people in one of the studies Brent had touted, Lombardi pointed out. In some of the studies, the scientists had not adjusted their work to properly account for exposures the study subjects had to pesticides other than glyphosate, and there were other shortcomings.

He didn't exactly call Brent a liar, but the implication was there. "These studies don't actually show an effect of glyphosate and getting cancer," Lombardi said, sounding like a father correcting the exaggerations of an errant child.

The jury also needed to know the truth about the International Agency for Research on Cancer, needed to understand that the authority of the group's findings had been vastly overstated, he said.

"You're going to hear testimony that they spent two days talking about glyphosate, and that's how they came to their conclusion," Lombardi explained. "Now, when you're talking for just two days, you obviously aren't doing your own testing. IARC . . . did not do any testing. They didn't go into a laboratory. They didn't do cell testing. They didn't do animal testing. They didn't do an epidemiology study. What they did was they reviewed publicly available testing. Some of it, not all of it, publicly available testing."

The jury should also know that IARC had not had the benefit of the latest Agricultural Health Study information, which showed no connection at all between glyphosate and non-Hodgkin lymphoma, Lombardi said. The updated data had not come out until just recently, well after IARC's classification of glyphosate as a probable carcinogen.

And when they thought about the IARC classification, he went on, the jurors should realize that IARC didn't say glyphosate definitely was cancer causing, just "probably." Moreover, the cancer group had said that there was only "limited" evidence in the studies of real people connecting glyphosate to cancer. It was also important for the jurors to know that the IARC scientists didn't evaluate the real-world risks to people; the cancer science group merely determined if substances were "cancer hazards," without taking into account how much of an exposure it might take for a person to develop cancer, Lombardi explained.

And finally, the jurors needed to know that it wasn't just glyphosate the group had declared a probable carcinogen; IARC had even classified very hot beverages as probable carcinogens, Lombardi said, an incredulous note in his voice. "IARC will not prove plaintiff's case."

Point by point, Lombardi told the jury that the events and the evidence Brent had laid out for them were but twisted versions of reality.

There was actually a "vast array of testing" that the EPA had evaluated dealing with both glyphosate and glyphosate formulations showing the safety of the products, the Monsanto attorney said.

As Lombardi spooled out Monsanto's defense, Brent kept a close eye on his adversary's presentation, taking notes as he followed along on the computer monitor situated atop the plaintiffs' table. If Brent was bothered by Lombardi's challenges to his credibility, it didn't show.

Seated at Brent's right shoulder, Dave reclined in his chair, a forefinger pressed to his cheek as he listened. Lee was quiet, displaying no emotion, but Dave could sense his client was growing weary.

Lombardi was rolling now. What about the story Brent had told about Monsanto and its consultant Dr. James Parry? Again, Brent had not given them the *whole* story, Lombardi told the jury. Under Brent's twisted version, Dr. Parry had been worried about Monsanto's herbicide formulations and urged the company to do cell tests to look into the potential genotoxic effects of the full formulations of glyphosate-based products, but Monsanto had pushed Parry aside in order to find an expert who would adopt the company narrative.

The truth, Lombardi told the jury, was that even though Monsanto decided not to work with Dr. Parry any further, the company did go on to publish a paper looking at the very issues that had concerned Parry.

"When counsel said that, that testing has not been done, that was not accurate," Lombardi told the jury before striding back to the defense table and pulling a thick document from a manila file. Handing the document to Brent, he then directed the jury's attention to the large screen outside the right front edge of the jury box displaying a PowerPoint presentation, where the first page of a scientific report appeared. The title was "Genotoxic Potential of Glyphosate Formulations: Mode of Action Investigations." The key finding of the published research paper was highlighted in yellow: glyphosate-based herbicides were "not genotoxic," according to the Monsanto scientists who were listed as authors of the research paper.

"That means they are testing the formulations," said Lombardi. "So the whole story? The evidence is a little different," Lombardi said, appearing outraged at what he implied was Brent's deceptive portrayal.

And what about that email from Donna Farmer that Brent had shown the jury? The one in which the Monsanto scientist wrote that the company had not done any carcinogenicity testing on Roundup? Though Brent made it sound nefarious, the truth was that Monsanto was simply following the guidelines set out by the EPA, and the agency wanted animal tests focused on the active ingredient, glyphosate, and not on the full product, Lombardi said.

Lombardi pointed to a slide of the email in question, enlarged for easier viewing on the screen. Brent had focused on the sentence in the email that said, "You cannot say that Roundup is not a carcinogen. . . . We have not done the necessary testing on the formulation to make that statement."

"He read this to you at a time when he was telling you how bad Monsanto is," Lombardi said. "Remember that?" But the jury needed to look at more than a snippet of information from that email; they needed to understand the entire context of the email, he said.

Farmer was a good scientist who was being "rigorously honest"in that email, and the only reason Monsanto had not conducted carcinogenicity testing on Roundup was that the EPA didn't require it, Lombardi emphasized. The regulatory agency's focus was on the active ingredient, glyphosate, not formulations such as Roundup.

"The bottom line here is that Roundup went on the market back in the '70s," Monsanto's lawyer said. "The EPA has looked at this product over and over again, has looked at 140-plus cell tests, has looked at 14 animal tests, has looked at all that epidemiology, and all the way through, the EPA has concluded that Roundup glyphosate-based products do not cause cancer and that no warning is necessary," Lombardi said.

The EPA's confidence in glyphosate products had been consistent and endured through generations of EPA scientists and administrators, he told the jury. "The science has been consistent that glyphosate is not carcinogenic."

Lombardi was ready to wrap up. Though Brent had taken nearly three hours of the jury's time, Lombardi was keeping his opening to well under two hours.

But he still had Brent's allegations of ghostwriting to address. "You've heard talk about something. Plaintiff's counsel called it ghost writing. . . . Do you remember that?" Lombardi asked the jury. "Well, let's just put it in context again."

The article Brent had told them about, the Williams, Kroes & Munro piece from the year 2000, was one in hundreds of studies and articles about glyphosate and was merely a review of other publications, not an original study by any means. Moreover, Lombardi pointed out, the authors had not hidden Monsanto's involvement; they had instead publicly thanked Monsanto scientists for their contributions to the article.

He used a yellow marker to highlight the words on the screen as he spoke.

"There's nothing about this article that obscures Monsanto's involvement in it," he said. "But the most important question is what is this article going to tell you about whether Mr. Johnson's cancer was caused by glyphosate? What is this allegation of ghost writing going to tell you about that? Nothing. Nothing. It will be irrelevant."

Lombardi was pacing now, spreading his arms wide, hands outstretched as if imploring the jury members to embrace his narrative.

"Now, why didn't Monsanto warn? Monsanto didn't warn because the science says that glyphosate-based products don't cause cancer. Monsanto didn't warn because that was the conclusion that the EPA had come to. The EPA had concluded that no warning was necessary. So Monsanto didn't warn because that's where the science took them."

One last point to make. He'd said it already, but Lombardi wanted to make sure this point was doubly clear.

"Mr. Johnson's cancer actually started well before he started his work at the school district," Lombardi said. "Mr. Johnson's symptoms showed up after he started working, a couple years after he started in that job. But the evidence is going to be that non-Hodgkin's lymphoma generally starts years before."

Lombardi paused a moment to allow the jury to take in his point.

"You can understand why Mr. Johnson might think it had something to do with the spray. But the fact is—the fact is—the scientific fact is that it did not."

All of the facts taken together, without the suggestive spin from Brent, made it clear that Johnson's cancer was not caused by Monsanto's glyphosate-based herbicides, Lombardi said emphatically.

"Thank you again for your attention today. It was a long time to sit and watch people talk," he told the jury with a chuckle. "But I appreciate it. Mr. Griffis and Ms. Edwards, and I look forward to presenting our case to you as we go forward. Thank you very much."

Brent let out a long sigh and looked at Dave. Damn, Lombardi was good. They all needed to talk, but not here in the courtroom. After gathering up their files, Dave, Brent, and the rest of the legal team walked slowly with Lee and Araceli the couple of blocks to the local law office they were using as a home base.

Lee had questions. Why was Lombardi saying Lee had cancer even before he worked at the school district, before he started spraying Monsanto's weed killers? Could that be true? Lee wanted to know.

Dave did his best to reassure him. While there were experts who said non-Hodgkin lymphoma typically took many years to develop, there was also evidence the disease could develop in a shorter time frame, even within months, particularly in a case like Lee's, in which his exposure had been extreme.

"Don't worry, this is all going according to plan," Dave told Lee. He complimented Lee and Araceli on their stoicism in the courtroom throughout the long day.

"You both did great," he told the couple. They should go find some dinner and get some rest, he said.

After saying goodbye to Lee and Araceli, the lawyers settled in for several more hours of work. Their jury consultant had put together a shadow jury—a group of people who mirrored the demographic makeup of the real jury—to offer their perceptions of the trial proceedings. Videos of the opening statements had to be assembled to give to the shadow jury that night for their input. This would continue throughout the trial. If something was not resonating with them, the chances were that it was not resonating with the real jury either, and adjustments to their presentations would need to be made.

It was going to be a long night.

CHAPTER 17

An Unusual Case

The first day of testimony opened easily enough, thank God, because Brent, Dave, and the rest of Lee's legal team were still tired from the prior long day and night. It was almost impossible to get more than a few hours of sleep during a trial.

To lead off the evidence and testimony, the team had decided to show jurors a two-and-a-half-hour-long video deposition of Mark Martens, a former director of toxicology for Monsanto.

Martens had never met Lee, of course, and had no direct knowledge about his specific condition. But Lee's lawyers determined the best approach for presenting their complicated case was to break up the evidence into two general sections. The first several days would be devoted to proving what they referred to as "general causation"—expert testimony and evidence that supported the allegation that Monsanto's glyphosate-based herbicide formulations such as Roundup could cause cancer. The second phase would be about specific causation—providing jurors with proof that Lee's exposures to Monsanto's products were a substantial cause of his disease. Martens's testimony was key for the first phase.

The Martens deposition focused on Monsanto's internal reaction in the late 1990s to news that Italian scientists had found concerning results with tests on Monsanto's glyphosate formulations. Company communications showed that Monsanto wanted to find an expert who would refute the findings and provide support for Monsanto's position that its products were safe. This was the Dr. James Parry story Brent had told the jury in his opening. Now he would show them the story was true.

The trial team would have preferred to have Martens appear in person; in fact, they wanted to bring several Monsanto executives to the stand to testify. Showing jurors a video is never as good as presenting a live witness. But Monsanto refused to agree, and the California court could not compel witnesses to travel from the company's home base in Missouri.

Aimee Wagstaff had conducted the deposition of Martens. In the video, she was seen pushing him into acknowledging that Monsanto executives had been worried about the genotoxicity studies. Under her prodding, Martens also admitted that Parry had been clear in telling Monsanto there were concerning indicators with glyphosate formulations when it came to carcinogenicity and that he had been insistent about the need for additional testing on health impacts.

Monsanto had declined to allow Parry to do that testing and ultimately ran tests using its own people within its own labs, never sharing Parry's concerns with the US Environmental Protection Agency (EPA) or any regulatory agency, Martens confirmed in the video deposition.

And after arguing the point, Martens finally reluctantly admitted that Monsanto had Parry sign a "secrecy agreement" that kept him from talking about the concerns he shared with Monsanto.

It was not blockbuster testimony. But it was a strong start.

Over the course of the next several days, Dave and Brent brought to the witness stand one scientist after another to dissect the studies linking

Monsanto's herbicides to cancer. In all, they called six scientists and doctors to testify for their side. Though Brent and Dave did the heavy lifting in questioning the witnesses and introducing evidence to the jurors, they were aided throughout by colleagues from multiple firms, including Michael Baum and Jeff Travers. Also lending a hand was Mark Burton, a San Francisco–based lawyer whose office was located just a few blocks from the courthouse. The team used Burton's conference room for convening strategy sessions before and after court.

Tim Litzenburg, Lee's lawyer from the beginning of the case, was noticeably absent from the proceedings. Though Tim had been the one to shepherd Lee through the depositions and had won his trust, Tim had lost the trust of Mike Miller and the other senior attorneys because the troubling behavior they had seen from Tim over the past several months was only growing worse. Tim missed several pretrial planning meetings, and the notes he sent to other members of the trial team were often incoherent. From the texts and emails he sent to firm members, it seemed Tim was more focused on using his new Corvette Stingray to pick up women than on preparing for the trial. Mike feared Tim might be using cocaine or other drugs.

They could have used Tim's help with the constant juggling act of witnesses and documents a trial demands, but there was no way they could let him go before the jury or even sit at the plaintiffs' table.

The drama outside the courtroom only mirrored the one inside as Lee's legal team put their scientific experts up on the stand and Monsanto's attorneys did their best to knock them down, trying to paint them as incompetent, corrupt, or deceitful. Monsanto also regularly peppered the plaintiffs' team with motions seeking to limit evidence and testimony, a strategy that forced the two sides into repeated arguments in front of the judge during breaks when the jurors weren't present.

One recurring argument was over Monsanto's insistence that there be no mention of the fact that California had decided that cancer warning labels should be placed on all glyphosate products sold in the state. Judge Suzanne Bolanos sided with Monsanto on that matter, as she did on several other matters limiting evidence. Both Brent and Dave felt the judge was favoring Monsanto in her rulings on evidence, but while it made their jobs harder, they also believed it made it more likely that a verdict in their favor would survive an appeal by Monsanto.

Another of Monsanto's requests turned out to be a boon for Lee's case, though the Monsanto team didn't know it. It came on the day Lee's dermatologist, Dr. Onaopemipo Ofodile, was due to testify. Ofodile had been a key early player in deciphering Lee's disease and referring him for cancer treatment. Dr. Ofodile was not an oncologist and had no expertise in cancer causation, but she had seen Lee more than two dozen times over two years.

When Brent and Dave talked with Dr. Ofodile that morning before court about her upcoming testimony, the doctor told them she had been reading a lot of information online about Monsanto's herbicides and was feeling uncertain about whether or not Lee's cancer was actually due to his herbicide exposure. If asked in court, she would answer with her truthful opinion: she was not sure his cancer actually was related to his exposure to Monsanto's herbicide.

Dread washed over Brent and Dave. It would be a big risk to put her on the stand. Their concern was confirmed by Mark Burton as the three men walked to the courthouse together to begin the day's proceedings.

"You can't call her," Mark said. "I know you guys like to gamble, but this is a nightmare. You should put that doctor on a plane to nowhere and tell the judge you have no witnesses today."

But they had to call her, Brent and Dave agreed. She was here. She was a key foundational witness to the facts of the development and spread of Lee's disease. They would just have to avoid asking her about what might have caused Lee's cancer. Monsanto's lawyers were not likely to want to open that door by asking for her opinion in their cross-examination. And even if they did, Brent would point out that she had no expertise to know if the herbicides were a factor. They'd figure it out. They'd be fine.

The problem was solved for them when they arrived at Judge Bolanos's courtroom and Monsanto's lawyers presented them with a freshly filed request to the judge to limit Dr. Ofodile's testimony. The company's attorneys were insisting that the doctor be barred from offering her opinion about what might have caused Lee's cancer. Neither side should be allowed to ask her if she thought glyphosate-based herbicides were to blame, Monsanto's attorneys demanded.

Brent and Dave did their best to hide their relief, agreeing to the limitation with as much feigned anger as they could muster. It was an unexpected—if unintended—gift from Monsanto. And they were grateful to accept it.

During her turn on the stand, Dr. Ofodile did what they had hoped she would do. She laid out for jurors the strange development and spread of the disease across Lee's body and all the treatments and procedures he had endured—without discussing her opinions on the cause. After Lee told her he was worried about continuing to spray Monsanto's weed-killing pesticides during his school district work, she had written a letter to Lee's employer requesting he not be exposed to things that could exacerbate his condition, Dr. Ofodile told the jury.

Lee's was an "unusual case" and also one of her "most severe cases," the doctor testified.

As they unspooled their arguments and evidence, Lee's lawyers referred again and again to the assorted internal Monsanto emails and other records that they said showed how Monsanto had spent years trying to stifle the science, manipulate regulators, and silence critics.

At any point, the company could have simply worked with regulators to put warning labels on its products, but instead, Monsanto did all it could to hide the risks of the herbicides, Lee's lawyers asserted.

One internal Monsanto email brought into evidence discussed concerns a company scientist had about the presence of formaldehyde in Roundup, along with traces of a carcinogenic substance referred to as N-nitroso.

A 2003 internal company presentation was also brought into evidence. Jurors saw how Monsanto noted all those years ago that surfactants used in its herbicides could be toxic.

Jurors were shown copies of multiple internal communications in which Monsanto discussed ghostwriting scientific papers and paying outside scientists to "edit & sign their names so to speak" to give the papers the air of independence. Jurors saw Monsanto's secret plan to "orchestrate outcry" against the International Agency for Research on Cancer (IARC) for classifying glyphosate as a probable carcinogen, and they saw records detailing Monsanto's meetings with government officials in Washington, DC, to try to counter the IARC classification.

Jurors saw EPA documents about a 1983 mouse study in which so many mice developed rare tumors after being dosed with glyphosate that several EPA scientists expressed concerns about the cancer-causing potential of the chemical—concerns that had largely been hidden from the world for more than thirty years. The jurors also learned that in response to those concerns, Monsanto officials wrote internally about their fear that regulatory action could have "serious negative economic repercussions" for the company.

Faced with the company's records, Monsanto's lawyers were forced to concede that the company had never conducted a twelve-month or longer chronic toxicity study of any of its glyphosate formulations sold in the United States as of June of 2017. Not only had Monsanto not done its own long-term toxicity testing, but there were also email discussions between Monsanto and industry allies about trying to head off a toxicity review of glyphosate by the US Department of Health and Human Services. Monsanto executives feared the review might agree with IARC's cancer concerns, the jurors learned.

Brent and Dave also introduced internal corporate emails discussing Monsanto's secret funding of the American Council on Science and Health, money given in exchange for the group's assistance in promoting glyphosate safety and deriding critics.

And jurors were shown an email thread that referred to Monsanto critics and discussed "being overrun by liberals and morons," who needed "taking out one at a time."

The presentation of the internal documents was woven into the testimony of the plaintiff's experts, such as Dr. Christopher Portier, who Brent brought to the stand to testify following the Martens video. Portier was a retired US government scientist with a lengthy résumé of scientific achievements, including leading a toxicology program at the National Institute of Environmental Health Sciences and participating as an "invited specialist" in the IARC glyphosate review. Portier spent four days on the witness stand testifying about his decades of experience with cancer risk assessments and his belief that glyphosate was a cancer-causing chemical.

"It's not absolute, but in my opinion, 90 percent or higher, I believe glyphosate is a human carcinogen," he told the jury. Roundup was as well, he testified. Portier explained details of the multiple studies he felt backed his conclusions and asserted that the EPA and European regulators had violated their own standards by failing to analyze the data appropriately. Portier had been so concerned about the EPA's failure to follow scientific guidelines in the glyphosate assessment that he sent the agency a lengthy analysis of the many "inappropriate" steps the agency had made, he told the jury.

"Why did you do it?" Brent asked the scientist.

"As I said earlier, my entire career has been about using scientific evidence to make decisions primarily about the carcinogenicity of compounds," Portier replied from the witness stand. "And this was just so amazingly wrong in the way they were doing it, not following their own guidelines, I just felt I had to say something about it." Portier had also challenged the safety findings of European regulators, writing an open letter to European officials telling them of flaws he said he found in the European risk assessment of glyphosate. Multiple tumors found in feeding studies with mice and rats had not been taken into consideration in the assessment, he determined.

In discussions of European regulators, jurors learned that the risk assessment in Europe had sections that had been simply copied and pasted from papers written by a group of scientists from various chemical companies that sold glyphosate, including Monsanto. Portier said that European regulators had considered only the rodent tumor data that the glyphosate industry told them to consider in finding no cancer risk.

Part of Portier's testimony was devoted to telling jurors about the studies that made Monsanto most nervous—those that found DNA damage in people who lived and worked in areas that were sprayed with glyphosate from the air.

And under Brent's questioning, Portier confirmed that he had been subject to personal online attacks because of his position about glyphosate.

The American Council on Science and Health, the group funded by Monsanto, had posted multiple negative articles about Portier on its website, saying he engaged in "scientific fraud," after the IARC classification. Other groups associated with Monsanto similarly had posted unfavorable commentaries about Portier, accusing him of unduly influencing other IARC scientists to skew the group's findings and of hiding the fact that he signed a lucrative litigation consulting deal for Roundup cases around the same time IARC was issuing its classification.

In cross-examining Portier for Monsanto, Kirby Griffis adopted a similar narrative, quizzing him about contacts and contracts with plaintiffs' law firms and implying that Portier's assertions about the cancer risk of Monsanto's herbicides were driven not by science but by financial interest. He presented Portier with an engagement letter showing Portier had signed on as an expert consultant on Roundup litigation on March 29, 2015, nine days after IARC announced its glyphosate classification.

"When you signed it, you immediately got a $5,000 retainer and are making $450 an hour for your work, right?" Griffis asked.

"That was the agreement," Portier said flatly.

Griffis hit the point again and again throughout his questioning of Portier, portraying the scientist as hiding his affiliation with plaintiffs' attorneys as he lobbied against regulatory findings of glyphosate's safety. He also painted Portier as suffering from inflated arrogance, believing that he knew science better than did regulatory agencies around the world.

Lee's lawyers watched the jury closely to try to gauge their reaction to Portier's testimony and Griffis's cross-examination but were unable to tell what the jurors were thinking.

Monsanto's attorneys were equally aggressive in cross-examining another of Lee's scientific experts, a Columbia University cancer expert named Alfred Neugut. As was the case with Portier, Neugut's expertise was hard to challenge. He specialized in medical oncology, treating cancer patients since 1980. He also had a busy academic life, teaching cancer epidemiology since 1982. And when it was his turn on the stand, he was emphatic about one key point: Monsanto's Roundup weed killer was clearly carcinogenic.

Monsanto's attorney George Lombardi did his best to paint Neugut as someone who was not to be trusted, someone motivated by the money he was making by testifying.

Was it correct, Lombardi asked Neugut, that in all his years of work with cancer, Neugut had never been familiar with glyphosate or worried even a little bit about the chemical until after he was retained by the lawyers suing Monsanto?

Neugut said he had been "a totally unbiased person with regard to the subject" when initially contacted by the lawyers, but he became convinced of the cancer risk after reading the research on glyphosate.

Lombardi would not let it go. His voice became louder and he stepped closer to the witness stand.

"What you did was you reached the opinion in this litigation that glyphosate caused cancer before you had read any of the glyphosate epidemiological studies, didn't you?" Lombardi insisted.

"Your honor!" Brent interjected with alarm. "Your honor, I don't know if this is intentional, but he's standing about four and a half feet away from my witness and shouting at him."

"I do not mean to raise my voice. But if my voice is too loud, your Honor, I'll do everything I can," Lombardi began.

"You can yell at me," Neugut interrupted coolly, eliciting smiles from the jurors.

"Doctor I have no intention to yell at you," Lombardi said. But as he pressed on, the hostility mounted again.

Neugut had not actually read all the relevant studies, had he? Lombardi asked. Hadn't he simply relied on the summary put together by the International Agency for Research on Cancer? And what if IARC was wrong?

Neugut responded that if he'd had any doubts about the science, he would have withdrawn as a witness. "I do have integrity and I wouldn't have sat up there and lied," he said.

Over and over Lombardi hammered at the doctor, accusing him of failing to answer questions or answering questions on the stand differently from the way he had during depositions taken before the trial. As Lombardi pressed, Neugut's anger became more apparent until he finally erupted, shouting, "Don't misquote me!" at Monsanto's attorney.

It was not the best day for Lee's case as Lombardi appeared to wear Neugut down with his barrage of questions and accusations.

Neugut was helpful enough under Brent's questioning, however, testifying that there was extensive research on glyphosate-based herbicides supporting the conclusion that the herbicides cause non-Hodgkin lymphoma.

"There are multiple studies of glyphosate and every other cancer on earth: Prostate cancer, breast cancer, colon cancer, whatever you like. All the other studies are negative," Neugut said. "The only type of cancer that repeatedly showed up with a causal connection to glyphosate herbicides was non-Hodgkin lymphoma. All the time, it's glyphosate and NHL."

Neugut's testimony was especially helpful for Lee's case when it came to addressing the epidemiology research referred to as the Agricultural Health Study, or AHS, which Monsanto touted as strong proof of no cancer connection to glyphosate. Though Monsanto asserted the study was more authoritative and robust than any other when it came to glyphosate and non-Hodgkin lymphoma, Neugut testified that the study had so many flaws in its methodology that it should be completely discounted.

Just as Dr. Beate Ritz had explained to Judge Vince Chhabria during the Daubert hearings in federal court, Neugut explained to the Johnson jurors that the AHS researchers had lost contact with tens of thousands of original study subjects and so had added in data based on what they inferred those subjects might have told them had they been able to re-connect for follow-up. The practice, known as imputation, was common in epidemiology, but the AHS imputation had been so skewed that it had introduced a 17 percent error rate, hopelessly invalidating the risk ratios.

Neugut made it clear that he thought the study was mostly worthless. But, if the study was to be given the merit Monsanto said it warranted, there was something jurors should know. While the AHS researchers concluded there was no overall association between glyphosate and non-Hodgkin lymphoma, the data did in fact show a significant association with an NHL subtype called mycosis T-cell lymphoma.

It was the same type of cancer that was killing Lee.

Another important witness for Lee's case was Dr. Chadi Nabhan, the medical oncologist from Chicago who had met with Lee, evaluated his condition, and discussed potential causes of his cancer.

In his opinion, Nabhan testified, Lee's exposure to Monsanto's Roundup and Ranger Pro products was a "major contributing factor" to the development of his disease.

It was impossible to ever pinpoint exactly how long a patient had to live, he said. But recent tests showed Lee's disease was progressing rapidly, and he was not responding well to chemotherapy.

"I don't think any physician should ever play God," Nabhan said. "I mean, we just don't know, but clearly the prognosis is bad. He has a disease that is progressing rapidly. So I, unfortunately, don't believe he has longer than December 2019 . . . and I hope I'm proven wrong."

CHAPTER 18

Fighting until the Last Breath

Lee didn't attend every day of the trial. Sometimes it was just too much to sit through. His lawyers were trying to do everything they could to make it easier for him. If he didn't want to make the drive back and forth to the apartment in Vallejo, they covered the costs of a hotel room for him and Araceli. But the couple had the boys to consider, and with the trial pushing from one week into another and then another, Lee didn't feel too guilty about missing some of it.

Finally, the day came when it was Lee's turn to take the stand. It was the third week of July; the jurors had been selected in mid-June, and by this time they were steeped in the science and structure of Monsanto's glyphosate business. They'd heard from most of the expert voices, and they'd heard from three of Monsanto's executives via video depositions.

Now they would hear from Lee.

And he knew just what to wear. The leather jacket was not quite orange and not quite bronze, and so ugly that the only place it belonged was the trash can, according to Araceli. But to Lee the coat was magnificent, his own suit of armor. He'd had the coat more than twenty years, longer than he'd known Araceli, longer than his children had been alive. He'd worn the coat to clubs back in the day when he was healthy and strong and the ladies all liked the way he looked. He had worn the coat to Las Vegas with his friend Daryl Waters, staying up all night, gambling and talking and planning for a long future. One sleeve had been slashed by some fool with a knife one dark night all those decades ago, but Lee had found someone to patch it. He loved the coat. And he didn't care what Araceli said, or anyone else for that matter. He was wearing the coat to court to face Monsanto.

Underneath the coat he wore a black button-down dress shirt layered over a soft white T-shirt. He put on one of his nicest pairs of pants and slipped his favorite stud earring into his left earlobe. His skin was bad; he had skipped the lotions and "grease" he usually applied to soften the scabs and scars. He wanted the jurors to see what he had to endure.

Araceli chose a sleeveless heather-gray dress for the occasion and combed her dark hair until it was straight and shiny. There would be reporters and cameras there. She and Lee would be the focus of so much attention. It almost took her breath away.

Before they put Lee on the stand, Brent and Dave wanted jurors to hear from Araceli. She was so nervous that they were not sure what, if anything, they would be able to get out of her. But she was the best person—other than Lee—to tell the jury about the toll cancer had taken on her family.

With Dave's gentle guidance and a reminder for her to speak loudly enough for jurors to hear, Araceli described how she and Lee had met in an algebra class at Napa Valley College and how she was instantly attracted to his good looks. She testified about their marriage, the raising of their two boys, and the times they had spent together as a family, snowboarding, watching and playing sports. Lee was vibrant, energetic, and engaged with his sons. Until he got sick, she said. Timidly at first and then gaining confidence, Araceli recounted how she had started working fourteen-hour days, five to seven days per week, when Lee could no longer work.

"I wanted to be able to help to ease off the stress for the bills and make sure that the kids had a place to live," she said.

"Was that hard on Lee when he couldn't work?" Dave asked.

"Tremendously." Araceli's voice quivered. "His job was everything. He had a great job. He had good insurance. He had—he had everything. I didn't have to work two jobs. I mean, he—he was fine. We were fine."

"How about now?" Dave prodded.

"It's very difficult. It's very stressful," she said, tears welling in her eyes. "It's just too much—too much for me to explain how I really feel."

The changes in her husband were more than just physical, Araceli explained. He was in so much pain, he became depressed, didn't sleep. He was angry a lot. The man she knew and fell in love with had changed.

"He did a lot of crying too, especially at night when he thought we were asleep," she said. "He wanted to be positive. You know, he tried to be positive. He wanted to be."

Dave had just one last question for Araceli: "When was Lee at his happiest that you've ever seen him?"

She answered easily. "Before he had cancer, we had nothing to worry about. We had no worries. No stress. Life was beautiful. Simple."

With Dave's direct examination completed, Monsanto attorney Sandra Edwards rose to address Araceli.

"Good morning, Mrs. Johnson," she said pleasantly. "Thank you for coming in today. But I have no questions for you."

The decision by Monsanto's lawyers to pass on questioning Lee's wife surprised no one on Lee's trial team. Her description of the loss of her once happy family life had clearly resonated with the jury. There was little to be gained and far too much to lose if the jurors perceived Monsanto's lawyers as bullying such a sympathetic witness.

It was time for Lee to take the stand. After being sworn in by the court clerk, he settled into the witness chair, tugging the leather coat tight around him as he tried to find a comfortable position. Araceli had been questioned for less than thirty minutes, but Lee knew he was facing hours of questioning, from his own lawyer and from Monsanto's.

"Thank you, Mr. Johnson," Dave began. "You just said your name is Dewayne Johnson. Do you go by Lee Johnson?"

"Yeah, I use Lee. I don't use Dewayne at all."

Dave was easing Lee in. "How are you doing today?"

"Okay," Lee replied.

Dave continued with the simple line of questioning, directing Lee to talk about where he grew up, his mom and large extended family of sisters and cousins, and then the family he had created with Araceli. Talking about his boys, Lee was effusive, pride filling his voice. His older son, Ali, was "super, athletic, strong, tall," playing multiple sports. He would be starting eighth grade in the fall and was so smart, and outgoing, a popular kid. His younger son, Kahli, was also impressive. He was less outgoing but more serious and reflective. After Lee got sick, Kahli would talk about growing up to become a chemist so he could make a potion to cure Lee's cancer.

Lee talked about his own love of sports; he had played golf until the pain and numbness in his hands made that impossible, he said. As Lee talked, Dave clicked through a series of photographs enlarged on the PowerPoint screen of Lee and his family in better times. He had Lee describe how life had changed because of his disease, how he couldn't play with his children anymore, how he struggled just to do small things around the apartment.

He asked Lee about his pain, sitting there in the witness stand. Was he feeling okay?

"I wouldn't call it okay," Lee answered. "I would call it that I've learned how to tolerate what I'm dealing with."

In conducting the direct examination, Dave's foremost goal was for the jurors to understand the depths of Lee's life so they could appreciate the losses he and his family were suffering. He asked Lee about his interest in writing; Lee had self-published two books and was working on a third. The books provided an outlet for his opinions and observations, Lee explained. The one he was currently working on was called *Face Value* and was an exploration of the misconceptions that came with stereotyping people by their appearance.

Over the course of two and a half hours, Dave led Lee through descriptions of his work for the school district, the protective gear he wore when spraying Monsanto's glyphosate-based herbicides, and the two incidents in which he wound up doused with the weed killer. With Dave guiding him, Lee recounted the confusion he felt when he started seeking medical treatment for the odd spots showing up on his body, and the frustration and lack of answers he found when he reached out to Monsanto not once but twice.

The first time he called the company, using a hotline phone number printed on the Monsanto herbicide bottle, a "nice lady" answered the line and listened to his concerns. She told him someone would call him back. But no one did.

Dave turned to the judge. "At this time, your Honor we move to publish Plaintiff's Exhibit 32." He handed a piece of paper to Lee. It was a copy of an email thread dated November 11, 2014. A Monsanto "product support specialist" named Patricia Biehl wrote to Monsanto physician Dan Goldstein about receiving the call. Lee had been "soaked to the skin" with the company's glyphosate-based Ranger Pro product and was "looking for answers" about whether the product might have caused his cancer, Biehl wrote. Goldstein wrote back: "I will call him. The story is not making any sense to me at all."

Even though he didn't hear from Monsanto after that call, Lee made a second call to the company in March of 2015. He was even sicker by that time, but he was still working and was growing increasingly worried about continuing to spray Ranger Pro at his job on a regular basis.

Monsanto noted the call in an incident report dated March 27, 2015, a copy of which Dave also introduced as evidence for the jury. The report read: "Caller states he's been using Ranger Pro as part of his job for 2 to 3 years. He has recently been diagnosed with cutaneous T-cell lymphoma. The caller's level of fear is rising over his continued use of Ranger Pro."

The incident report was dated just a few days after the International Agency for Research on Cancer had classified glyphosate as a probable human carcinogen with a positive association to non-Hodgkin lymphoma. Lee did not know about the IARC classification when he made the call, and Monsanto did not tell him about it.

"Did anyone ever tell you that the International Agency for Research on Cancer had concluded that Roundup and glyphosate was a probable human carcinogen?" Dave asked.

Lee answered quietly. "No."

"Did anybody ever call you back, Mr. Johnson?" Dave pushed.

"No one called me back," Lee said, slumping slightly in his chair.

"Mr. Johnson, if they had told you Roundup was a probable human carcinogen or could cause non-Hodgkin's lymphoma, would you have continued to spray Ranger Pro?" Dave asked.

"I would not have sprayed Ranger Pro on school grounds and anywhere else if I knew it was causing illness to people," Lee said, his voice hardening. He didn't want to appear angry, but it was hard to keep his emotions in check.

Dave decided it was time to move on. Time for more photos of Lee's damaged skin. One by one, Dave displayed close-ups of the sores that marked Lee's body: several on his hand, many more on his legs, arms, and stomach. Even one on his eyelid.

He had never had any skin problems before, Lee testified. He had, he said wistfully, "100 percent beautiful skin," until the disease set in.

With Dave prompting him, Lee talked about how the cancer would seem to retreat for a while after treatment but then would roar back without warning, erupting in new lesions and inflaming others. Lee described how just when he thought certain spots were healing, they would instead become infected. It seemed he was constantly on antibiotics. His appearance got so bad at times that strangers would gawk at him in public, he said.

"It's so tough," he said. "You know when you can't work, you can't provide for your family. The pain that I have to go through, all of that stuff is very tough and hard to deal with."

Lee was facing another round of chemotherapy and dreading the increased suffering he knew the treatment would trigger.

"I'm getting to the point where I'm really tired of going through the whole thing of chemo and all of that because it really takes everything out of you," he said. "I'm not feeling good about it at all."

Dave realized it was time to wrap up. "Do you have an understanding as to what your outlook is, your prognosis?" he asked. He hated these questions.

Lee took a moment before answering. "You know, I think that because I have the attitude of beating cancer, that I was, sort of, in denial until this case," he said. "I think that I was just on, 'I'm not dying from cancer. I've got to figure it out. I've got to keep myself healthy. I've got to exercise. I have to drink right, eat right and try to be as healthy as I can to beat this thing.' Now, it's pretty scary. So I know, in reality, I am not better. And I'm not getting any better."

"Are you going to keep fighting?" Dave asked.

"I'll keep fighting until the last breath," Lee said, determination in his voice. "You know, until my time's written in the sky, I'll be fighting."

Cross-examining Lee for Monsanto was not an easy assignment, and Sandra Edwards knew she had to tread delicately. She would gain no support from the jurors by trying to discredit Lee, as her co-counsel had endeavored to do with the expert witnesses for Lee's case. Edwards's goal was to be respectful and sympathetic but to show jurors it was ludicrous to think that Lee's cancer had developed within the short time he worked at the school district. He had started at the district only in

2012. Non-Hodgkin lymphoma was a disease that many experts said took decades to develop.

"Good afternoon Mr. Johnson. Thanks for being here today," she began.

"You're welcome," Lee answered.

Edwards led off her questioning by asking Lee about his duties at the school district, his use of Ranger Pro on weeds on school grounds, and the small amount of Ranger Pro he would mix with large amounts of water to prepare the spray. Wasn't a typical tankful of spray only about 1 to 2 percent of the active chemical ingredient and roughly 98 to 99 percent water? Edwards asked.

Lee didn't have the percentages memorized but agreed generally the mixture was largely water with a smaller percentage of the active ingredient.

Edwards asked him about the protective gear he wore, pointing out that it appeared he had been "very careful" to avoid coming into contact with the chemicals. Then she turned to the onset of his disease, asking Lee to recall when he told doctors he first developed a "rash." It was the fall of 2013, wasn't it? she asked.

Lee did not remember. He just didn't. Edwards could ask as many different ways as she wanted, but he simply was not able to recall the specific time periods that these lawyers found so critical to his case. It could have been 2013 or 2014 or the fall or spring or summer. Lee's memory of that time was fogged over. Even during the depositions he gave months before the trial, his memory had failed him. He blamed the cancer treatments.

Then Edwards turned to the multiple doctor visits Lee had made; she wanted to make it clear that of all the many doctors who had helped to treat him, none told Lee that Monsanto's herbicides were to blame.

"Your current oncologist is Dr. Truong at Kaiser; right?" Edwards asked. "And she hasn't told you what caused your mycosis fungoides; right?"

"I've asked her," Lee replied. "And yeah, she hasn't told me."

"And then you saw a dermatologist at UCSF. Do you remember Dr. Pincus?" Edwards continued.

"Yes."

"All right. And she didn't tell you whether there was a cause to your mycosis fungoides either; right?" Edwards pushed.

"They say the same thing. They all say the same thing," Lee answered, growing irritated.

"All right," Monsanto's lawyer persisted. "And by 'they' does that also include Dr. Kim, the doctor down at Stanford?"

"Yes. Yes." How much longer did she want to do this, Lee wondered.

"All right. And so she hasn't told you what caused your mycosis fungoides either?"

"No," Lee said again. He was sick of this bullshit. "They all say that they don't have any scientific evidence that proves that that's what caused it. So that's what they told me. They don't know what causes lymphoma. They just try to treat me as doctors, is what they try to do. They didn't really go into the cause or where I got it from."

"Okay. All right," Edwards said. She had accomplished all she could. "Thank you very much for your time, Mr. Johnson. I appreciate it."

And with that, Lee was done.

"Thank you Mr. Johnson," said Judge Bolanos. "You may be excused."

CHAPTER 19

The Last Word

Lee's testimony had gone very well, his legal team agreed. But it wasn't going to win the case for them. They had to present more evidence: more science, more internal documents from Monsanto's files, and more proof that Monsanto cared only about its profits and not about the potential risks of its herbicides.

One highlight of their case that Lee's lawyers hoped would resonate with jurors was a video of Monsanto toxicologist Donna Farmer answering questions during a deposition taken before the trial began. Farmer had been with Monsanto since 1991 and was a high-profile public defender of the safety of the company's herbicides. Mike Miller had taken Farmer's deposition, questioning her repeatedly about records he believed showed Monsanto was cavalier in the face of scientific evidence that its weed killers could cause cancer.

Mike relished turning witnesses' own words against them, and with Farmer he had ample ammunition. Even though his injuries from the kiteboarding accident were still healing and he couldn't be at the trial in person, through the video Mike was very much present.

"All right," he said as the video began. The camera was trained only on Farmer, but Mike's Virginia accent was clearly heard. "Now, ma'am, as a Monsanto employee and a person with your particular skills and expertise that we've been discussing about, even you, Donna Farmer, cannot say that Roundup does not cause cancer, true?"

"Roundup does not cause cancer," Farmer said, shaking her long ringlets of hair back and forth. "There's no data that supports that statement."

"All right, ma'am." Mike handed Farmer a document. "Now this is a document, a copy of an e-mail, sent by you, right, ma'am? Donna Farmer?"

"Yes," Farmer said, looking down at the paper.

"Okay. And it was sent by you on September 21, 2009, right?" Mike continued. "And in that you say this: 'You cannot say that Roundup does not cause cancer. We have not done the carcinogenicity studies with Roundup.' Did I read that correctly?" Mike sounded incredulous.

"Yes you did read that correctly," Farmer said. "But," she raised her forefinger in the air, stammering a bit as she tried to formulate her answer: "I want to point out that I should have—in other e-mails that I have done—is that what we talk about is while we have not done carcinogenicity studies with Roundup per se, we have data on glyphosate."

Farmer steadied herself. "We don't believe the surfactants—they are not carcinogenic. So normally what I would say is that when you put those two together, even though we haven't done these carcinogenicity studies, um, that there is no evidence that Roundup would be carcinogenic."

Mike read the email aloud again. "You said, 'You cannot say that Roundup does not cause cancer. We have not done the carcinogenicity studies.' How long has Monsanto been selling Roundup? Since 1974? Thirty-five years, and no studies on whether Roundup caused cancer?" Mike made it clear he thought it astounding that the company had not done such testing.

But Farmer appeared unfazed. "As I was saying, we are not required to do chronic carcinogenicity studies on the formulated product, but we are on the active ingredient. If you look at other e-mails of mine, you would find that I would put that in there that we have no evidence of carcinogenicity with glyphosate, we have no evidence with the surfactant. Therefore, even though we haven't done any carcinogenicity studies with Roundup, we would not have any evidence to support that it says it would cause cancer." It was her mistake for failing to make that clear in the email, Farmer said.

Changing course, Mike quizzed Farmer on why internal Monsanto documents showed she added a section on genotoxicity to the draft of a scientific paper supporting glyphosate safety that appeared to be independent of Monsanto. It was another example of ghostwriting, according to Mike.

"If a scientist looks at the article, he doesn't know that the genotoxic section was written by a Monsanto employee, right?" Mike asked. "The only thing that's hidden is that it was cut and pasted by a Monsanto employee?"

There was nothing wrong with what she had done, Farmer insisted.

"I wanted to make sure they had the full range of information available to them that they may not have been aware of," she said. "Everyone knows that Monsanto—they talk about us in their credits. It's a very large document. So these are only just a few sections in a very, very large document."

Mike hammered on and on at Farmer, forcing her to acknowledge an "inoculation plan" Monsanto put in place to counter the International Agency for Research on Cancer's glyphosate classification, including the company's strategy to "orchestrate outcry" against IARC.

"It was simply a way to defend glyphosate globally," Farmer said.

More damning for Monsanto than Farmer's deposition was the video deposition of Monsanto physician and clinical toxicologist Dan Goldstein. Goldstein, who started working for Monsanto in 1998, was responsible for handling consumer safety complaints for Monsanto. It was Goldstein who had been notified of Lee's concerns, not just once but multiple times.

Again, Mike Miller had taken the deposition, trying to make clear that Goldstein was well aware of numerous scientific studies linking glyphosate-based herbicides to non-Hodgkin lymphoma and still had seen little need to issue any warnings. Goldstein was so familiar with the scientific literature associating glyphosate with cancer that he and others within Monsanto had predicted that IARC would classify the weed killer as a possible or probable carcinogen, Mike pointed out. And yet Goldstein had never called Lee back, never warned him of even a potential risk.

When Mike asked Goldstein about Lee's pleas to Monsanto to help him understand if the chemicals he was spraying could be harming him, Goldstein said he didn't recall the details of Lee's situation. He was sure, however, that he would not have warned Lee even if they had communicated because concerns that Monsanto's products caused cancer were "not supported by the science."

Mike tried to drill home his point: "But, Dr. Goldstein, let me ask you if you're aware of this, sir: When he wrote you on November 11, 2014, he was not terminal yet. He continued to spray glyphosate. He got no information from anyone at Monsanto. He later became terminal after continuing to spray the glyphosate. Are you aware of that, sir?"

Goldstein kept his answer brief: "I have not seen his medical records."

Lee hadn't been the only one reaching out with concerns about his health, Mike made clear. The same month Lee called Monsanto, one of Monsanto's own employees—a worker at the company's Roundup manufacturing plant in Muscatine, Iowa—notified Monsanto's occupational nurse that he had been diagnosed with non-Hodgkin lymphoma. The worker wrote that he had irregular blood counts while working at the plant and he was wondering if his cancer diagnosis was related to working around all the chemicals at the Monsanto plant.

Monsanto had not reported that worker's cancer or his inquiry to the US Environmental Protection Agency. But didn't federal law require that type of information to be reported to regulators? Mike asked.

"So here we have a gentleman that worked around glyphosate, had abnormal blood counts while working around glyphosate, reports he has non-Hodgkin's lymphoma, and you, sir, the medical safety officer, decide not to report it?" Mike asked Goldstein.

Goldstein replied that the employee had not made an allegation that his cancer was related to chemical exposure; he had merely asked a question, and thus legally the information did not have to be reported to the EPA.

Mike also pressed Goldstein about the money Monsanto had given to the American Council on Science and Health (ACSH) and his email discussion with colleagues about how financially supporting ACSH would be helpful in countering public concerns about the IARC glyphosate cancer classification. ACSH had in the past promoted the safety of tobacco and downplayed cancer concerns with smoking, so was not the perfect ally. But it was useful. ACSH did not disclose Monsanto's funding to the public and so appeared to be an independent scientific group when it proclaimed glyphosate safety and criticized the international cancer scientists. The group was so valuable to Monsanto, Goldstein had written in an email, that the company could not afford to lose its support for glyphosate. "You WILL NOT GET A BETTER VALUE FOR YOUR DOLLAR than ACSH," Goldstein had written.

Mike did his best to make his point unequivocal for the jury: at the same time that Lee Johnson was seeking truthful information from Monsanto about the potential cause of his disease, Monsanto was secretly paying a front group to provide disinformation to the world.

Mike additionally pushed Goldstein on internal emails that showed Goldstein had engaged in his own version of ghostwriting. The Monsanto doctor had written draft op-eds to be given to people outside the company to sign and send to newspapers supporting glyphosate safety, Goldstein admitted under Mike's questioning. Readers would never know the op-eds came from Monsanto.

Over the course of multiple days, Dave and Brent continued to present the jury with internal Monsanto documents—some dating back decades—in which Monsanto executives discussed ways to promote the safety of glyphosate-based herbicides while also avoiding long-term cancer testing of the products. The company's creation of a "scientific outreach network" of seemingly independent scientists who could be deployed to defend glyphosate was documented. Monsanto's cozy connections to officials at the EPA, and more discussions of ghostwriting papers proclaiming glyphosate as safe, were also documented in the evidence.

Jurors also saw a recent internal memo detailing internal concerns that Monsanto stood to lose significant revenues if school districts stopped spraying the company's glyphosate-based herbicides amid the cancer controversy. "School districts are another big risk with the healthy schools act and increased attention," the report stated.

The video of Mike deposing Monsanto toxicologist William Heydens, the company's product safety assessment strategy lead, was another high point for Lee's case as jurors saw Heydens struggle to explain away the company's practice of ghostwriting papers supporting glyphosate safety.

In order to help the jury keep the litany of cancer studies straight, Dave and Brent presented what they called "tumor charts." Jurors saw that time after time, in experiment after experiment, laboratory animals developed tumors when exposed to glyphosate-based herbicide. One scientific paper had particular resonance for Lee's case; the authors of the study had written that the research results "suggested that glyphosate has tumor promoting potential in skin."

Before concluding the presentation of their direct evidence, Dave and Brent wanted to make sure the jury knew just how wealthy Monsanto had become peddling its herbicides and other products. Monsanto's lawyers argued that the company's financial position was not relevant to the case; they especially did not want jurors to learn that Bayer AG had paid $63 billion in June to acquire the company. But Judge Suzanne

Bolanos agreed that Brent could read two simple sentences to the jury: "As of the first quarter of 2018, Monsanto's net worth was $6.6 billion. And among Monsanto's assets, cash and cash equivalents were valued at $3.1 billion."

Brent and Dave had taken eleven days to make their case. In contrast, Monsanto's lawyers took only four days presenting their side. After all, they had already challenged each of the witnesses testifying for Lee, cross-examining them and questioning their credibility. The ghostwriting allegations were easily explained away as nothing more than cherry-picked phrases taken out of context, Monsanto's lawyers insisted. The same was true for the other records Lee's lawyers said showed dishonest activities by Monsanto, according to the company's attorneys.

As far as the science went, studies allegedly showing links between glyphosate and cancer were falsely presented by Lee's lawyers as more solid than they actually were, Monsanto's lawyers told the jury. Their own scientific and medical experts took turns on the witness stand testifying that the best science available proved there was no cancer risk with the use of the company's herbicides.

One of Monsanto's was Harvard University cancer epidemiologist Lorelei Mucci, who had testified at the Daubert hearings. As a star witness for the defense, Mucci told jurors about numerous flaws she said she had found in the studies Lee's lawyers presented. According to Mucci, one of the most reliable studies was the 2018 update to the Agricultural Health Study (AHS) that had found no association between glyphosate and non-Hodgkin lymphoma but had come out only after the IARC classification of glyphosate. The witnesses who had testified that the AHS study was marred by a lack of follow-up with thousands of its subjects were simply wrong, Mucci said.

Under questioning by Monsanto lawyer George Lombardi, Mucci testified that after taking into consideration a large body of epidemiologic evidence, she was quite certain that there was "no causal association between exposure to glyphosate-based herbicides and NHL risk."

Also testifying for Monsanto was Canadian medical researcher Warren Foster. Foster had experience in toxicology and exposure studies with environmental contaminants and at one time had served on a working group for IARC. While Mucci had focused on the human studies, Foster's testimony was specific to the animal studies regarding glyphosate.

According to Foster, Lee's experts had "misapplied and over-interpreted" the statistical data in the animal studies they presented to the jury. With proper analysis, he testified, the data showed no "compound-related effects."

"My ultimate conclusion," Foster told the jury, "is that since glyphosate is not a rodent carcinogen, it doesn't support the hypothesis that it could be a human carcinogen."

And just as Lee's lawyers had made use of video depositions, Monsanto's lawyers showed the jury a video deposition of Aaron Blair, the epidemiologist from the National Cancer Institute whom Monsanto blamed for some of its woes. Blair had chaired the IARC working group on glyphosate and, according to Monsanto, had withheld critical data from the working group that showed glyphosate did not cause cancer. Some of the data had become part of the updated Agricultural Health Study, showing that glyphosate had no tie to NHL. There was also information from other North American epidemiology analyses, and had Blair included it all in the data being considered, the IARC scientists would have seen a reduced relative risk from the epidemiology evidence, Monsanto's lawyers argued.

In the video deposition, Blair admitted he hadn't shared certain preliminary research data with the IARC group as they evaluated glyphosate. He said that was because the data were not final, not reviewed or published, and thus not appropriate for consideration. But he acknowledged that inclusion of the data would have lowered the relative risk seen in the epidemiology evaluated by IARC.

By the time Monsanto's lawyers finished with their last witness, it was August, and the two sides had been wrestling through the trial proceedings since mid-June.

The time had at last come for closing arguments. Lee's side would go first, followed by Monsanto's lawyers. And finally, because the burden of proof lay with the plaintiff, Lee's lawyers would get to address the jury again. They would have the last word.

~

Brent had been practicing his closing argument for months. He knew exactly what he wanted to say and how he wanted to say it. Mike and Dave and others on the trial team all had weighed in, cautioning him to leave jurors with a message that resonated but didn't overreach. He should ask for hefty damages, sure, but not too much.

There was also some concern that Brent might not be able to keep his emotions in check. The young lawyer litigated with a ferocious intensity that the team knew helped him connect with jurors, but Brent didn't have a lot of trial experience. He would have to tread carefully.

"Mr. Wisner—when you're ready," Judge Bolanos prompted.

Brent rose from his seat, facing the judge, and loudly—perhaps too loudly—took in and let out a long breath. Here we go, he thought.

"May it please the court," he addressed the judge. Pivoting toward Monsanto's table of attorneys, he acknowledged his adversaries. "Counsel," he said. Lombardi nodded back.

Brent then turned to the jury. "Hi, everyone. . . . At the beginning of this trial, I told you this case was about choice and the fact that Monsanto, by not warning, deprived consumers in California and Mr. Johnson of the right to make an informed choice about what chemicals he exposed himself to, and in this case, what chemicals he actually exposed to children in the Benicia School District. But as this case has unfolded, it's occurred to me that this isn't just about the choice that was robbed from my client. It's also about the choices that Monsanto made," Brent said, pointing to the table where Monsanto's lawyers sat. They were busy taking notes, not looking at Brent.

Monsanto had made so many bad choices, Brent went on. The company's scientists chose to ghostwrite science to make its products appear safe; they chose not to share Dr. Parry's concerns about their herbicides with the EPA; they chose not to do long-term carcinogenicity tests on their products. They chose not to call Lee back.

And, Brent said, despite all the scientific studies showing ties between glyphosate and cancer, despite the IARC cancer classification, "Monsanto made a choice to not put a cancer warning on the label."

Brent's voice grew louder, his anger apparent. "That is a choice that reflects reckless disregard for human health. It is a choice that Monsanto made and today is their day of reckoning."

The volume ticked up another notch. "Every single cancer risk that has been found had this moment, every single one, where the science finally caught up, where they couldn't bury it anymore, where the truth got shown to 12 people sitting in a jury box making a true and honest decision, and that is this day."

Brent pointed again at the table where Monsanto's lawyers sat, mute. "This is the day Monsanto is finally held accountable."

The jury could send a message to Monsanto, Brent continued. They could say, "Monsanto, no more. Warn. Call people back. Do the studies that you needed to do for 30 years. . . . And if you return a verdict today that does that, that actually changes the world. . . . I told you all at the beginning of this trial that you were part of history, and you really are, and so let me just say thank you."

With the aid of the PowerPoint presentation, Brent flipped through a few images of Lee, who would be starting another round of chemo in a few weeks, Brent reminded the jury. "He won't make it to 2020 absent a miracle," Brent said.

How much was Lee's life worth? Brent asked the jury. There were his real economic costs: his lost income, his health-care costs, and then the future economic costs and losses he faced. But there were also non-economic costs, the pain and suffering, the disfigurement, the emotional distress, and other intangible harms his family was facing even now and had been ever since his diagnosis. Monsanto should pay Lee $39.2 million for all that he had lost and would lose.

Finally, there were punitive damages. Monsanto had ignored Lee's calls at the very time that their own scientists were predicting IARC would classify glyphosate as a possible or probable human carcinogen. They had shown disregard not just for Lee but for all Monsanto customers. The company had continued to target schools for sales of its glyphosate-based herbicides, even after the IARC cancer classification, Brent reminded jurors.

Punitive damages were designed to punish, to deter future bad conduct, and Monsanto's conduct warranted a harsh punishment, according to Brent. Think of it, he told the jurors: Monsanto executives were no doubt sitting in a conference room in the St. Louis company headquarters just waiting for the phone to ring and tell them they'd won. They likely had a bottle of champagne chilling on ice waiting for a celebration, he said.

Lombardi was incensed. "Your Honor, I object," he interjected. "This is supposed to be about the evidence. This is complete fantasy."

But Brent continued: "The number that you have to come out with is the number that tells those people . . . 'We have to change what we're doing.' Because if the number comes out and it's not significant enough, champagne corks will pop."

Lombardi objected again, and Judge Bolanos had also had enough. "Mr. Wisner, please do not engage in speculation," she admonished.

Brent moved on to the math he wanted the jurors to consider. Monsanto had $3.1 billion in cash. At a 2 percent interest rate, it would make $62 million per year. Lee had been exposed in 2014 and would likely die by 2020. Those six years of suffering should cost Monsanto every dollar it had made in interest on its cash for those six years, plus just a little more, he said.

Brent directed the jurors' attention to the PowerPoint screen, where large red numbers blazed out from a stark black background: $373,000,000.

"That's a number that makes people change their ways. That's a number that sends a signal to Monsanto and everybody that works there." Brent paused. "Your verdict will be heard around the world."

In contrast to Brent's heart-tugging, champagne cork–popping imagery, Lombardi made clear from the outset that his closing argument would be about facts, not feelings. He started by apologizing to the jury for the "long haul" and reminding them that after all they'd heard, the case boiled down to answering just one key question: whether or not Lee's cancer was caused by Monsanto's weed killers.

And the answer—he asserted with a confident smile—was an easy no. There was a wealth of scientific evidence dating back decades supporting the safety of Roundup and Ranger Pro herbicides, Lombardi said. The EPA fully backed the safety of glyphosate, as did other regulators.

"Forty years of this product on the market. Forty years of this product being regulated. Forty years of scientific studies ranging from human to animal to cell. The evidence is clear," he said. "The message from that evidence is clear, and it's that this cancer was not caused by Ranger Pro."

Though Lee had not made it to every day of testimony, he was there for the closing arguments and watched quietly as Lombardi continued.

"It's not my burden to show you that. It's the plaintiff's burden. They have to show you that actually it's the case that throughout that entire time, Ranger Pro caused cancer. They have to show you"—Lombardi's hand sliced through the air repeatedly as he emphasized his points—"for some of their claims that the whole world thought, the whole scientific community thought, Ranger Pro caused cancer, and there's absolutely no proof of that."

As for the evidence that Dave and Brent had laid out—well, they were "allegations in search of proof," either designed to play to the jurors' emotions or just flat-out wrong, Lombardi said, striding back and forth in front of the jury. They made a big deal out of the fact that Monsanto's Dan Goldstein had not called Lee back, and, yes, Goldstein should have called Lee back, he said. But that did not make him a bad person, and the lack of a call had no impact on Lee's health.

What about those allegations of ghostwriting? Those were built on "snippets" of documents pushed by people who "ignored the truth," Lombardi continued. When Monsanto was involved in writing papers, that was disclosed in a footnote, not hidden, as Lee's lawyers alleged.

And it was absurd to believe that Lee could have gotten his cancer from Roundup exposure, since he was diagnosed so soon after starting his job. Everyone knew it took years, sometimes decades, for non-Hodgkin lymphoma to develop. Lee couldn't even remember correctly when he first noticed changes in his skin, Lombardi pointed out.

In the end, the hints of scandal, the rhetoric about bad conduct at Monsanto, had nothing to do with whether or not Lee's cancer was caused by his exposure to the company's herbicides, Lombardi said, summing up. Thanking the jurors for their time, Lombardi urged them one last time to put aside any sympathy for Lee and decide the case "fairly and on the facts."

Then Brent stood up again to address the jury one last time. He led jurors back through key evidence, entreating them to remember how Monsanto had buried Dr. Parry's concerns; how people who had been sprayed with glyphosate in Ecuador were found to have DNA damage; how animal studies had shown that mice and rats dosed with glyphosate developed tumors; how human studies in multiple countries had shown that farmers using glyphosate-based herbicides had elevated rates of non-Hodgkin lymphoma; and how Monsanto had never seen fit over forty years of selling its herbicides to do a long-term carcinogenicity test on its products.

He reminded them of the studies showing the danger of the surfactant that Monsanto used in its Ranger Pro herbicides, the same herbicide Lee had used at the school district.

"At the end of the day, the evidence is actually overwhelming. Other than hiding behind the EPA, Monsanto has quite literally no defense," said Brent. "So do the right thing. Go back in that deliberation room, answer those questions, talk it out, figure out the truth. Because the truth is it causes cancer. It caused Mr. Johnson's cancer. And these guys," he paused, pointing to Monsanto's table of lawyers one more time, "need to be held accountable."

CHAPTER 20

Verdict

Sitting together in the jury box week after week, many of the jurors had become friends. They took coffee breaks together, celebrated birthdays with cupcakes, and forged a Friday's food-truck-for-lunch tradition. But during all those many long days, they had not been allowed to discuss the details of the case. Now they could.

Armed with their notebooks, along with evidence binders and individual instructional packets provided by the judge, the group decided the best way to tackle the mountain of information they'd been given was to go back through the key points one by one. The windowless conference room designated for their deliberations came with two large whiteboards mounted on the walls and a pad of poster-size adhesive sheets of paper. The jurors created a summary of what they had learned from each witness on the pages, pasting them onto the walls around the room in the order of the testimony.

Seated at rectangular tables arranged end to end, the jurors took turns discussing the pieces of evidence they found compelling as well as the arguments they found lacking. The evidence binders did not include the details of the scientific studies discussed at trial, which frustrated some jurors. But they did contain the internal Monsanto emails.

Monsanto's ghostwriting activities were particularly disturbing to many of the jurors, as was the lack of responsiveness to Lee when he reached out to the company. And the words of Monsanto's own scientists—asserting they had done all the testing they were required to do—did not sit well with several jurors. Why hadn't they done more? Why hadn't they done long-term cancer testing of the formulated products?

In his closing argument, Monsanto attorney George Lombardi had told the jury the case came down to the one key question—Had the company's weed killers caused Lee's cancer? But it was actually more complex than that. There were multiple, fairly technical questions in the verdict form that dealt with degrees of liability and negligence. And there were questions about the science, and then questions dealing with damages, if the jury found damages were warranted. The verdict form contained seventeen questions in all.

Jury members were barred from seeking out any information not presented during the trial. They could not search the internet or look to newspapers or other news outlets for insight. They could not seek the opinions of their friends or family members. They were strictly to focus on the evidence introduced by the opposing sides. Any juror violating those rules could be held in contempt of court and face sanctions; Judge Suzanne Bolanos had made that clear.

She had left them with a few other admonishments: Monsanto was entitled to the same fair and impartial treatment an individual would receive. The burden of proof required that in order to prevail, a party had to persuade the jury that what they were claiming was "more likely to be true than not true."

And, finally, the jury would need to determine whether or not Lee's exposure to Monsanto's herbicides was a "substantial factor" in causing his cancer. They should understand that phrase—"substantial factor"—had to be more than a remote or trivial factor, but it did not have to be the sole cause.

It was a lot to work through. They didn't want to rush it.

～

Brent could not remember ever feeling this nervous. He had been so confident in the courtroom, so sure of his case. But this waiting game was wearing on him. During the course of the trial, he had thought he was getting positive vibes from some jury members. One in particular, who Brent thought of simply as "the old guy," had smiled at Brent during a break in the proceedings, and during one passing encounter in a courthouse hallway had whispered to Brent, "You're killing them!" But who knew how the other jury members felt? What were they thinking? How long would they take?

One day passed, and then another. The jury had some questions, wanted some things read back to them, including testimony from one witness from each side. And then it was Friday, August 10. Verdicts often came down on Fridays. Could this be the day?

Brent thought back to a brief private exchange he'd had with one of the many members of Monsanto's extended legal team one day outside the courtroom. The lawyer had acknowledged to Brent that the company knew Lee's lawyers might prevail, but if Brent and Dave somehow did manage to pull out a win, it would most likely be inconsequential. They'd be lucky to get a couple million dollars. "There's winning, and then there's winning," Brent recalled the lawyer saying smugly.

Brent was in the courthouse hallway giving an interview to a French television crew when he got the word. The jury was back. They needed to notify Lee right away. The judge would announce the verdict in thirty minutes.

As he made his way to the courtroom in silence, Brent saw the same juror—the one he called "the old guy"—who had earlier given him the words of encouragement. The man had no smile for Brent today. He appeared glum and kept his eyes on the floor as Brent passed.

That was it, Brent thought. They had lost.

He had known Monsanto would be tough to beat. He had known their case had its challenges. But, damn, he thought these jurors saw what he saw, a corrupt company that didn't care if it killed people with its chemicals.

Brent began to run through a mental checklist of all the people he had let down: the partners on his legal team, especially Mike Miller, who had entrusted him to help Dave with the historic case; thousands of plaintiffs around the country, whose claims would effectively be scuttled with a loss here today; and, most painfully, Lee and Araceli. He had hoped to win them enough money to allow Araceli to quit working, so the family could spend time together for however long Lee had left to live.

Brent replayed his closing argument in his mind; where had he lost the jurors, he wondered. Had he gone too far with the champagne-on-ice comment? Had he been too glib? Too certain? He wanted to cry.

As Brent tried to steady himself, Dave and the rest of the team waited impatiently for Lee to arrive. He was always late, they had learned that; but they didn't think he'd be late to hear his own verdict.

Lee had not wanted to hang around the courthouse all day, so he had taken a drive to the historic Coit Tower, a 210-foot-tall landmark that offered 360-degree views of the city and the nearby waterfront. The tower was situated in a park at the tip of a steep and winding road carved out of the wealthy Telegraph Hill neighborhood. The area boasted some of the city's most expensive mansions and was a place where Lee had never dared to even dream of living. Until now. As he took in the lush landscape of flowers and trees planted to please the millionaires who lived there, he thought for the first time about what a verdict in his favor might mean. Brent had said they might get hundreds of millions of dollars. Was it possible Lee could one day afford a mansion? Nah, he thought, shaking his head. That wasn't for him. He just hoped the jury would award him enough to take care of some medical bills, and maybe there would be enough to allow him to seriously look at doing that bone marrow transplant the doctors had been talking about.

Suddenly his cell phone rang; it was his friend Daryl Waters checking in. No word yet, Lee told him. But before they could hang up, another call buzzed in. It was Pedram Esfandiary, calling from the courthouse. The jury was back, Pedram told him. Lee needed to get back to the courthouse immediately. Lee jumped in his car and sped the three miles back to downtown. Pedram was waiting for him and rushed him into Judge Bolanos's courtroom, which Lee saw was already packed with reporters and spectators. Michael Baum sat with Mark Burton and Bobby Kennedy in the front row. Noticeably absent was Araceli. They had not known there would be a verdict today, and she had stayed in Vallejo to work and take care of the boys.

Brent sat down first. He had no words to say. Dave sat to his right, then Lee. Pedram joined them, taking a seat at Lee's right. They all needed to be ready to help Lee face the decision, whatever it might be.

One by one, the jury members filed into the courtroom, taking their seats without a word. The bailiff announced the entrance of Judge Bolanos and, once she was seated, handed her the completed jury form. Silently, the judge read through the form as the courtroom waited.

She turned a page, still reading to herself. Then she turned another page, and another. The verdict form the jurors had been given to fill out contained several yes-or-no questions on each page. If the jurors had decided to answer the questions in favor of Monsanto, they were to ignore and skip over several questions. But if they decided the case in favor of Lee, they had to answer every question. Brent noted that it seemed to be taking the judge quite a while to go through the pages. Did that mean every question was answered? Brent's heartbeat picked up a pace. The judge kept reading silently, turning another page. Ah, that was a good sign. Brent took a deep breath. His hopes started to lift.

"I will now read the verdict in the matter of Dewayne Johnson, Plaintiff, versus Monsanto Company, Defendant," the judge began. "We the jury answer the questions submitted to us as follows: With the claim of design defect: One, are the Roundup Pro or Ranger Pro products ones about which an ordinary consumer can form reasonable minimum safety expectations? Answer: Yes.

"Did Roundup Pro or Ranger Pro fail to perform as safely as an ordinary consumer would have expected when used or misused in an intended or reasonably foreseeable way? Answer: Yes. Was the Roundup Pro or Ranger Pro design a substantial factor in causing harm to Mr. Johnson?

"Answer: Yes."

Lee leaned into Dave. "What does it mean?" he asked.

"I don't know how much yet, but it means you're getting something," Dave whispered back excitedly.

Seated to Lee's right, Pedram started to smile.

The judge kept reading. On every point, the jury had found in Lee's favor. Every single point. Yes, the potential risks of Monsanto's herbicides presented a "substantial danger" to people using them, the jury determined. Yes, Monsanto failed to warn of the risk. Yes, the lack of warning was a "substantial factor" in causing harm to Lee. And yes, Monsanto had known, or should have known, that its herbicides were dangerous or likely to be dangerous. Would a reasonable manufacturer under similar circumstances have warned of the danger? The jury answered yes.

Brent could barely contain his excitement. To his right, Dave leaned back in his chair as relief and anticipation washed over him. The only question left was how much the jury was going to make Monsanto pay.

The judge kept reading. The jury had decided that Monsanto owed Lee for his past and future economic losses and his pain and suffering for a total in compensatory damages of $39.2 million, the judge said, reading from the verdict form. It was exactly what Brent had asked for and a big win. But was there more? Brent had also asked for the jury to punish Monsanto with hefty punitive damages. Had they?

"With regard to punitive damages," Judge Bolanos continued to read. "Did you find by clear and convincing evidence that Monsanto acted with malice or oppression in the conduct upon which you base your finding of liability in favor of Mr. Johnson? Answer: Yes.

"Was the conduct constituting malice or oppression committed, ratified or authorized by one or more officers, directors or managing agents of Monsanto acting on behalf of Monsanto? Answer: Yes."

The judge paused just for a moment. "What amount of punitive damages, if any, do you award to Mr. Johnson?

"Answer: $250 million."

Tears began to flow from Brent's already moistened eyes. A total award of $289.2 million. He thought back to the conversation with Monsanto's lawyer about the difference between winning small and winning big. "There's winning, and then there's winning." Goddamn right, he thought. There was no question which type of win this was. He turned his head, hoping the television cameras could not catch the emotions playing out over his face.

Monsanto's lawyers—Sandra Edwards, Kirby Griffis, and George Lombardi—looked on grimly from the defense table. They asked the judge to poll the jurors. Was there any divide at all, or was it unanimous? One after one, the jurors answered the queries of the judge. It was a unanimous decision.

Lee covered his face with his hand. He couldn't believe it. Pedram reached over, laying a hand on his back.

As the judge called the proceedings to a close, Brent stood to face the jury one last time, his cheeks damp with tears. "Thank you," he mouthed quietly to them. "Thank you."

The next couple of hours flew by in a rush of press interviews and congratulatory calls and texts. People Lee had never met wanted to shake his hand, to hug him, to take a picture with him. As was the tradition after successfully concluding a case, Dave and Brent decided the occasion called for a lavish celebratory dinner.

Lee knew he should want to celebrate too. He certainly was grateful for all the work the team had put in. But he was also exhausted and overwhelmed, and he could feel the pain beginning to envelop him, as it typically did at the end of a long day. He said his goodbyes, climbed into his car, and steered carefully onto the highway. He had to get home, home to Araceli and his boys.

EPILOGUE
A Leaf That Doesn't Die

It's autumn in Napa, California, and Lee and his family are settling into a new home. The neat, cream-colored two-story house is near the good schools Araceli wanted, and offers enough space for each boy to have his own bedroom and for a large white sectional sofa to wrap around the great room. The old orange couch is gone, left behind along with the dark and cramped apartment Lee hated so much.

It's not the grand mansion Lee dreamed of that day the jury handed down its verdict in San Francisco. But it is a real family home with four bedrooms, plum and cherry trees out back, and block after block of quiet neighborhood streets for the boys to explore on their bikes.

The beveled-glass front door sits underneath a graceful turret lined with high windows that welcome in the sunshine. A swirl-shaped glass chandelier reflects the warm rays across the cherry-stained wood floors. Lee doesn't want to shut out the light these days.

He's still dying; at least, that is what the doctors tell him. But Lee doesn't believe them. He's lived longer than they told him was possible, longer than his attorneys and Monsanto's had told the court was likely.

"I'm not giving up on my life. If I give up, I know it's going to be worse for me," he tells me as we walk together along a tree-lined path in his new neighborhood.

His pain is still constant, though he won't say it's growing worse because he doesn't know how it could be worse. He starts each day the same way—shuffling into the kitchen to make himself a bowl of cereal to help keep the pain pills from making him nauseated. He washes down the pills with a glass of water mixed with heaping spoonfuls of powdered vitamin C.

Flakes of skin follow him wherever he goes; the new floors are coated with the fine powdery bits of it.

Lee did not immediately receive any money from Monsanto. A month after the verdict, the company's lawyers filed a motion for a new trial, arguing that the jury had acted on emotion instead of evidence and that the damages awarded to Lee were excessive and unconstitutional.

Judge Suzanne Bolanos seemed to agree, indicating in a "tentative" ruling that she was inclined to order a new trial. She questioned whether or not Brent's statements that the jurors would be "changing the world" if they found in Lee's favor were too prejudicial. And she determined that there was no evidence that Monsanto acted "despicably." She also wrote in her tentative ruling that Lee's lawyers failed to prove evidence of "malice" on the part of Monsanto.

The jury members were outraged when they read news of the judge's intention, and several were angry enough to write personal letters imploring her not to reject their carefully considered verdict.

Robert Howard, juror number 4, wrote: "The possibility that, after our studious attention to the presentation of evidence, our adherence to your instructions, and several days of careful deliberations, our unanimous verdict could be summarily overturned demeans our system of justice and shakes my confidence in that system."

Juror number 1, Gary Kitahata, also wrote to the judge: "Our verdict was not flawed or inflamed by either passion or prejudice. You may not have been convinced by the evidence, but we were. I urge you to respect and honor our verdict and the six weeks of our lives that we dedicated to this trial."

A week after receiving the jurors' letters, the judge reversed course, issuing a permanent order that left the jury verdict intact but sharply reduced the monetary award from $289 million to $78 million.

That was not the end of it, of course, but merely another beginning. Monsanto filed an appeal seeking to throw out the jury award altogether. Lee then cross-appealed for restoration of the full $289 million jury award. In July of 2020, the appellate court affirmed Johnson's victory, saying his lawyers had presented "abundant" evidence that Monsanto's Roundup products had caused his cancer and that there was "overwhelming evidence that Johnson has suffered, and will continue to suffer for the rest of his life, significant pain."

The appeals court said, however, that though it sided with Johnson, he could recover only $20.5 million from Monsanto because of a provision in California law that provides less money for someone with a short life expectancy than for someone expected to live many years with their injury. The reduction was a sharp disappointment to Lee and Araceli. After legal fees and taxes are deducted, they would be left with very little money if and when Monsanto actually paid the damage award. With that in mind, Lee appealed the reduced verdict to the California Supreme Court in August of 2020, seeking restoration of the $250 million punitive damage award. Monsanto also appealed, again trying to reverse the verdict. But the state's high court refused to review the case, leaving Lee with the win but also owed a much smaller award.

Two other trials followed Lee's, and in each case, the juries found the evidence of Monsanto's wrongdoing sufficient to award large punitive damages, though in each case the judges lowered the damage awards substantially. Lawyers for Monsanto appealed those verdicts, and the cases are pending as of this writing.

As for the tens of thousands of other plaintiffs who filed lawsuits also claiming their cancers were caused by Roundup, Monsanto's German owner, Bayer AG, agreed in June of 2020 to pay out $10 billion to settle close to one hundred thousand claims brought by cancer patients and their families. Bayer had threatened to file for bankruptcy if it could not find a way to end the litigation. Many plaintiffs were angered by the deal because though the lawyers stood to make millions of dollars in fees, individual plaintiffs on average would receive relatively little, some less than $100,000. Soon after its announcement, the settlement deal became stymied with complications, and it is unclear as of this writing how many cases will actually be resolved and how much money will ultimately be paid out by Bayer.

Another on the long list of disappointments for Lee has been the fate of his first lawyer, Tim Litzenburg. A little more than a year after Tim was barred from helping represent Lee at trial and then separated from The Miller Firm, he was arrested and charged by the US Department of Justice on federal charges of extortion. Prosecutors said he and another lawyer tried to extort $200 million out of a company (not Monsanto) involved in the glyphosate supply business. In June of 2020, Tim pled guilty to a reduced charge of one count of transmitting interstate communications with the intent to extort. Litzenburg was sentenced to two years in prison for the scheme.

While Lee waits for a payout from Monsanto, his lawyers have helped him arrange a loan of sorts, an advance against the money he could receive once his case is finally concluded. This type of funding is popular in legal circles but can also be highly exploitive of vulnerable individuals, requiring huge fees on top of repayment of the advance once the plaintiff receives a jury award or a settlement. Some funders require repayment nearly double the amount advanced, though if the plaintiff loses an appeal, they then are not required to repay the advance.

It's a gamble by both parties, and though Lee liked to gamble, he didn't like feeling exploited. It took him nearly a year after the trial ended to move forward and secure a small advance against his jury award, just enough to pay some bills and buy the house for Araceli and the boys. He needed to make sure they were taken care of.

The peace and comfort he has finally found have been a long time coming, Lee says. In those first few weeks and months after the verdict, people he barely knew and people he didn't know at all barraged him with requests for money. A woman he refers to as a "voodoo priestess" somehow obtained his cell phone number and called at all hours of the day and night claiming she could heal him. The stress was overwhelming.

But on this fall day, as we walk, the stress is long gone. We come upon an aging farmstead that at first appears abandoned, but then we see it is not. A scattering of clucking hens and a woolly alpaca greet us. It's a charming find amid the suburbia. Lee decides he doesn't like the dust and the smell, however, and so we resume our stroll along the shady sidewalk.

He is in a reflective mood. "I don't want to leave my boys without their foundation, what they need," he says. "No one wants to leave their family. But I'm not afraid to die. I've been loved my whole life. And that's a beautiful thing."

Since winning the trial against Monsanto, Lee has become known around the world, held up as an inspirational voice in a global battle against chemical corporation corruption. Activist organizations have flown him to Canada, to New York City, to Hawaii, to speak about this cancer and the dangers he believes come with the use of herbicides. Several communities have started taking a critical look at the use of pesticides in public spaces, and some have stopped using glyphosate entirely.

With the attention has come interest in Lee's songs, the ones he has written about dealing with his disease. He's performed his music for audiences arranged by the activists, and he was able to make a music video. A lot of people want to hear what he has to say.

"I didn't ask for it," he says of the attention that has come his way. "I didn't hope to get famous. I expected to maybe get rich and famous from being a rapper, but this, this is a lot bigger than what I could have done with music. You can only just set out to do good; you can't always control how that happens."

He stops walking for a moment and looks back toward the street where his new house sits, where his boys wait for us to return. "It would be cool if my kids could look back one day and say, 'My dad made history. My dad stood up for himself and for us.'"

I ask what other lessons he hopes his boys will carry with them.

"I would tell my boys that pain can make you stronger, because real strength comes from within," Lee answers. "And to always try to do the right thing, help people when you can, and try to always be positive." He pauses to make sure his words are precise. "And to prepare for the worst, but enjoy the good times because you never know when the bad times are coming."

We stop walking to rest in the shade for a moment. Lee reaches a scarred hand to a low branch and slowly strokes a silky green leaf.

"I know I am supposed to face this, to accept this, the death thing," he says. "But maybe I don't have to. Maybe I'm supposed to survive . . .

"Maybe I'll be the leaf that doesn't die."

A Note on Sources

I cannot recall the exact moment I realized I wanted to write a book about the events surrounding the Lee Johnson trial. But in the fall of 2015, as I sat at my desk writing a story for Reuters about the first Roundup litigation filings, it was immediately clear to me that an epic legal battle lay ahead.

Over the course of reporting this book, I also became deeply fascinated by the imperfect and paradoxical nature of the mass tort system in the United States. I learned that too often the plaintiffs at the heart of the legal actions—people injured or killed by dangerous or defective products or practices—wind up as mere pawns on a chessboard in a game where the real winners are the attorneys who reap riches from every case won and the corporations that often escape with relatively mild punishments.

It is a highly imperfect system that can clog courts with thousands of claims for each problem product and each person harmed. But it also is the only avenue for justice offered to those who suffer the consequences of a lax regulatory system that protects corporations over consumers. Without the hard work and commitment of plaintiffs' attorneys such as the people described in this book, injured individuals stand almost no chance of achieving compensation and the companies pushing dangerous products escape accountability.

The contents of this book are true. They are based upon countless hours spent over five years of observing, interacting with, and interviewing the key individuals involved not just in the Johnson case but also in the national mass tort Roundup litigation, including the leaders of the legal team who cumulatively represented more than fifty thousand plaintiffs. I conducted interviews with lawyers, expert witnesses, and Johnson trial jurors and spent many hours with Lee and his family. I studied documentary evidence files, video depositions of witnesses, and transcripts of court proceedings, and I was present at many of the events recounted in these pages. I am, in fact, the journalist described in chapter 9 downloading the Monsanto Papers and reposting them on a nonprofit organization's website so they could easily be shared and read by other journalists and members of the public. The website was that of the nonprofit U.S. Right to Know.

Monsanto's attorneys, sadly, did not respond to requests for interviews, so their words and actions are based upon transcripts of proceedings, video recordings of proceedings, my own observations of them in and outside of court, and notes of meetings they engaged in that I was able to obtain.

The quotes drawn from courtroom testimony and depositions are all taken from written transcripts and video transcripts. The quoted conversations that took place outside of courtrooms and are recreated in these pages were either witnessed by me or recounted to me as the best recollections of the individuals involved in them, with each exchange confirmed by multiple involved parties.

The database of documents produced by Monsanto in discovery included 2,552,033 documents and 15,989,111 pages, though much of that database remains sealed. The total case file for the Johnson trial consisted of 80,000 pages of exhibits, binders, and documents, and the trial transcript amounted to more than 5,000 pages. I've been through almost all of it.

The case titled *Dewayne Johnson v. Monsanto Company* was filed on January 28, 2016, in the Superior Court of California for the County of San Francisco. A copy can be found here: https://usrtk.org/wp-content /uploads/2016/09/Dewayne-Johnson-lawsuit.pdf.

Many of the court documents, discovery documents, and transcripts from the Johnson case and the broader Roundup litigation can be found in one or all of the following document databases.

Baum Hedlund Aristei & Goldman. *Dewayne Johnson v. Monsanto Company* records. https://www.baumhedlundlaw.com/toxic-tort-law/monsanto-round up-lawsuit/dewayne-johnson-v-monsanto-company/#transcripts.

University of California, San Francisco. "Chemical Industry Documents: Roundup Products Liability Litigation." https://www.industrydocuments.uc sf.edu/chemical/results/#q=(case%3A%22Roundup%20Products%20 Liability%20Litigation%22)&h=%7B%22hideDuplicates%22%3 Atrue%2C%22hideFolders%22%3Atrue%7D&subsite= chemical&cache =true&count=373.

University of California, San Francisco. "Chemical Industry Documents: USRTK Agrichemical Collection." https://www.industrydocuments.ucsf .edu/chemical/results/#q=(collection%3A%22USRTK%20Agrichemi cal%20Collection%22)&h=%7B%22hideDuplicates%22%3Atrue% 2C%22hideFolders%22%3Atrue%7D&subsite=chemical&cache=true &count=1824.

U.S. Right to Know. "Monsanto Papers: Roundup (Glyphosate) Cancer Cases: Key Documents & Analysis." https://usrtk.org/monsanto-papers/.

The following additional resources also were useful to me.

American Association for Justice. Accessed June 29, 2019. https://www.justice .org/advocacy.

American Cancer Society. "Key Statistics for Non-Hodgkin Lymphoma." Accessed March 8, 2019. https://www.cancer.org/cancer/non-hodgkin-lym phoma/about/key-statistics.html.

American Cancer Society. "Non-Hodgkin Lymphoma Risk Factors." Accessed March 8, 2019. https://www.cancer.org/cancer/non-hodgkin-lymphoma /causes-risks-prevention/risk-factors.html.

Andreotti, Gabriella, Stella Koutros, Jonathan N. Hofmann, Dale P. Sandler, Jay H. Lubin, Charles F. Lynch, Catherine C. Lerro, Anneclaire J. De Roos, Christine G. Parks, Michael C. Alavanja, Debra T. Silverman, and Laura E. Beane Freeman. "Glyphosate Use and Cancer Incidence in the Agricultural Health Study." *Journal of the National Cancer Institute* 110, no. 5 (May 2018): 509–16. https://doi.org/10.1093/jnci/djx233.

Associated Press. "Eli Lilly Settles Zyprexa Lawsuit for $1.42 Billion." January 15, 2009. http://www.nbcnews.com/id/28677805/ns/health-health_care/t/eli-lilly-settles-zyprexa-lawsuit-billion/#.XGdcpuhKjcs.

Bayer AG. "CEO Werner Baumann at the Annual Stockholders' Meeting of Bayer AG: Bayer Is Making Good Progress Strategically." Press release, May 25, 2018. https://www.investor.bayer.de/en/news/archive/investor-news-2018/investor-news-2018/bayer-is-making-good-progress-strategically/.

Bayer AG. "European Commission Conditionally Approves Bayer's Proposed Acquisition of Monsanto." Press release, March 21, 2018. https://www.investor.bayer.de/en/news/archive/investor-news-2018/investor-news-2018/european-commission-conditionally-approves-bayers-proposed-acquisition-of-monsanto/.

Brennan, Vince. "Grant, Other Executives to Leave Monsanto after Bayer Acquisition Closes." *St. Louis (MO) Business Journal*, May 7, 2018. https://www.bizjournals.com/stlouis/news/2018/05/07/grant-other-executives-to-leave-monsanto-after.html.

Campaign for Accuracy in Public Health Research. "Most Comprehensive Study Ever to Be Conducted on Glyphosate Finally Published." Accessed January 15, 2020. https://campaignforaccuracyinpublichealthresearch.com/most-comprehensive-study-on-glyphosate-finally-published-ahead-of-major-eu-vote/.

Christophi, Helen. "Yelling Breaks Out during Roundup Cancer Link Trial." Courthouse News Service, July 18, 2018. https://www.courthousenews.com/yelling-breaks-out-during-roundup-cancer-link-trial/.

City of Creve Coeur, Missouri. "Creve Coeur History." Accessed May 25, 2019. https://www.creve-coeur.org/220/History.

Cornell Law School, Legal Information Institute. "Rule 45. Subpoena." Accessed May 11, 2019. https://www.law.cornell.edu/rules/frcp/rule_45.

Crowson v. Davol, Inc. Case No. A-03-CA-668-SS, slip op. (W.D. Tex. June 10, 2004).

Dickerson, Linda. "Perspectives: Head of Data Firm Says 'What Gets Celebrated Gets Done.'" *Pittsburgh (PA) Post-Gazette*, May 31, 2003. https://www.post-gazette.com/business/businessnews/2003/06/01/PerspectivesHead-of-data-firm-says-what-gets-celebrated-gets-done/stories/200306010019.

DRI. "And the Defense Wins." April 17, 2013. https://www.hollingsworthllp.com/uploads/23/doc/media.9130.pdf.

Elkins, Arthur A. Jr., Office of Inspector General, US Environmental Protection Agency. Letter to Ted W. Lieu, US House of Representatives, May 31, 2017. https://www.documentcloud.org/documents/3853786-EPA-OIG-Letter-to-Ted-Lieu.html.

Fisk, Margaret Cronin. "Welcome to St. Louis, the New Hot Spot for Litigation Tourists." Bloomberg, September 29, 2016. https://www.bloomberg.com/news/articles/2016-09-29/plaintiffs-lawyers-st-louis.

Gillam, Carey. "Monsanto Says Panel to Review WHO Finding on Cancer Link to Herbicide." Reuters, July 14, 2015. https://news.yahoo.com/monsanto-says-expert-panel-review-finding-cancer-herbicide-184600564.html.

Gillam, Carey. "New 'Monsanto Papers' Add to Questions of Regulatory Collusion, Scientific Mischief." *Huffington Post*, August 1, 2017. https://www.huffpost.com/entry/newly-released-monsanto-papers-add-to-questions-of_b_597fc800e4b0d187a5968fbf.

Gillam, Carey. "Praise & Polo Shirts—More Evidence of Scientific Influence Seen in Newly Released Monsanto Papers." U.S. Right to Know, April 30, 2019. https://usrtk.org/monsanto-roundup-trial-tacker/praise-polo-shirts-more-evidence-of-scientific-influence-seen-in-newly-released-monsanto-papers/.

Gillam, Carey. "Something to Chew On." U.S. Right to Know, March 1, 2019. Posted by Gary Ruskin. https://usrtk.org/monsanto-roundup-trial-tacker/something-to-chew-on/.

Gillam, Carey. "US Lawsuits Build against Monsanto over Alleged Roundup Cancer Link." Reuters, October 15, 2015. https://www.reuters.com/article/us-usa-monsanto-lawsuits-idUSKCN0S92H720151015?feedType=RSS&feedName=everything&virtualBrandChannel=11563.

Gillam, Carey. *Whitewash: The Story of a Weed Killer, Cancer, and the Corruption of Science*. Washington, DC: Island Press, 2017.

Goldstein, Matthew. "As Pelvic Mesh Settlements Near $8 Billion, Women Question Lawyers' Fees." *New York Times*, February 1, 2019. https://www

.nytimes.com/2019/02/01/business/pelvic-mesh-settlements-lawyers
.html.

Hakim, Danny. "Monsanto Emails Raise Issue of Influencing Research on Roundup Weed Killer." *New York Times*, August 1, 2017. https://www.ny times.com/2017/08/01/business/monsantos-sway-over-research-is-seen-in -disclosed-emails.html.

Howard, Robert. Letter to Judge Suzanne Bolanos, October 2018. https://usrtk .org/wp-content/uploads/2018/10/Juror-Howard-letter-to-judge-Bolanos -letter-copy-2.pdf.

Hsu, Tiffany. "Johnson & Johnson Told to Pay $4.7 Billion in Baby Powder Lawsuit." *New York Times*, July 12, 2018. https://www.nytimes.com/2018/07 /12/business/johnson-johnson-talcum-powder.html.

"In Defense of Scientific Integrity: Examining the IARC Monograph Programme and Glyphosate Review." Transcript of hearing by the Committee on Science, Space, and Technology, US House of Representatives, February 6, 2018. https://docs.house.gov/meetings/SY/SY00/20180206/106828/HHRG -115-SY00-20180206-SD004.pdf.

Kamp, Jon. "Five Years after Cancer Warnings, Some Hospitals Still Use Hysterectomy Tool." *Wall Street Journal*, April 9, 2019. https://www.wsj.com/ar ticles/five-years-after-cancer-warnings-some-hospitals-still-use-hyster ectomy-tool-11554814802.

Kendall, Brent, and Jacob Bunge. "U.S. to Allow Bayer's Monsanto Takeover." *Wall Street Journal*, April 9, 2018. https://www.wsj.com/articles/justice-de partment-to-allow-bayers-acquisition-of-monsanto-after-company-conces sions-1523297010.

Kitahata, Gary. Letter to Judge Suzanne Bolanos, October 14, 2018. https://usrtk .org/wp-content/uploads/2018/10/Juror-Kitahata-letter-to-judge.pdf.

Leiser, Ken. "Hundreds Protest outside Monsanto Headquarters in St. Louis." *St. Louis (MO) Post-Dispatch*, October 13, 2013. https://www.stltoday.com /news/local/metro/hundreds-protest-outside-monsanto-headquarters-in-st -louis/article_74d8c4e4-8870-5f72-a57a-cfba1e286820.html/.

Lesser, Benjamin, Dan Levine, Lisa Girion, and Jaimi Dowdell. "How Judges' Secrecy Has Added to Toll of Opioids and Other Products." Reuters, June 25, 2019. https://www.insurancejournal.com/news/national/2019/06 /25/530417.htm.

Liss, Samantha. "Merger Puts Spotlight on Monsanto's Charitable Giving." *St. Louis (MO) Post-Dispatch*, September 15, 2016. https://www.stltoday.com /business/local/merger-puts-spotlight-on-monsanto-s-charitable-giving /article_8021a5ea-b0e4-58c8-841d-461f61000548.html.

Monsanto Company. "Once Again, EPA Concludes That Glyphosate Does Not Cause Cancer." Press release, May 2, 2016. https://monsanto.com/news -releases/once-again-epa-concludes-that-glyphosate-does-not-cause -cancer/.

Morrow, David J. "Fen-Phen Maker to Pay Billions in Settlement of Diet-Injury Cases." *New York Times*, October 8, 1999. https://www.nytimes.com /1999/10/08/business/fen-phen-maker-to-pay-billions-in-settlement-of -diet-injury-cases.html?pagewanted=all.

National Organization for Rare Disorders. "Rare Disease Database: Mycosis Fungoides." Accessed January 10, 2019. https://rarediseases.org/rare-diseases /mycosis-fungoides/.

Nelson, William B. Jr. "Goliath." In *Eerdmans Dictionary of the Bible*, ed. David Noel Freedman and Allen C. Myers. Grand Rapids, MI: Eerdmans, 2000.

Neslen, Arthur. "Monsanto Banned from European Parliament." *Guardian*, September 28, 2017. https://www.theguardian.com/environment/2017/sep /28/monsanto-banned-from-european-parliament.

Nicklaus, David. "Bonus and Stock Lift Monsanto CEO's Pay to $19.5 Million." *St. Louis (MO) Post-Dispatch*, December 21, 2017. https://www.stl today.com/business/columns/david-nicklaus/bonus-and-stock-lift-mon santo-ceo-s-pay-to-million/article_fc7f785f-d967-5e10-abb0-ff67ffc86 da4.html.

O'Hagan, Sean. "Toxic Neighbour: Monsanto and the Poisoned Town." *Guardian*, April 20, 2018. https://www.theguardian.com/artanddesign/2018/apr /20/mathieu-asselin-monsanto-deutsche-borse-anniston-alabama.

Oyez. "*Cipollone v. Liggett Group, Inc.*" Accessed March 17, 2019. https://www .oyez.org/cases/1991/90-1038.

Pollack, Andrew. "Takeda Agrees to Pay $2.4 Billion to Settle Suits over Cancer Risk of Actos." *New York Times*, April 28, 2015. https://www.nytimes.com /2015/04/29/business/takeda-agrees-to-pay-2-4-billion-to-settle-suits-over -cancer-risk-of-actos.html.

Public Health Law Center at Mitchell Hamline School of Law. "Minnesota Litigation and Settlement." Accessed June 21, 2019. https://publichealthlawcen ter.org/topics/tobacco-control/tobacco-control-litigation/minnesota-litiga tion-and-settlement.

Rossman, Sean. "Emails Show Monsanto Tried to 'Ghostwrite' Research." *USA Today*, March 16, 2017. https://www.usatoday.com/story/news/nation-now /2017/03/16/emails-show-monsanto-tried-ghostwrite-research/9924 8950/.

Saul, Michael, and Celeste Katz. "John Edwards Exposed as Cheating Lowlife, Serial Liar in Book 'The Politician' by Andrew Young." *New York Daily News*, January 26, 2010. https://www.nydailynews.com/news/politics/john -edwards-exposed-cheating-lowlife-serial-liar-book-politician-andrew -young-article-1.183195.

Schuessler, Todd. "Creve Coeur to Keep Protesters off Median near Monsanto." *St. Louis (MO) Post-Dispatch*, May 12, 2014. https://www.stltoday.com/news /local/govt-and-politics/creve-coeur-to-keep-protesters-off-median-near -monsanto/article_7d1c6f7b-016a-5430-aeda-7d4c3b86c1c8.html.

Semmens, Brice X., Darius J. Semmens, Wayne E. Thogmartin, Ruscena Wiederholt, Laura López-Hoffman, Jay E. Diffendorfer, John M. Pleasants, Karen S. Oberhauser, and Orley R. Taylor. "Quasi-Extinction Risk and Population Targets for the Eastern, Migratory Population of Monarch Butterflies (*Danaus plexippus*)." *Scientific Reports* 6, no. 23265 (March 21, 2016). https: //doi.org/10.1038/srep23265.

Skin Cancer Foundation. "Squamous Cell Carcinoma Overview." Accessed January 10, 2019. https://www.skincancer.org/skin-cancer-information/squa mous-cell-carcinoma.

Smith, Peter Andrey. "Where Science Enters the Courtroom, the Daubert Name Looms Large." Undark, February 17, 2020. https://undark.org/2020 /02/17/daubert-standard-joyce-jason/.

Stern, Simon, and Trudo Lemmens. "Legal Remedies for Medical Ghostwriting: Imposing Fraud Liability on Guest Authors of Ghostwritten Articles." *PLoS Medicine* 8, no. 8 (August 2, 2011): e1001070. https://doi.org/10.1371 /journal.pmed.1001070.

Tamma, Paola. "EU Agencies Accused of Cherry-Picking Evidence in Glyphosate Assessment." Euractiv, October 10, 2017. https://www.euractiv.com

/section/agriculture-food/news/eu-agencies-accused-of-cherry-picking -evidence-in-glyphosate-assessment/.

University of California, Division of Agriculture and Natural Resources, State-wide Integrated Pest Management Program. "Little Mallow (Cheeseweed) (*Malva parviflora*)." Accessed May 14, 2019. http://ipm.ucanr.edu/PMG /WEEDS/little_mallow.html.

University of California, San Francisco, Drug Industry Documents. "Actos Litigation Documents." Accessed March 27, 2019. https://www.industrydocu ments.ucsf.edu/drug/collections/actos-litigation-documents/.

University of California, San Francisco, Industry Documents Library. "Truth Tobacco Industry Documents." Accessed March 23, 2019. https://www.industry documentslibrary.ucsf.edu/tobacco/research-tools/litigation-documents/.

Upadhye, Anand. "California Code of Civil Procedure 36(d) regarding Preferential Trial Date in Torts/Products Case." Casetext, June 1, 2015. https://case text.com/analysis/kileut6bm33xflxr-california-code-of-civil-procedure-36d-regarding-preferential-trial-date-in-tortsproducts-case.

US Environmental Protection Agency, Office of Chemical Safety and Pollution Prevention. "Glyphosate: Report of the Cancer Assessment Review Committee." Memorandum, October 1, 2015. http://src.bna.com/eAi.

Washington University in St. Louis. "Monsanto Laboratory of the Life Sciences." Accessed March 12, 2019. https://wustl.edu/about/campuses/dan forth-campus/monsanto-laboratory-life-sciences/.

Weinstein, Henry. "Sanctions Ordered in Tobacco Case." *Los Angeles Times*, November 18, 1997. https://www.latimes.com/archives/la-xpm-1997-nov-18 -fi-54941-story.html.

Wikipedia. "John Edwards." Accessed March 3, 2019. https://en.wikipedia.org /w/index.php?title=John_Edwards&oldid=883594806.

Williams, Gary, Marilyn Aardema, John Acquavella, Sir Colin Berry, David Brusick, Michele M. Burns, Joao Lauro Viana de Camargo, David Garabrant, Helmut A. Greim, Larry D. Kier, David J. Kirkland, Gary Marsh, Keith R. Solomon, Tom Sorahan, Ashley Roberts, and Douglas L. Weed. "A Review of the Carcinogenic Potential of Glyphosate by Four Independent Expert Panels and Comparison to the IARC Assessment." *Critical Reviews in Toxicology* 46, sup1 (2016): 3–20. https://doi.org/10.1080/10408444.2016 .1214677.

Williams, Gary M., Robert Kroes, and Ian C. Munro. "Safety Evaluation and Risk Assessment of the Herbicide Roundup and Its Active Ingredient, Glyphosate, for Humans." *Regulatory Toxicology and Pharmacology* 31, no. 2 (April 2000): 117–65. https://doi.org/10.1006/rtph.1999.1371.

Wisner, Brent. Letter to Arthur A. Elkins Jr., Office of Inspector General, US Environmental Protection Agency, August 1, 2017. https://usrtk.org/wp-content/uploads/2017/08/Exhibit-Letter-from-plaintiffs-attorneys-to-OIG.pdf.

Wolfe, Jan. "Litigators of the Week: Eric Lasker and Rosemary Stewart of Hollingsworth LLP." *American Lawyer*, March 7, 2013. https://www.hollingsworthllp.com/uploads/23/doc/media.959.pdf.

World Health Organization. "The Tobacco Industry Documents: What They Are, What They Tell Us, and How to Search Them." Accessed July 12, 2019. https://www.who.int/tobacco/communications/TI_manual_content.pdf.

World Health Organization, International Agency for Research on Cancer. "About IARC." Accessed February 17, 2019. https://www.iarc.fr/cards_page/about-iarc/.

World Health Organization, International Agency for Research on Cancer. *Evaluation of Five Organophosphate Insecticides and Herbicides.* IARC Monographs vol. 112, March 20, 2015. https://www.iarc.fr/wp-content/uploads/2018/07/MonographVolume112-1.pdf.

World Health Organization, International Agency for Research on Cancer. *Some Drugs and Herbal Products: Pioglitazone and Rosiglitazone.* IARC Monographs vol. 108, September 2015. https://monographs.iarc.fr/wp-content/uploads/2018/06/mono108-12.pdf.

Several court cases separate from Johnson's case provided additional information for this book. The following are some of the relevant documents from those cases.

Arias, et al. v. DynCorp, et al., 928 F. Supp.2d 10, 2013 WL 821168 (D.D.C. February 19, 2013).

Bessemer v. Novartis Pharm. Corp., No. MID-L-1835-08-MT (N.J. Super. Ct. 2010), aff'd, No. L-1835-08, 2012 WL 2120777 (N.J. Super. Ct. App. Div. June 13, 2012).

Edwin Hardeman v. Monsanto Company. Filed February 2, 2016. Case No. 3:16-cv-00525-VC. US District Court of the Northern District of California.

Elaine Stevick and Christopher Stevick v. Monsanto Company. Filed April 29, 2016. Case No. 3:16-cv-02341-VC. US District Court for the Northern District of California.

Jones v. Velsicol Chem. Corp., 625 N.Y.S.2d 934 (N.Y. App. Div. 1995).

Phyllis Kennedy v. Monsanto Company. Filed December 31, 2015. Circuit Court of Camden County. Case No. 16CM-CC00001.

Roundup Products Liability Litigation. Brief in Support of Plaintiffs' Motion for Transfer of Actions to the Southern District of Illinois. US Judicial Panel on Multidistrict Litigation. July 27, 2016. Case MDL No. 2741, Document 1-1.

Roundup Products Liability Litigation. Declaration of R. Brent Wisner in Response to Pre Trial Order 28. Re: Case No. 3:16-md-02741-VC. August 14, 2017. https://usrtk.org/wp-content/uploads/2017/08/Declaration-of-Brent -Wisner.pdf.

Roundup Products Liability Litigation. Monsanto Company's Application for Emergency Relief. Case No. 3:16-md-02741-VC. August 2, 2017. https: //usrtk.org/wp-content/uploads/2017/08/Monsanto-emergency-relief -motion.pdf.

Roundup Products Liability Litigation. Pretrial Order No. 45: Summary Judgment and Daubert Motions. Case No. 3:16-md-02741-VC. July 10, 2018. https://usrtk.org/wp-content/uploads/2018/07/Daubert-order.pdf.

Roundup Products Liability Litigation. Protective and Confidentiality Order. Judge Vince Chhabria. Re: Case No. 3:16-md-02741-VC. December 9, 2016. https://usrtk.org/wp-content/uploads/bsk-pdf-manager/2019/08/Chha bria-Protective-Order-Dec-2016.pdf.

Roundup Products Liability Litigation. Transcript of Daubert Hearing Proceedings. Case No. 3:16-md-02741-VC. March 6, 2018. https://usrtk.org/wp -content/uploads/2018/03/Monsanto-Daubert-hearing-transcript-180 306VC.Vol_.2.pdf.

Roundup Products Liability Litigation. Transcript of Daubert Hearing Proceedings. Case No. 3:16-md-02741-VC. March 9, 2018. https://usrtk.org/wp -content/uploads/2018/03/MDL-Daubert-hearing-transcript-March-9 .pdf.

Roundup Products Liability Litigation. Transcript of Proceedings. Case No. 3: 16-md-02741-VC. August 24, 2017. https://usrtk.org/wp-content/uploads /2017/08/Aug-24-2017-transcript-document-dispute-hearing.pdf.

Roundup Products Liability Litigation. Transcript of Proceedings. Case No. 3:16 -md-02741-VC. November 9, 2017. https://usrtk.org/wp-content/uploads /2017/11/Transcript-of-Nov.-9-2017-case-management-conference.pdf.

Roundup Products Liability Litigation. Transcript of Teleconference. Case No. 3:16-md-02741-VC. August 9, 2017. https://usrtk.org/wp-content/uploads /2017/08/Aug.-9-2017-Teleconference-Transcript.pdf.

Roundup Products Liability Litigation. Video of Proceedings. Case No. 3:16-md-02741-VC. March 5, 2018. https://www.uscourts.gov/cameras -courts/re-roundup-products-liability-litigation.

Teri Michelle McCall v. Monsanto Company. Filed March 9, 2016. Case No. 3: 16-cv-05749-VC in the US District Court for the Central District of California. https://usrtk.org/wp-content/uploads/2017/02/Teri-McCall-law suit.pdf.

The Miller Firm. "Monsanto Roundup Lawsuit." Accessed February 21, 2019. https://millerfirmllc.com/roundup-lawsuit/.

The Miller Firm, LLC v. Timothy Litzenburg. Filed February 4, 2019. Orange County Circuit Court. Case No. CL 18001118. https://usrtk.org/wp-con tent/uploads/2019/12/Miller-v-Litzenburg-First-Amended-Complaint -1-1.pdf.

United States Judicial Panel on Multidistrict Litigation. Transcript of Hearing. September 28, 2016. Case No. ILS/3:16-cv-00823, Document 18.

United States Judicial Panel on Multidistrict Litigation. Transfer Order. Case No. 3:16-cv-02741-VC.

Acknowledgments

I have met very few people in my life who demonstrate the steady strength and quiet determination that Lee Johnson has shown in his battle with cancer. I am so grateful to him for allowing me to witness his struggle and for sharing with me not only his story but also his friendship. I thank Lee for bringing me into his home to meet his beautiful family and for enduring my endless questions over many visits. I hope that I have adequately conveyed in these pages what a remarkable individual he is.

Araceli Johnson also has my gratitude for allowing me many hours of her time and for sharing with me the mix of emotions she has endured amid the turmoil Lee's cancer brought to her family. She is a strong woman trying to prepare herself for a future without her husband and to prepare her children for a future without their father.

I also am forever grateful to the many other cancer patients who told me of their own battles with the disease, their hopes for survival, and their anger and frustration with a regulatory system that allows cancer-causing chemicals to quite literally poison our planet. This book is dedicated to all of those who suffer from this dreadful disease and those whose lives have been lost.

As in everything I do, I must thank my husband, Don Kelley, and my children, Ally, Andrew, and Ryan, for loving me and supporting my work. My father, Chuck Gillam, deserves much gratitude, as do so many other friends and colleagues who assured me the writing was worthwhile during the times when I was doubtful.

Many of the lawyers named in the book have my appreciation for their patience and professionalism as I followed their work both in and outside of courtrooms these past few years.

And finally, thank you to Emily Turner, my editor at Island Press; David Miller, president of the publishing house; Sharis Simonian, Island Press production manager; and all the other talented Island Press team members who made this book happen.

And finally, I say thank you to the growing number of enlightened individuals who understand the dangers chemicals such as glyphosate pose to our health and who are toiling away in their communities to create a healthier world for us all. There is no more time to waste.

About the Author

Investigative journalist Carey Gillam has spent more than twenty years reporting on the health and environmental impacts of the agrochemical industry, including seventeen years working for the Reuters news agency. Her 2017 book about pesticide dangers, *Whitewash: The Story of a Weed Killer, Cancer, and the Corruption of Science*, won the 2018 Rachel Carson Environment Book Award from the Society of Environmental Journalists and has become a part of the curriculum in several university environmental health programs.

Gillam's reporting and writing have led her to become recognized as an international expert on corporate control of agriculture and the health and environmental impacts of a pesticide-dependent food system. She was asked to testify about her findings in 2017 before the European Parliament in Brussels, Belgium, and was an invited speaker at the World Forum for Democracy in Strasbourg, France, in 2019. She also has been a featured speaker at events throughout North America, Australia, the Netherlands, Brussels, and France.

Gillam left Reuters in late 2015 and became research director for the investigative nonprofit group U.S. Right to Know, whose mission is to provide the public with information about often-hidden practices and policies that shape the food system. She also writes occasionally for the *Guardian* news outlet.

Gillam resides in Overland Park, Kansas, with her husband, three children, and one very large and much-loved dog.

Index